I0793075

IMAGES
of America

Pacific Northwest's Whaling Coast

On the Cover: The Bioproducts Company flensing team prepares to flense another whale. From left to right are Alva Elliot, harpooner; Harold Cunningham; Orvo Puppo; Mark Dozier, "flening expert" from California; Lyle Anderson; and Richard Carruthers, president of Hvalfangst Whaling Oregon and Bioproducts Inc. Flensing is a Norwegian term referring to cutting the fat and blubber off whales.

IMAGES
of America

Pacific Northwest's Whaling Coast

Dale Vinnedge

ARCADIA PUBLISHING

ISBN 978-1-4671-3257-2

Published by Arcadia Publishing
Charleston, South Carolina

Printed in the United States of America

Library of Congress Control Number: 2014941230

For all general information, please contact Arcadia Publishing:
Telephone 843-853-2070
Fax 843-853-0044
E-mail sales@arcadiapublishing.com
For customer service and orders:
Toll-Free 1-888-313-2665

Visit us on the Internet at www.arcadiapublishing.com

Contents

Acknowledgments

I wish to acknowledge the assistance of Jeff Smith, the director of the Columbia River Maritime Museum (CRMM) in Astoria, Oregon. He assisted in finding and making available photographs from the museum's collection. The Bioproducts photographs came from Richard Carruthers and family, and are on deposit with the CRMM. Carruthers was the president of Bioproducts Inc. and Hvalfanst Whaling Oregon, the two companies that caught and processed whales from Oregon and Washington in the 1960s.

I would also like to acknowledge the work of Robert Lloyd Webb, who published *On the Northwest* in 1988. That book was my primary source for research on whaling in British Columbia and surrounding areas. I would like to thank the volunteers and staff at the Vancouver Maritime Museum, the Columbia River Maritime Museum, and local libraries and museums for their interest in developing works in maritime history, and also my editors at Arcadia Publishing.

Unless otherwise noted, all images are from the author's collection.

INTRODUCTION

There were several styles and methods of whaling in Pacific Northwest waters. The earliest whaling was practiced by natives from the coasts of British Columbia and Washington. There was also early whaling from Alaskan coastal waters, but the type of whales and the methods of whaling were different.

Information does not exist to show that Oregon natives went whaling. They did, however, utilize drift whales for meat and fat. Whaling was practiced off the coasts of Oregon and Washington by Yankee whalers returning from the Arctic every year from the 1850s. Whalers were known to occasionally anchor in protected bays and harbors on their way south to San Francisco and Hawaii for refitting every fall.

After 1900, modern whaling methods using steel catchers and harpoon guns were being established in British Columbian, southern Alaskan, and Washington waters. This development continued until whaling was ended in the 1970s. Whaling in British Columbia was done from Vancouver Island, and there were quite a few whaling stations scattered around the island. Southern Alaska had several stations, with the most utilized at Akutan on the Aleutian Islands. In Washington, whaling operated in roughly the same timeframe as in British Columbia and Alaska. The Bay City station sent catchers to Oregon waters who whaled to near the California border.

The use of whale meat for human consumption was experimented with in the first half of the 20th century. Whale meat was made available to butchers and restaurants and had some success, particularly during the war years when beef was not available. Even though it was supported by governments with fliers, articles, and even recipes, when World War II ended and beef became available again, the market for whalemeat waned.

One

Early Shore Whaling

From the 1850s to the 1890s, shore whaling was a common practice in California—from Crescent City in the north, to the tip of Baja California in the south. They used boats powered by sail and oars. Whales were chased in whaleboats, and, once the whales were harpooned, the whalers would stay fast with stout ropes. As the whale tired, the whalers would catch up and try to lance it and kill it. After the whale died, they would tow it back to a land station, where tryworks were used to process the whale.

Whaling off of British Columbia began in the 1860s, with a company started by Thomas "Welcome" Roys and James Dawson. Dawson, who was from Scotland, and a partner named Warren attempted to take whales in through Saanich Inlet in 1866, though this effort ended in failure. They managed to harpoon three whales, but, due to bad weather, lost all three. Dawson tried again with a new partner—a sea captain named Abel Douglass—and, according to Robert Webb, two Californians named Bruce and Woodward. The group acquired a small schooner named the *Kate* and began whaling in Saanich Inlet. They used bomb lances to capture whales. These were state of the art in 1868, when the operation began. They set up tryworks on Saanich Island, and the operation did moderately well that year. They acquired another ship, the *Industry*, to bring down oil. In 1868, they brought out about 100 barrels of oil for sale.

In 1869, the Dawson and Douglass Whaling Company moved its equipment to Cortez Island. Later, the *Kate* was damaged when it ran up on a rock. The season was ultimately disappointing and ended with only 14 whales taken. In 1869, the operation joined forces with the Lipsett Whaling Company and formed the Union Whaling Company, which lasted only about six months and landed only four whales. Dawson and Douglas then reorganized their company in June 1870. Lipsett went on to establish the Howe Sound Company and organized a group of men to go to Howe Sound in the summer. In 1871, Dawson and Lipsett joined forces again to form the British Columbia Whaling Company, while Douglas and Strahan sailed aboard the *Industry*. The companies returned with 20 and 15,000 barrels of oil respectively, but, due to poor prices at the time, the season was deemed a failure.

Thomas Roys was a well-known whaling captain who had discovered bowhead whales in the Bering Strait in 1848. He had also invented his own type of whaling harpoon, and a device for raising whales that had sunk to the bottom. Roys made two cruises for whales, sailing in the 83-foot *Emma* in the summer and fall of 1868. He reported bad weather and problems with his equipment upon returning to Victoria. Roys went on to form the Victoria Whaling Adventurers Company. He whaled from several locations, but had trouble with fog and broken equipment. Finally, the *Emma* broke a propeller and was towed back to Victoria. Within a week, the company had been disbanded.

Roys returned to Victoria in early 1860 and sent the *Emma* to Barclay Sound, where a building and a tryworks were built. Roys had trouble with the weather for two months and tried other locations, but still did not fare well. Captains Roys and Dawson retired and Douglass never whaled again, but he had success in other businesses. The whales were given a rest for the next few years. There may have been a few attempts to go whaling in that period, but none were notably successful. It would take an equipment upgrade to revitalize the local whaling industry.

Another whaling operation was started in 1879, when the Northwest Trading Company built a shore-based whaling station at Killisnoo. In 1878, a large number of finback whales were observed in the bay, off of the new trading post. Whaling was again attempted in 1880, and seems to have continued until 1882, when a whaling bomb exploded on a boat and killed Tith Klane—a local Indian medicine man who was employed by the Northwest Trading Company. After his death, the local tribe demanded reparations in the form of 200 blankets. The company refused the payment and called upon the US Navy—then serving as the government of Alaska—to mediate. The situation led to the "shelling of Angoon" on October 26, 1882. In 1973, the federal government finally paid $90,000 in reparations for the shelling incident. This incident led to the formation of local civil government in 1884, and eventually to Alaska's statehood.

The local whaling industry faded after 1871, and while there may have been several applications for whaling licenses up until 1900, none were issued. A few whalers probably sailed in the area on their way to or from Alaska, and there may have been some native whaling, but the industry had effectively died.

The whales of importance to the local industry are seen in this illustration. From top to bottom are the sperm whale, the sulphur-bottom whale (or blue whale), and the humpback.

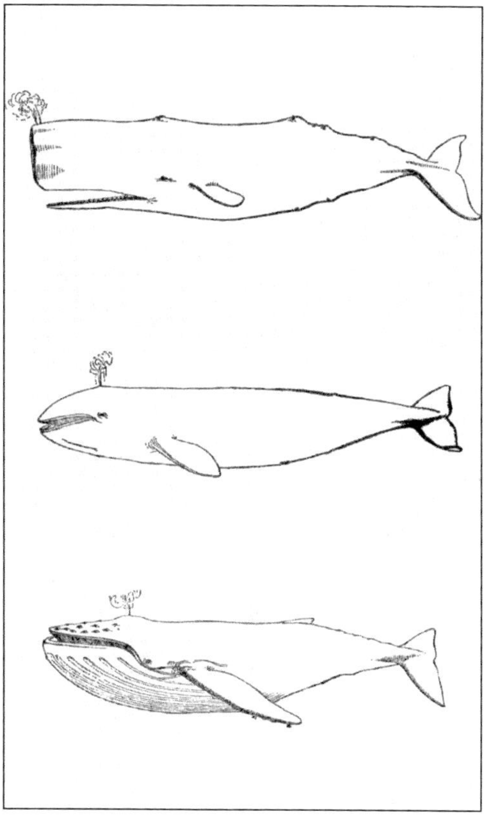

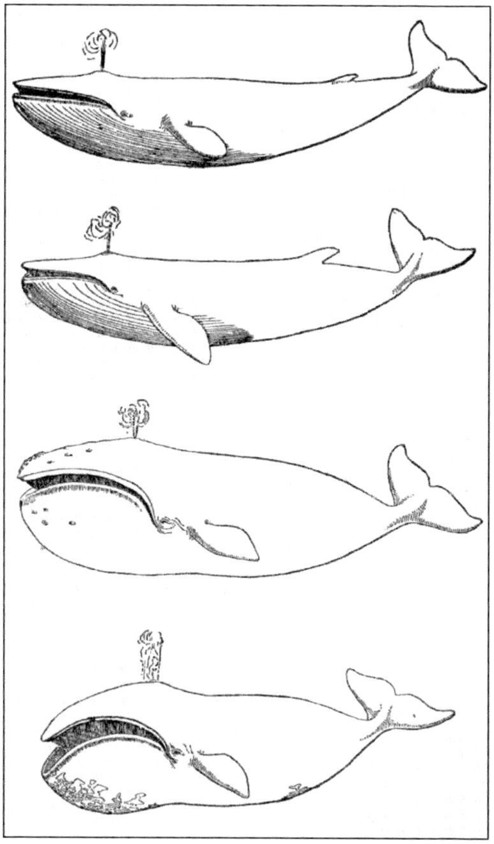

Further important fishing whales are, from top to bottom, the fin whale (top two), the bowhead, and the right whale.

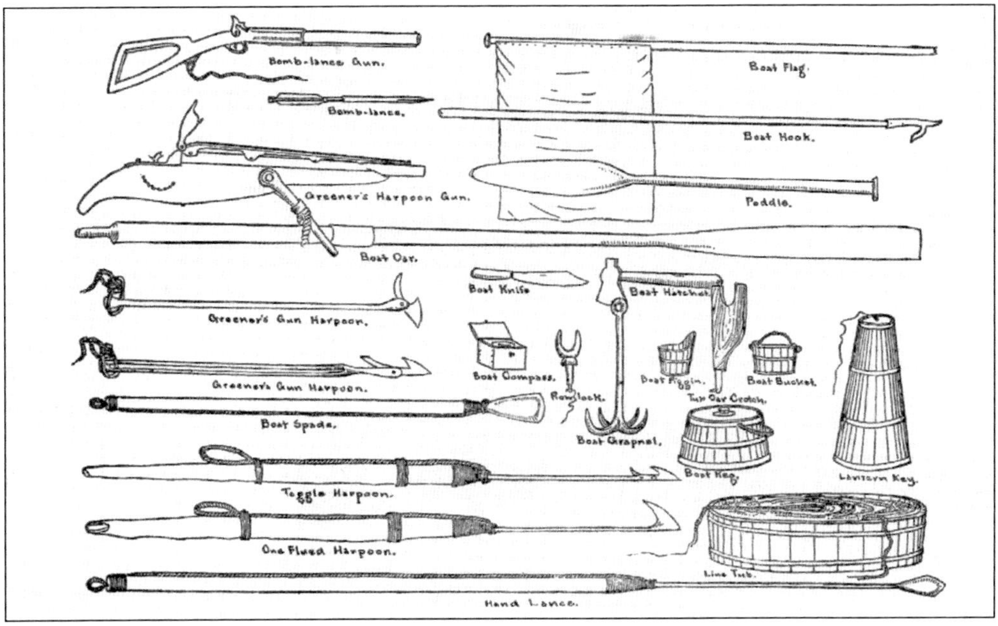

Several pieces of common, traditional whaling hardware are pictured here.

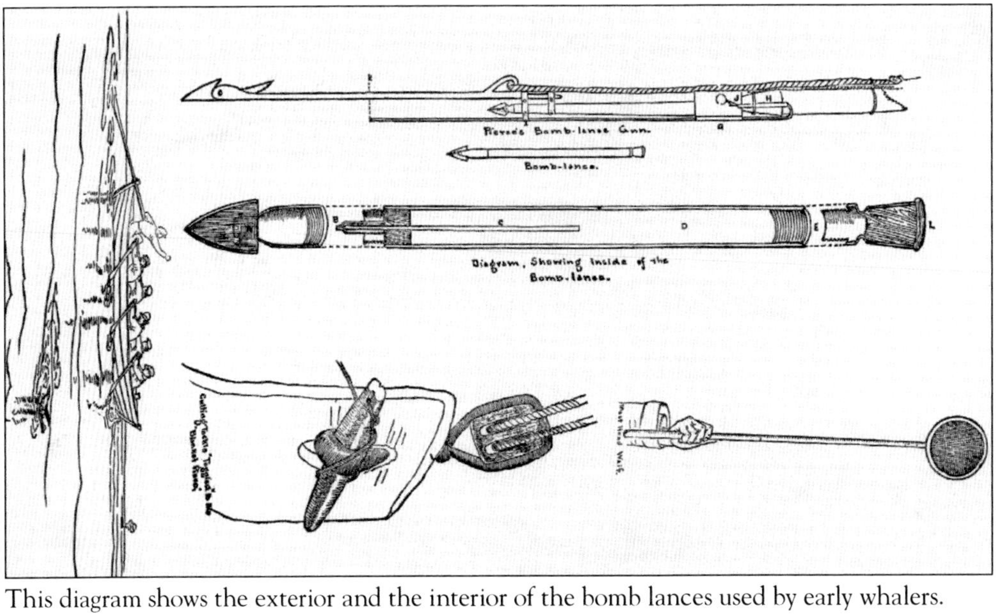

This diagram shows the exterior and the interior of the bomb lances used by early whalers.

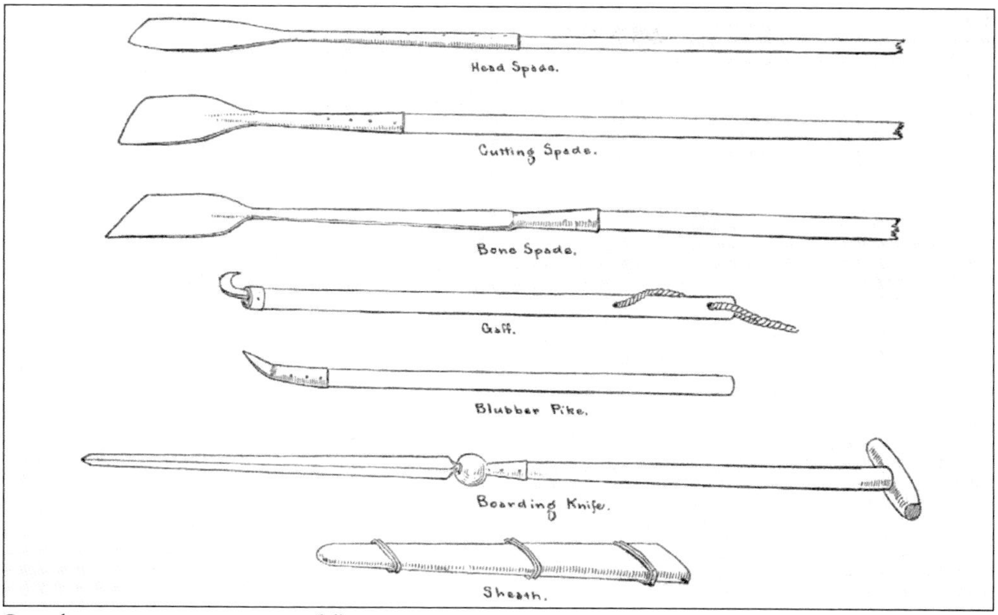

Seen here are various pieces of flensing equipment, including the head spade, cutting spade, bone spade, gaff, blubber pike, and the boarding knife with its sheath. These tools made for messy work.

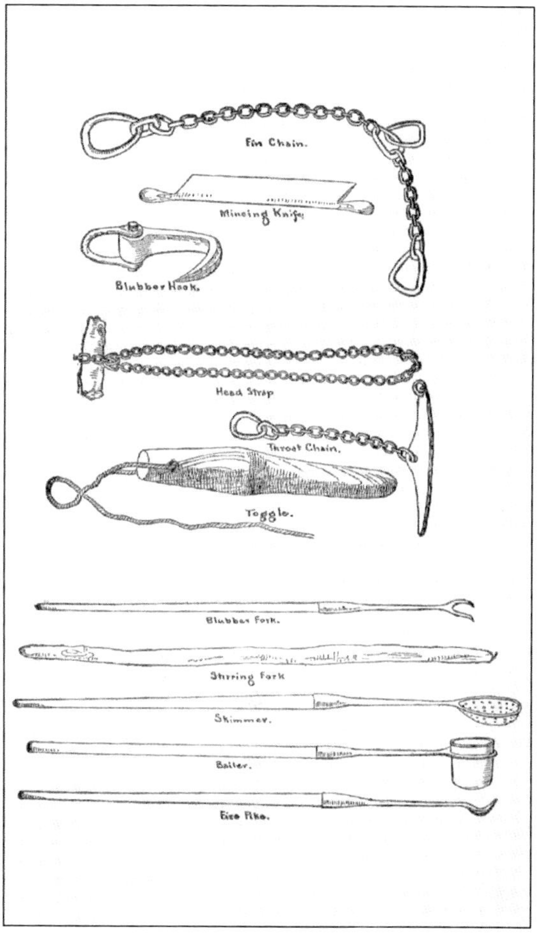

Pictured here are some mincing knives, along with various other tools of the trade.

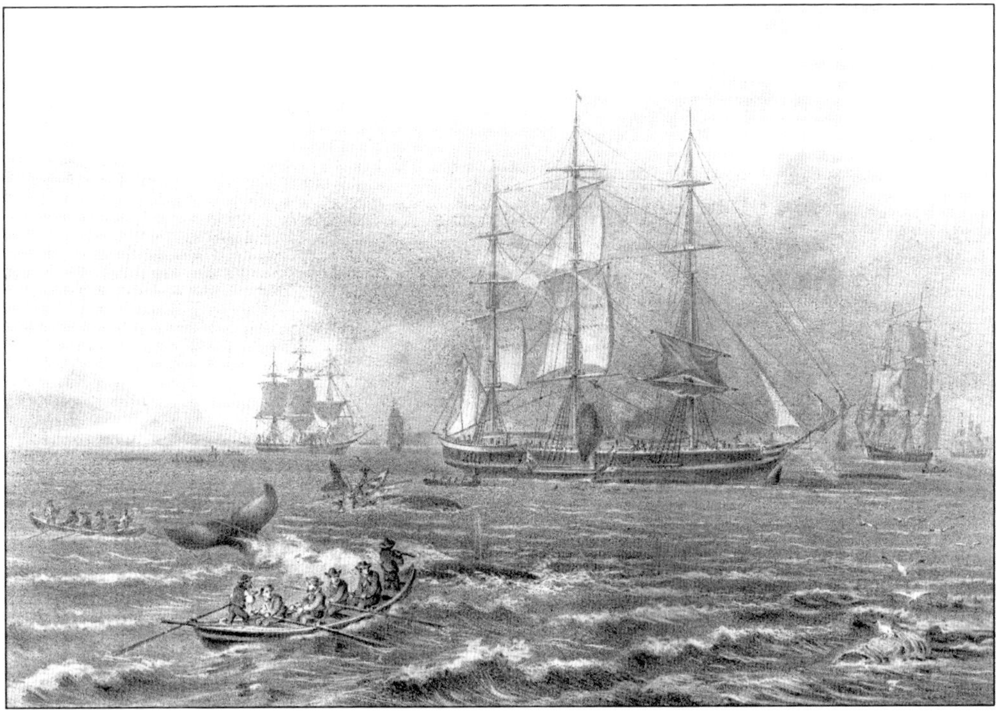

This beautiful illustration, *A Northern Whaling Scene*, first appeared in Charles M. Scammon's 1847 work, *The Marine Mammals of the North-Western Coast of North America, Together with an Account of the American Whale-Fishery.*

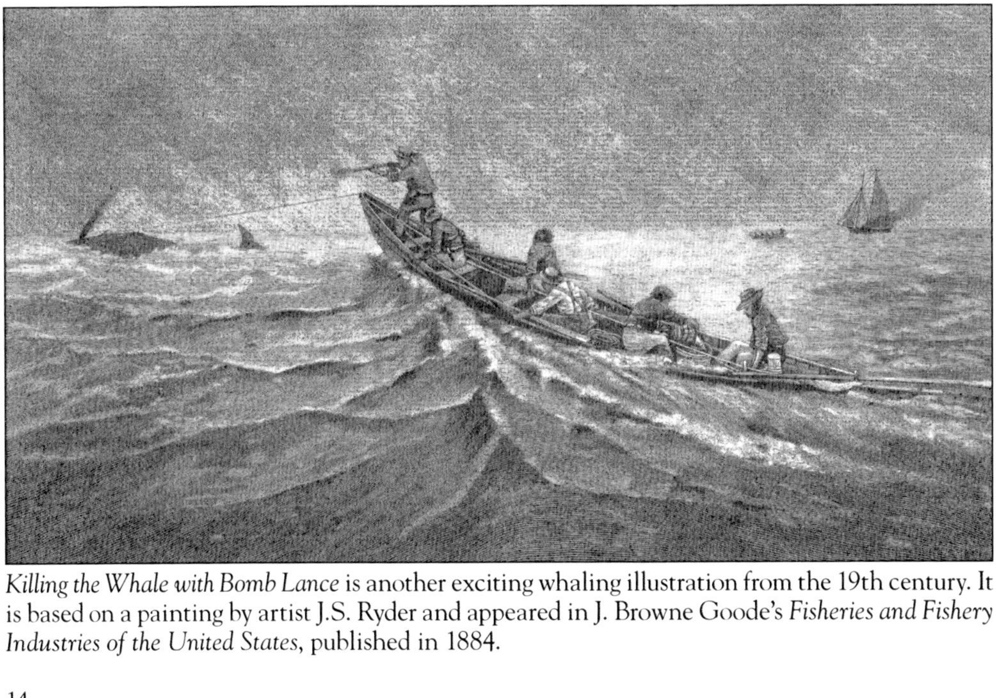

Killing the Whale with Bomb Lance is another exciting whaling illustration from the 19th century. It is based on a painting by artist J.S. Ryder and appeared in J. Browne Goode's *Fisheries and Fishery Industries of the United States*, published in 1884.

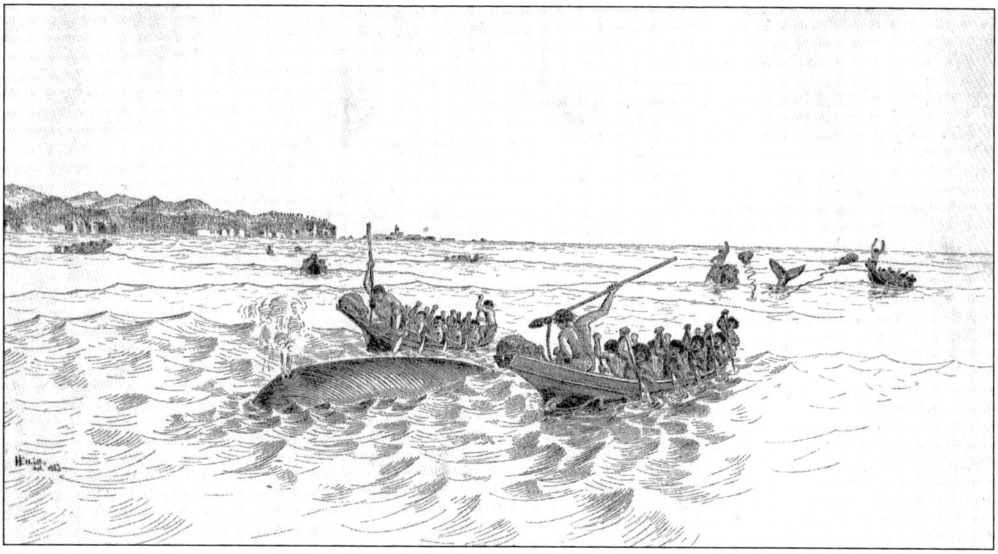

This drawing by H.W. Elliot, *The Whale Fishery*, is also from Goode's 1884 study. The Makah Indians used spears with bone or stone points. They whaled in groups, so that multiple boats would throw spears. These spears were tied to sealskin floats, which were dragged by the whale. The whale would eventually be caught and killed. It would then be towed back to shore for flensing.

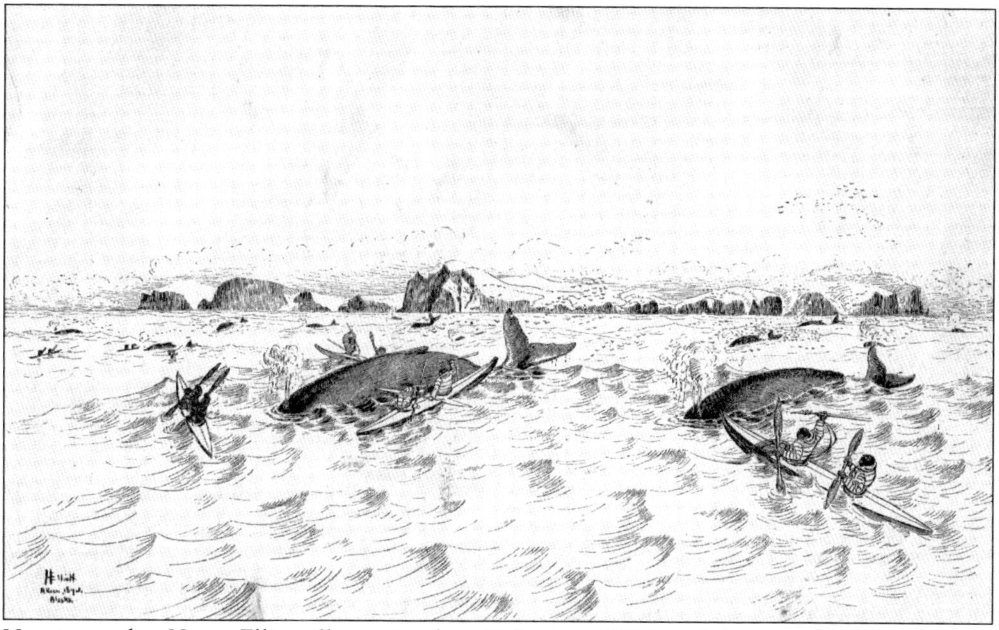

Here is another Henry Elliott illustration from *Fisheries and Fishery Industries of the United States*. The Aleuts were known to whale completely differently from the Makah, and used Aconite poisoning with their whales. The whales would die and rise to the surface after two or three days. The Aleuts tended to hunt individually for their whales.

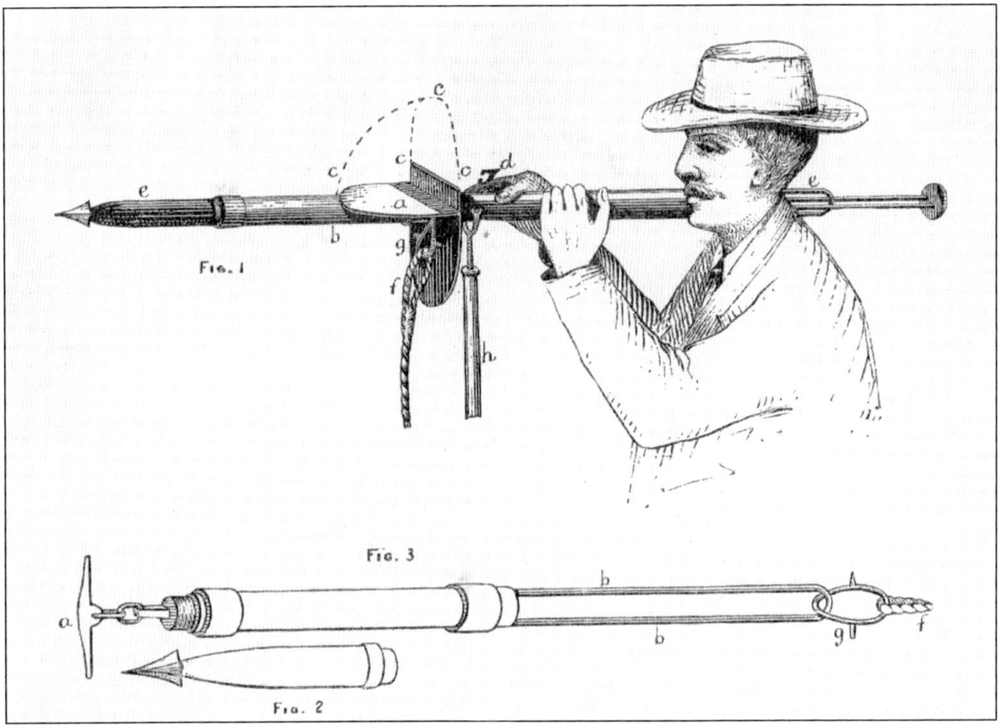

This illustration shows Thomas "Welcome" Roys and his shoulder mounted bomb gun. This gun was sold, with little success, to some early whalers. Other gun designs proved more effective.

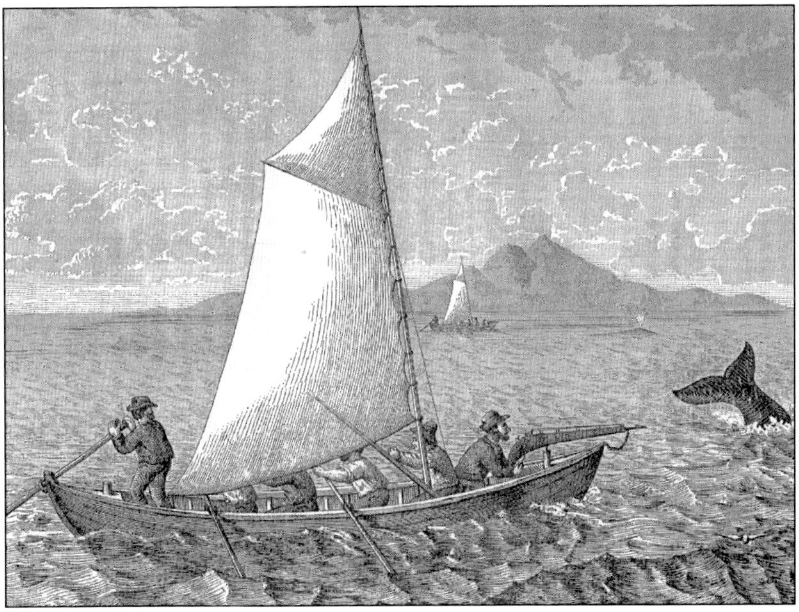

This illustration depicts a whaleboat with a Greener harpoon gun mounted on its bow.

Two

Oregon Whaling

The native Indians of coastal Oregon left little evidence to indicate that they were active whalers. They are better known for utilizing dead whales that drifted close to shore, using the whale's flesh and blubber for food and oil. In 1856, a whale in the possession of some Indians at Coos Bay was found to be in a state of decay that indicated it had been dead before it came ashore. Even though the smell was bad, the Indians were pleased to have the food—as some of the children were showing signs of starvation. Whaling ships operated frequently off of the Oregon coast, especially from late summer to early fall. Any whales that had been struck but escaped and later died could wash ashore and provide a bounty for people and animals inhabiting the area.

In 1848, the whaleship *Maine*, of Massachusetts, was directed by her owners to enter the Columbia River and unload its cargo at Astoria, after two years cruising around the North Pacific. This was to be the first location on the west coast where whale products could be obtained. At the time, Astoria was the largest city on the northwest coast, as Seattle was still small and San Francisco was under Mexican control and at war with the United States.

The text *The Works of Hubert Howe Bancroft, Volume XXX, History of Oregon, Vol. II 1848–1888* relates a little information about the *Maine*, stating that, "the close of the period was marked by the wreck of the whaleship Maine, Captain Netcher, with 1,400 barrels of whale-oil, 150 of sperm-oil, and 14,000 pounds of bone. She had been two years from Fairhaven, Mass., and was a total loss." According to James A. Gibbs, in his book *Pacific Graveyard*, the *Maine* was a 294 ton vessel and wrecked on Clatsop Spit on August 25, 1848. Further, in Alexander Starbuck's *History of the American Whale Fishery*, it can be gleaned that the *Maine* was owned by E. Sawin and sailed on August 11, 1846, for the Indian Ocean and northwest whaling grounds. Starbuck's text agrees with the other information above, but asserts that 6,500 pounds of whalebone was sent home on another ship, most likely from Hawaii, where the *Maine* spent her off-season winters. No other whaling ships attempted to cross the Columbia River bar and bring whaling products directly into Astoria.

After 1900, whaling stations were placed along the coastline at intervals that were determined to be sufficient for whale populations to recover. Whaling stations were not established in Oregon, however, and those established in Washington sent ships as far south as Cape Blanco—which has a lighthouse near Port Orford, close to the south end of Coos Bay. The whales were towed back to the Grays Harbor Station near Aberdeen, Washington. Newspaper stories note that Oregon whaling carried on from 1911, with a new feature being established in 1924. William Schupp, of the American Pacific Whaling Company of Grays Harbor, signed a contract in early 1924 to lease three docks in Empire, near the mouth of Coos Bay. In early May, the company began to tow whales into Coos Bay Harbor, where they were collected and taken in groups to the Washington station. Beginning in early May 1924, whales were taken north by the whalers *Moran*, *Aberdeen*, and *Westport*, or the tugs *Roosevelt* and *Ambassador*. The *Roosevelt* and the *Ambassador* were local ships hired for towing. The *Roosevelt* was built for Cmdr. Robert Peary in 1905 in preparation for his second attempt to reach the North Pole. By 1923, the *Roosevelt* was owned by the Washington Tug and Barge Company of Seattle.

The *Roosevelt* was built to Peary's specifications, particularly in how she dealt with ice. This enabled Peary's 1906 push to longitude 87°06'—then the international record for the farthest distance traveled north. The ship was badly damaged by ice, however, and limped home. In 1908, the repaired *Roosevelt* again bore Peary north, to Cape Sheridan on Ellesmere Island. This position allowed for Peary's successfully reaching the Pole in April 1909. When Peary no longer had use for the ship, the *Roosevelt* was used for commercial shipping. She ran aground near the Panama Canal, sank, and lies there still.

Empire's whalers soon encountered a problem, however: The whales that were brought in began to smell terrible in short order. This prompted a group of citizens to file for an injunction against the company. In a month, after the company brought in 60 whales in 60 days, the smell was said be noticeable six miles from town. The injunction was approved temporarily, with the company agreeing to remove the whales in a timely manner. The whales were kept out of Empire, and the company used the open harbor at Port Orford to collect its whales for shipment to Bay City.

The following is the story of a whale that landed on a beach in Southern Oregon on Sunday, August 21, 1938. It was a sperm whale that was disposed of except for its skeleton, which was displayed for at least 10 years at Randall's Shore Pines Cottage Park, five miles South of Waldport, Oregon. This story was printed and handed out free to anyone who asked for it. The whale had its tongue missing, which was correctly attributed to its being taken by killer whales. The story has been shortened to the pertinent information:

> Tillie, of Tillacum Beach, 5 mile South of Waldport, Oregon, is a whale. Or more correctly, she was a whale when she landed on the beach early Sunday morning, August 21, 1938. (She also was known as the Yachats whale, but is the same whale as Tillie). Now she is but a skeleton. It is believed that she met with an untimely end. These deductions are based upon the fact that she arrived on the beach minus her tongue. Experts tell us that is a sign of a conflict with the deadly "killer whale," a smaller but vicious creature. We have no way of telling how old Tillie was when she died, but she was plenty old when she landed here. It took no brain work to determine that. The nose knows.
>
> As she lay on the beach that sunny August morning she measured about fifty feet in length and it is estimated that she weighed about forty tons. She must have been a big baby though, for there was considerable blubber in her make-up. A fertilizer company took care of that part of her carcass and rendered it out into oil. In so doing they also rendered a very helpful service for us in the task of extricating her skeleton, for the blubber is a layer of fat several inches thick just under her tough black hide. At that, the deboning process was no small job, but with the aid of hand axes, crow bars, a tow car and cable, some clothes pins for the nose and a couple of good high tides we succeeded in getting the skeleton out a piece at a time. After a curing period they were reassembled so that we are now able to present to you Tillie, unadorned.

Other whales were stranded and became garden ornaments. Postcards show a 21-foot jawbone with six men standing on it near Tillamook, Oregon.

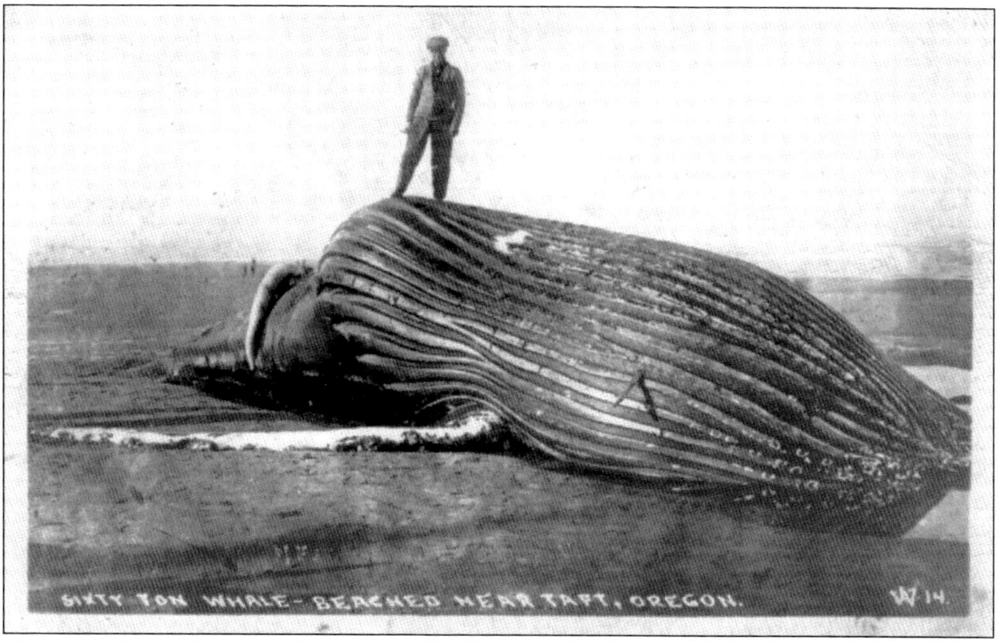

This is a 60-ton whale, beached near Taft, Oregon. This humpback whale died at sea and was not harpooned by whalers. The iron pole seen in the whale is there to prevent it from drifting back into the ocean at high tide.

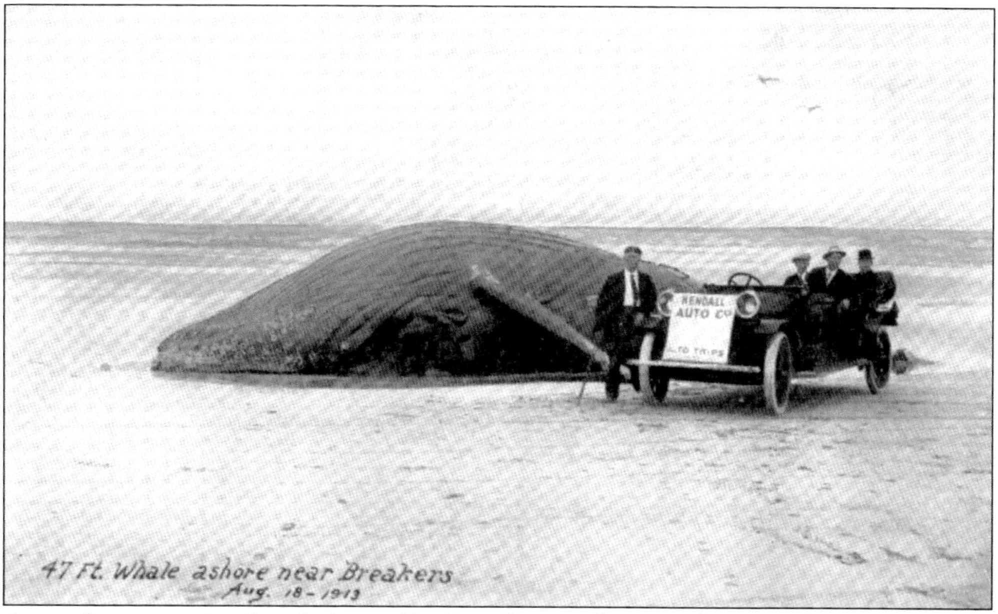

As people come to visit this whale near Breakers, Oregon, they saw advertising for Kendall Motors. The company still exists today—no doubt due to their creative advertising.

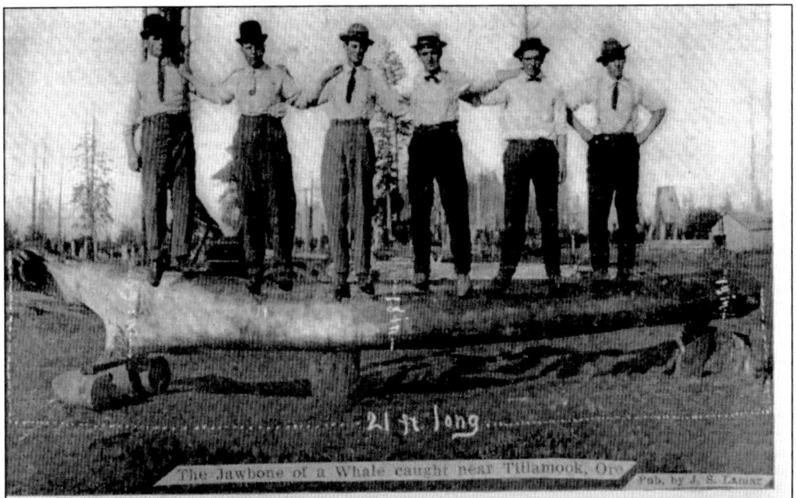

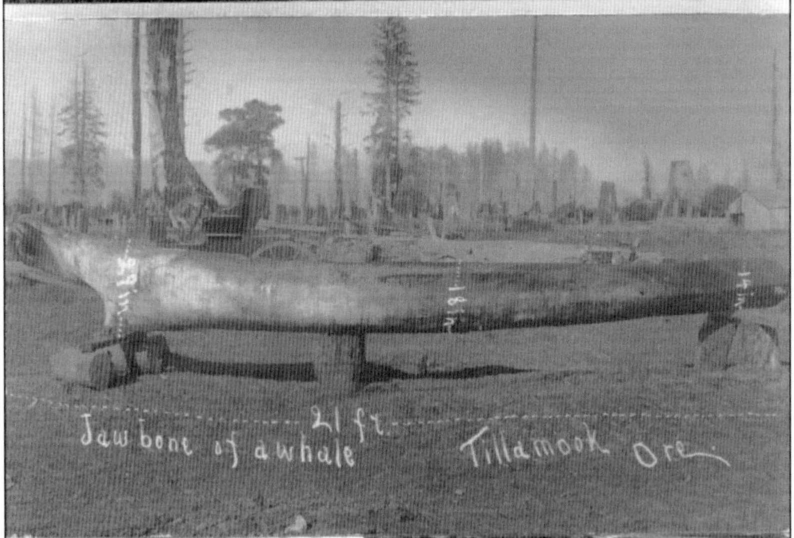

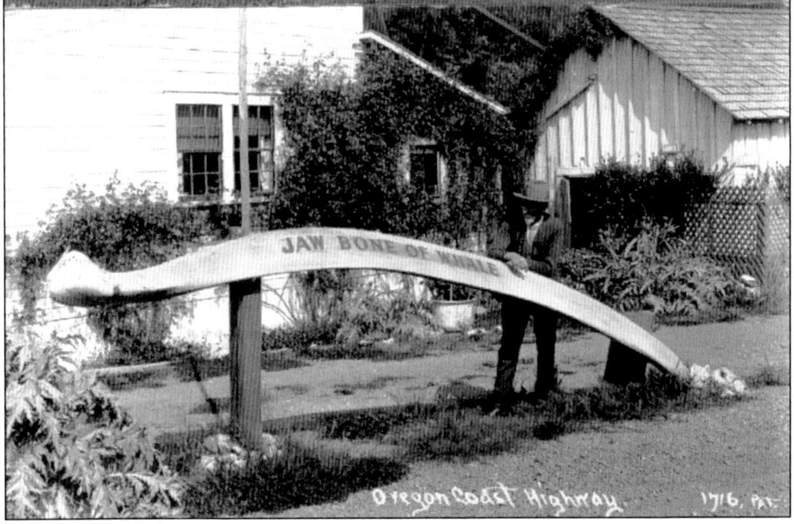

Here are three different photographs of whale jawbones being used to decorate property in Oregon. The top two are different photographs of the same jawbone, while the bottom appears to be a different jawbone and location. The whale in the first two pictures was called Tillie, because it was caught near Tillamook, Oregon.

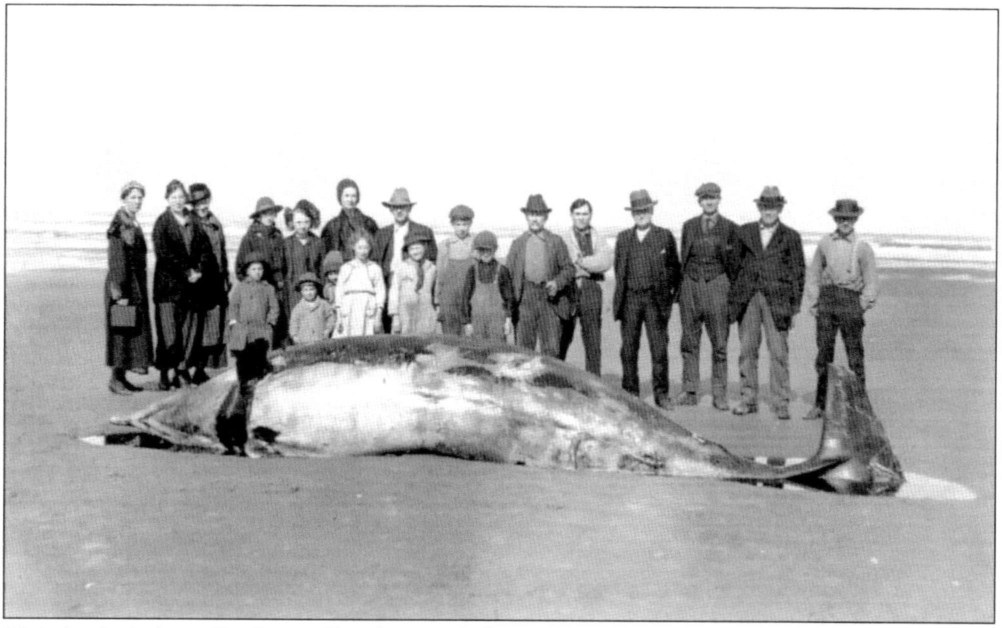

This dead whale on Rockaway Beach, near Tillamook, provided quite the photo opportunity.

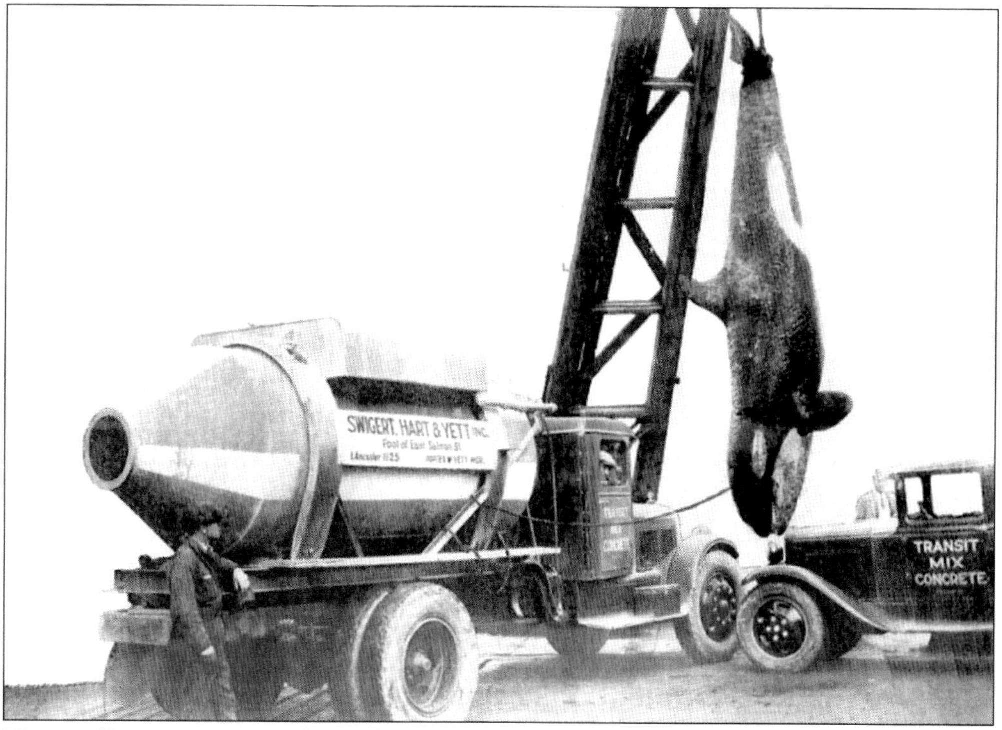

This small orca swam 110 miles up the Columbia River before turning south on the Williamette River toward Oregon City. Unfortunately, he noticed the bridges above him and would go no farther up or down river. The animal was then shot by some locals, who embalmed the body and carted it all over the area. People were charged a small amount to see the whale.

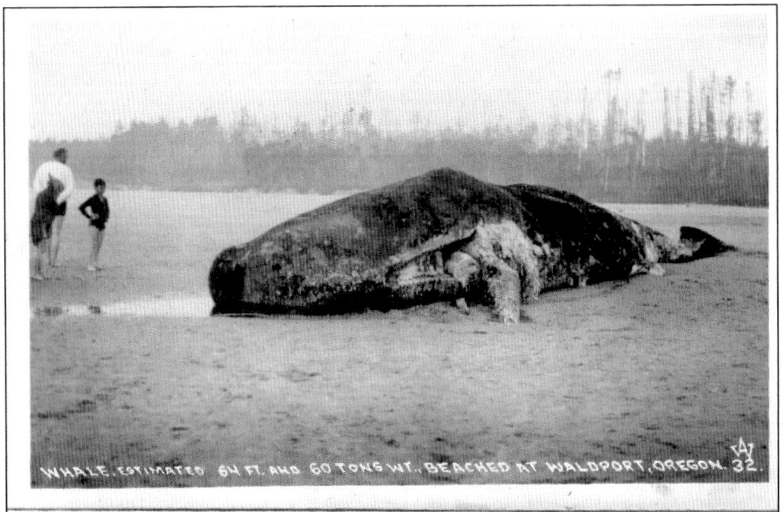

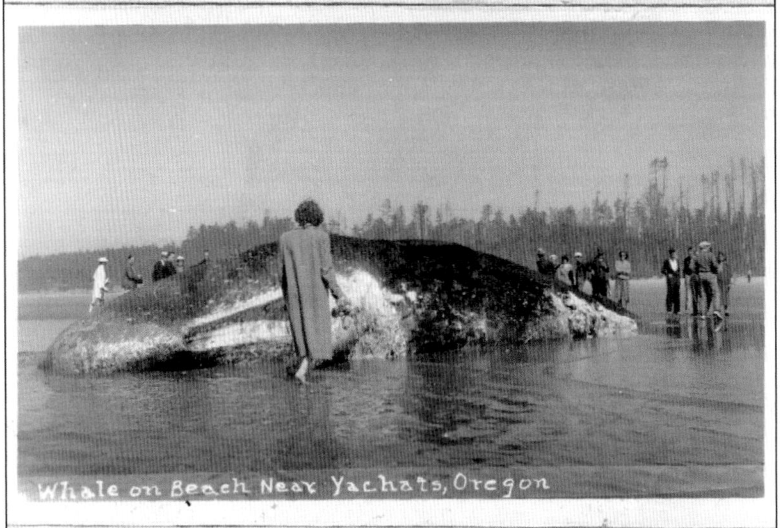

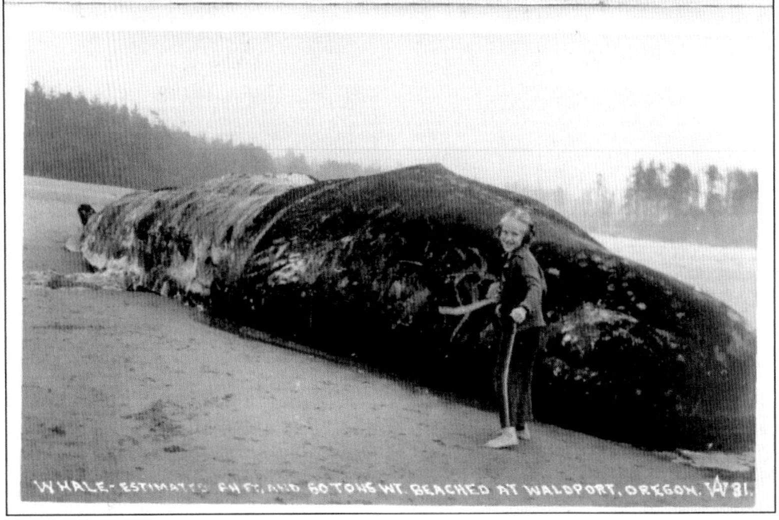

These three photographs all show the same whale, which became popular in the Yachats area. The whale was buried in the sand on the beach.

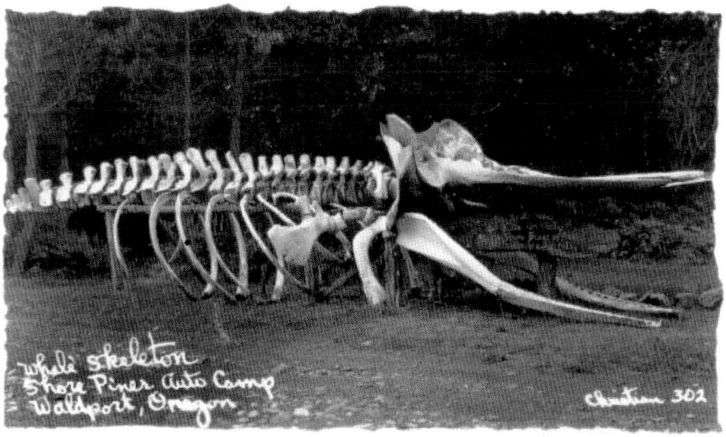

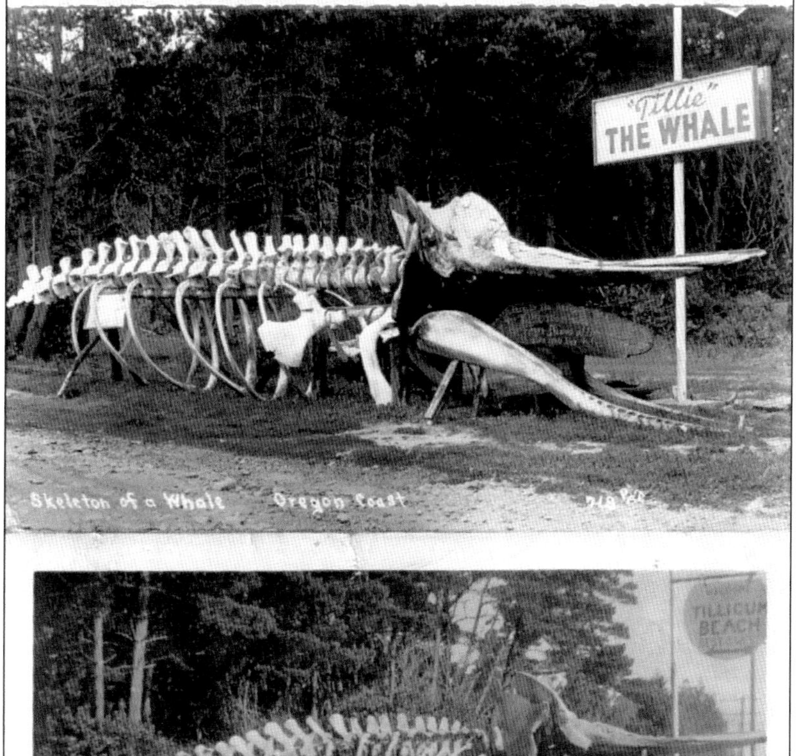

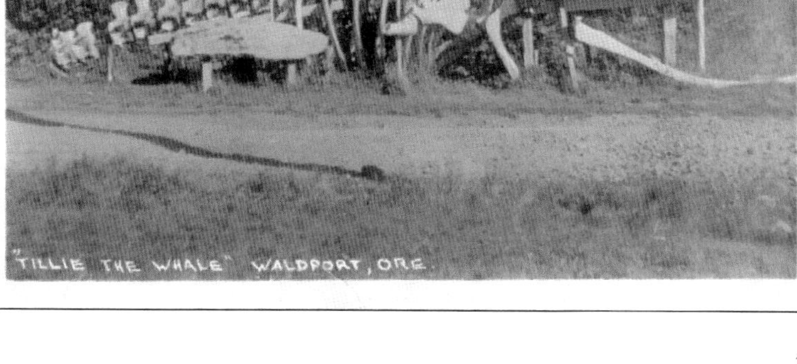

These three photographs show the Yachats whale after it was dug up. The skeleton was put together in front of an auto park for trailers, and is now called Tillie the Whale—for Tillicum Beach, where it was found.

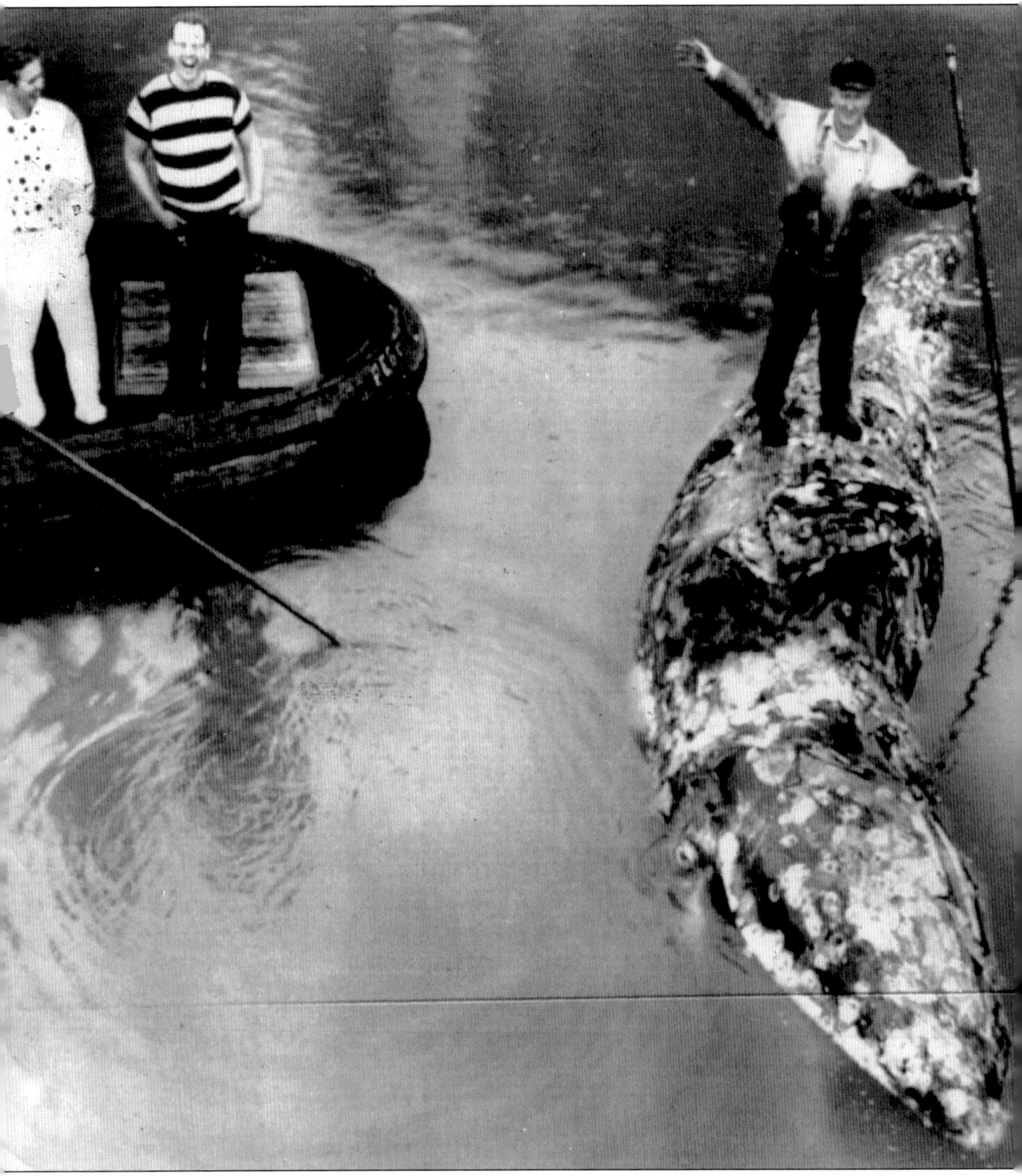

Pictured here is a rare whale that made its way up the Columbia River, became stranded, and died.

Three

Bioproducts Inc.

In the early 1960s, whaling was proving profitable in California, particularly in the pet food industry. The pet food market actually increased the total value of the whales that were being brought in, due to the depressed markets for whale meal and oil. This California operation influenced people from Oregon to start whaling. *Offbeat Oregon History*, an online magazine, said of the operation, "the 1961 venture was more than a bit bizarre, looked at from a modern perspective. It was a coming-together of the need of Oregon mink growers for large volumes of cheap protein, and the need of the National Aeronautics and Space Administration for large volumes of whale oil."

The whaling operation, which is believed to be the only one of its kind in Oregon, was started in Hammond in 1961. The operation was a joint project between Bioproducts Inc.; the Oregon Fur Producers Association, of which Charles Smith of Seaside was president; and manager Merv Hille, of Astoria. Eben Parker purchased a 95-foot trawler named the *Tom & Al* to convert into a whaler. The *Tom & Al* sailed from the company's Hammond site, just inside the Columbia River and west of Astoria. Frank Parker, Eben's brother, was the harpooner on the *Tom & Al*. The 50-millimeter harpoon gun and its mount were installed by the Astoria Marine Construction Co. The gun was tested by Richard Carruthers and Alva Elliot—a former naval gunner working for Bioproducts—in May 1961.

In *My Days At Bioproducts*, Lyle Anderson says that, "We fitted out and sent out, one at a time, the *Tom and Al* skippered by Eben and Frank Parker; an ex-minesweeper, skippered by McCroskey, the *Halawai*, renamed the *Tonquin*, skippered by Pete Peterson." About the guns, he said, "We had two guns, a 50 millimeter gun with pointed harpoon heads, and a 90-millimeter gun with armor-piercing harpoon heads." While these harpoons weren't armor piercing, they had a tip with an explosive charge inside. It was designed to enter the whale and detonate a few seconds later. The charge was designed to kill the whale—hopefully on the first shot—depending on where the harpoon hit the whale's body.

The whales were towed to Warrenton and flensed by the company's subsidiary, Hvalfangst Oregon. The prime meat would be ground into mink food, and the blubber rendered into oil. In *Warrenton, 1791–1992*, Lyle Anderson said, "Oil was sold to the Mount Hood Soap Company in Portland, the bones were dried and ground up for flower bulb fertilizer, and vitamin A was obtained from the liver. The loins were chunked, cooled, ground, sacked, and frozen for dog or mink food. A few whale knick-knacks were sold to the curious procession of visitors."

In an article in the September and October 1961 issue of *The Northwest*, the author states that, "When the first whale, a 43 foot sperm, was towed up to the slipway on the evening of 24 the crews of Hvalfangst Oregon, who were to flense and cut up the huge beast and the Bioproducts crew whose task it would be under Chemist (Lyle) Anderson's direction to conserve all parts of the whale, except the meat taken for mink feed, were literally appalled by the tasks ahead."

Marv Hille and Frank Smith, the manager and superintendent of the Oregon Fur Producers Association, had the problem of quickly hauling, cooling, grinding, and freezing the 13,000 pounds of meat and were more than a little concerned by the job ahead of them. All went well, however. Flensing and cutting were done properly and promptly, which was attributed to chief flenser Marquette "Mark" Dozier. He had come north from Richmond, California, seeking a position with the new whaling company, and Warrenton was lucky to have so experienced a man in its employ. At the time, he was the only employee who had any whaling experience.

The Northwest also reported on the story of the first whale brought in by the company, which almost ended in disaster: "The first whale as it was winched to the top of the slipway a shackle broke, a three quarter inch steel 'straw' line snapped, flipping a workman head-over-heels in the process; fortunately he was not seriously hurt. Sparks flew, and the whale slid back into the water like an express train, breaking off two dock pilings before it was stopped against other pilings and the *Tom and Al*, which had been standing by."

According to Anderson, in *Warrenton, 1791–1992,* the operation received 13 whales in five years: "3 Sperm whales and two humpback whales in 1961, one finback whale in 1962, five finback whales in 1963, one sperm whale in 1964, and one finback whale in 1965." The 1965 season proved to be the last for Oregon whaling. After five years, the operation had been determined to be a failure. Some reasons offered for this were there not being enough whales in the area; of those that were found, the whales would spoil due to internal gasses on the long trip to port; and the market for whale parts was not what it once was. Further, the fish reduction machinery that purchased for the venture wasn't suitable to handle whale meat; the whales were always landed at off times, requiring too much overtime pay; and it was not satisfactory to own or contract a killer boat. Finally, the United States and its people were becoming more interested in conservation, which rendered whaling an unpopular occupation and business.

The Mt. Hood Soap Company bought the whale oil that was produced by Bioproducts Inc. between 1961 and 1965. The company used to make various brands of bar and laundry soap. Formed in 1902 as the Mt. Hood Soap and Soda Co., the company currently manufactures sustainable cleaning products and is a subsidiary of Swisher Hygiene. Tom Mulflur has been running the company since 1995.

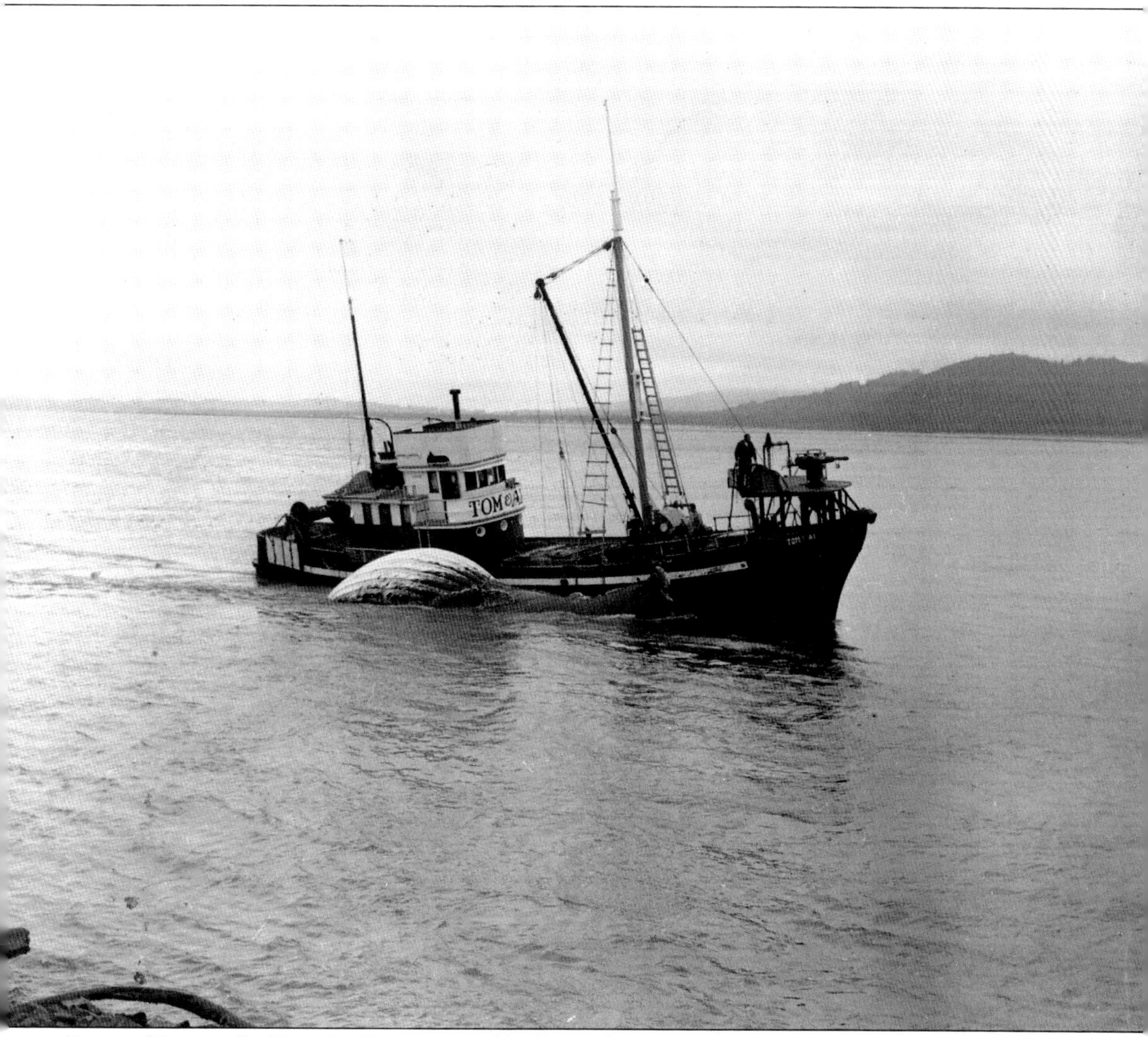

Pictured here is the *Tom & Al*, a converted halibut fishing boat that was used by Bioproducts Inc. of Oregon as a whaling boat. The harpoon gun on the bow was fired by the harpooner into the whale. The harpoon carried an explosive head that was designed to kill the whale on the first strike. This did not always happen, and the boat had to get close enough to a fleeing whale to harpoon it a second time. The whale in the photograph is connected to the boat by the harpoon line. (Courtesy the Columbia River Maritime Museum.)

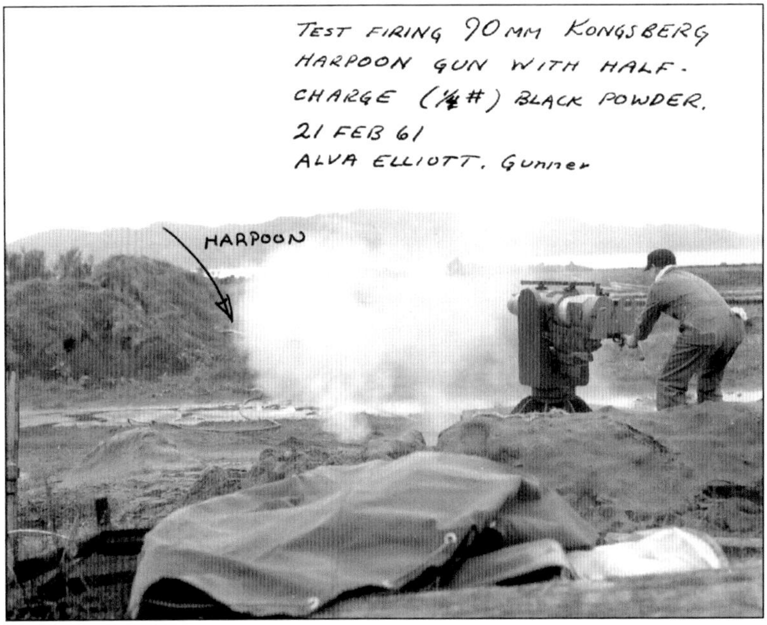

The note on the photograph reads: "Test firing 90 mm Kongsberg harpoon gun with half-charge (¼ #) black powder. 21 Feb 61. Alva Elliott, gunner." (Courtesy the Columbia River Maritime Museum.)

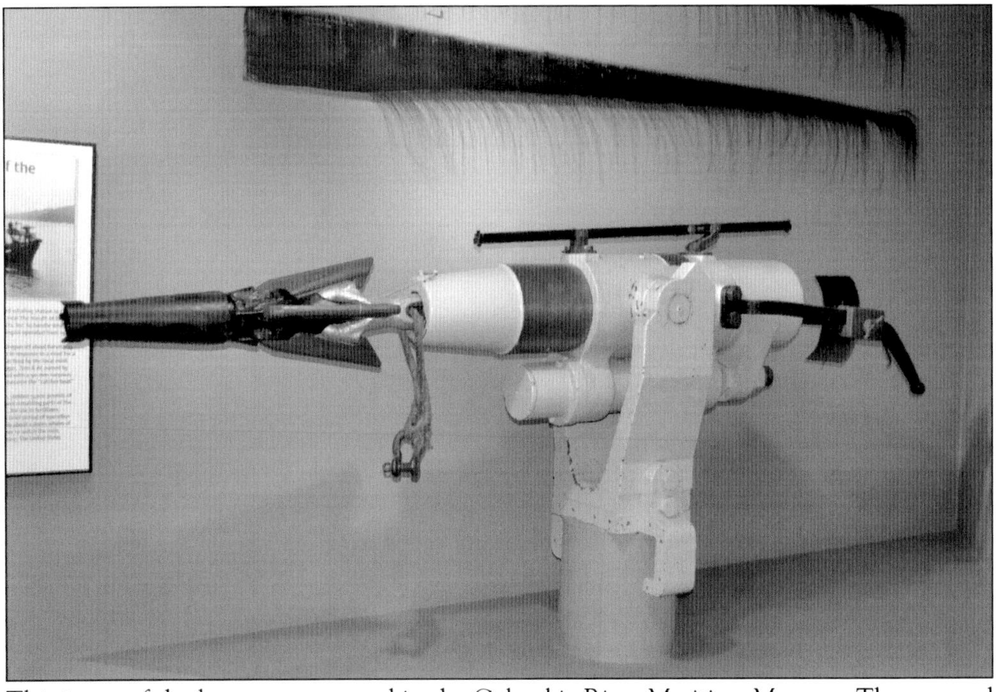

This is one of the harpoons mounted in the Columbia River Maritime Museum. The gun and harpoon are shown below long pieces of whale baleen. Most of the baleen whales taken by Bioproducts Inc. were humpback whales. Toothed whales, like sperm whales and the orca, do not have baleen. Most of the toothed whales taken by Bioproducts Inc. were sperm whales.

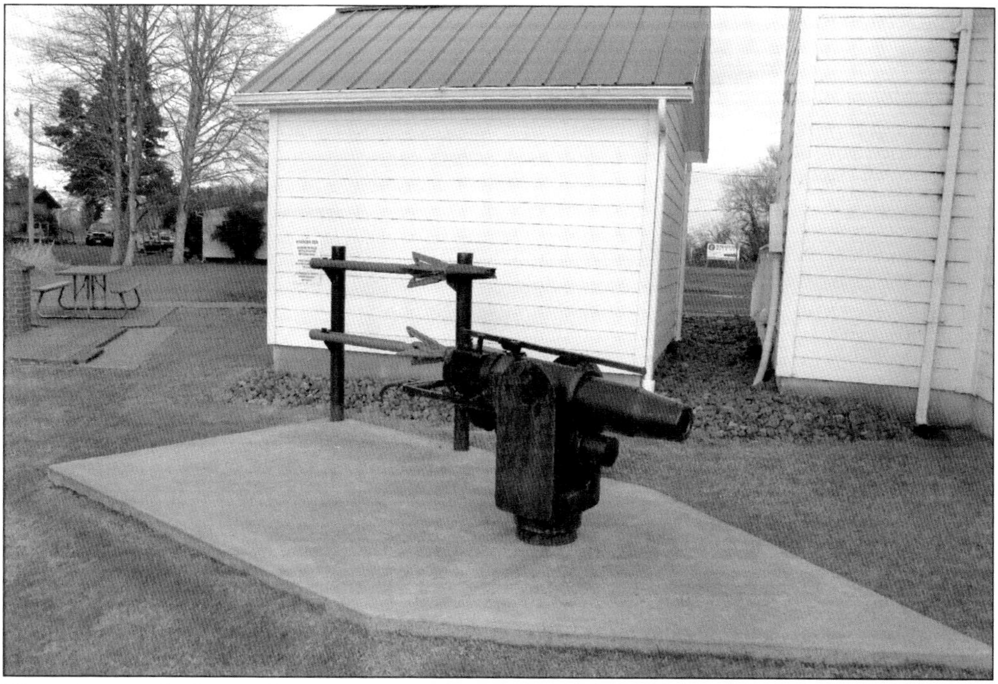

This photograph shows a harpoon gun and two harpoons, which were donated to the lighthouse park in Warrenton, Oregon. They are mounted next to a prominent intersection in town.

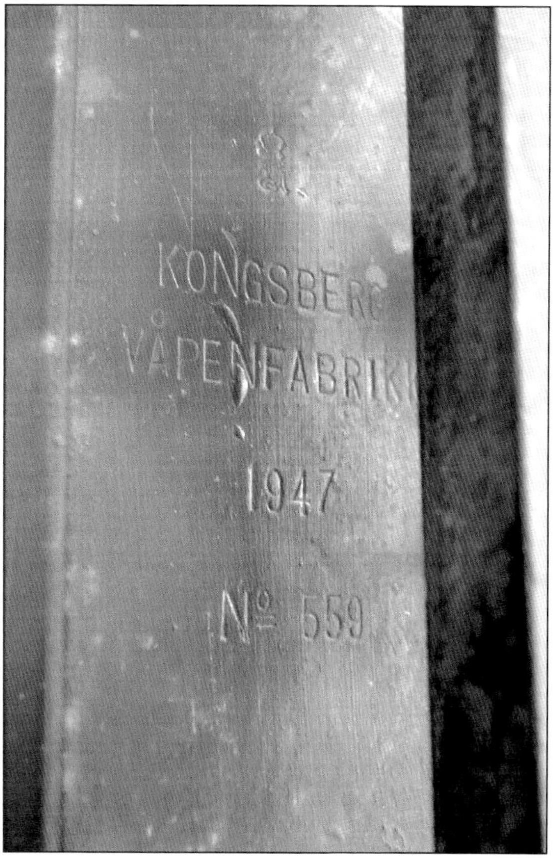

This photograph shows the identification plate on the gun. It reads, "Kongsberg Våpenfabrikk, 1947, No. 559." The guns were already 15 years old when they were purchased by Bioproducts Inc. They were probably used by another whaling company and sold in used condition by the company, or a broker that handled whaling gear.

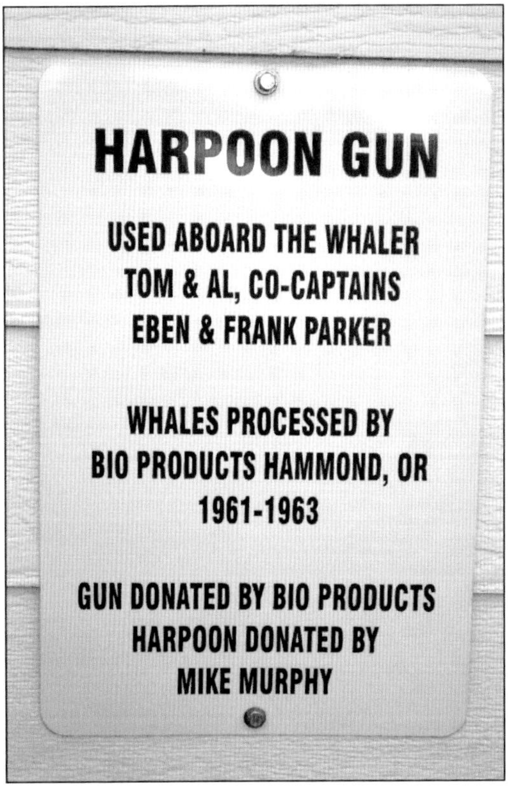

This sign is on display at Lighthouse Park in Warrenton. Eben and Frank Parker were co-owners of the *Tom & Al* and were paid for their efforts on a per-whale basis. The whales caught by the *Tom & Al* were actually processed between 1961 and 1965.

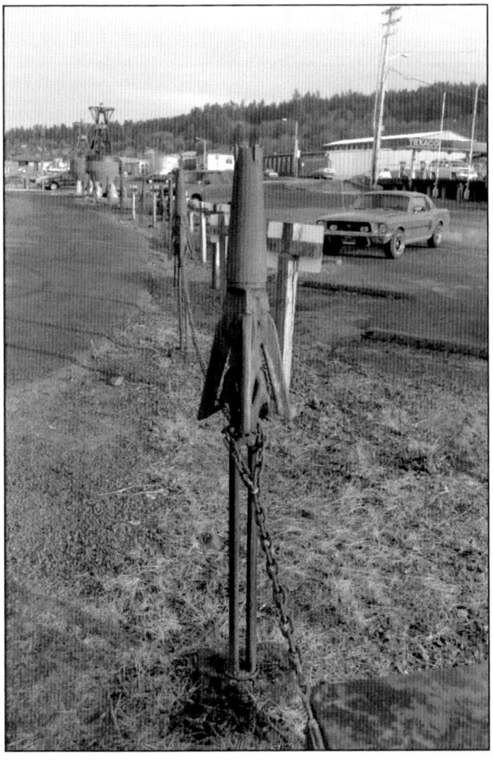

This line of whaling harpoons—connected with steel chain-links—is used to separate a Navy parking lot from a small road next to the Columbia River Maritime Museum. The harpoons are identical to the two at Lighthouse Park, and may have been leftover from Bioproducts Inc. How they came to be used at this Navy parking lot is a mystery.

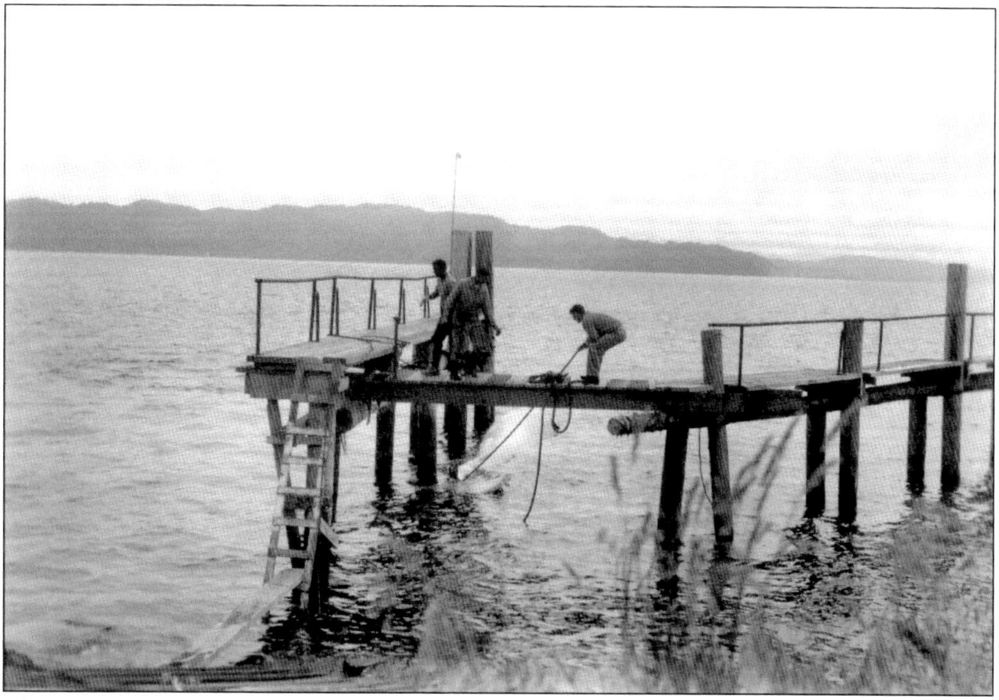

This is the dock on the Columbia River that whales were tied to when the *Tom & Al* brought them in. There is a whale on the line here, and it is being maneuvered toward shore so it can be brought onto land for flensing.

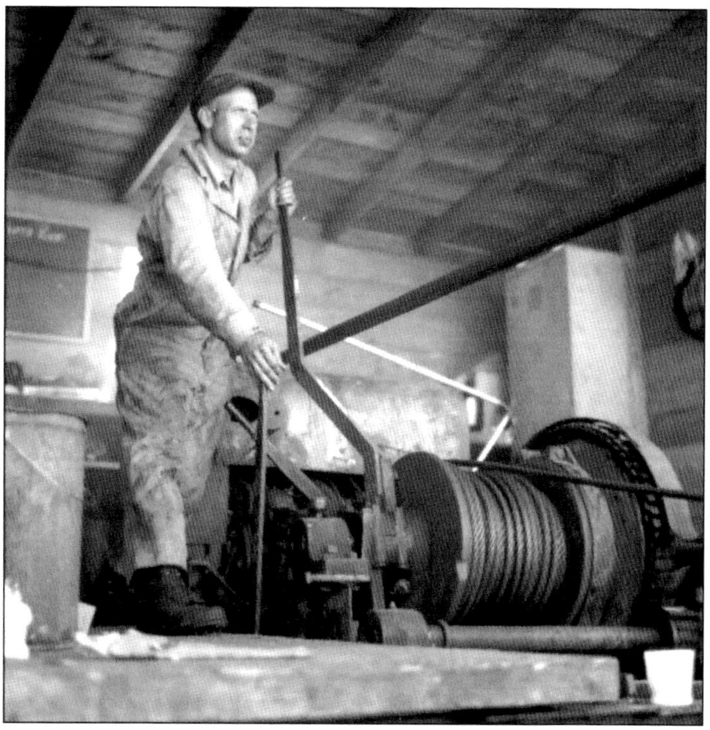

The whale was attached to a winch and slowly drawn up a ramp until it was ideally located for flensing.

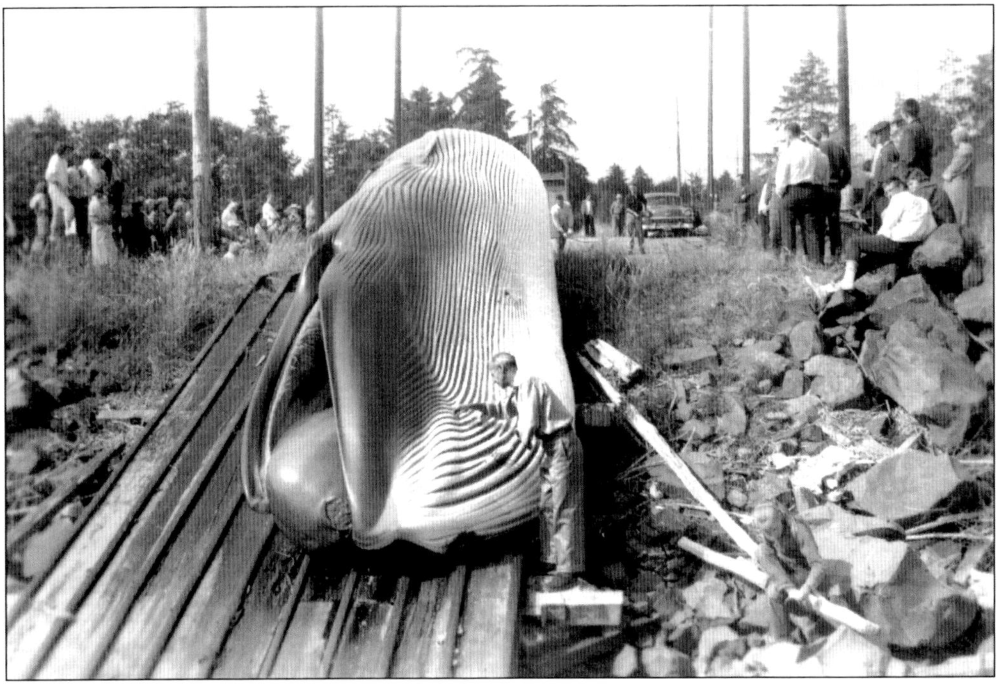

This finback whale is being dragged up a wooden ramp toward the flensing area. Note that the tongue has swollen due to the gasses released as the whale decomposes. The same whale is pictured below farther up the ramp and being used for a photo op.

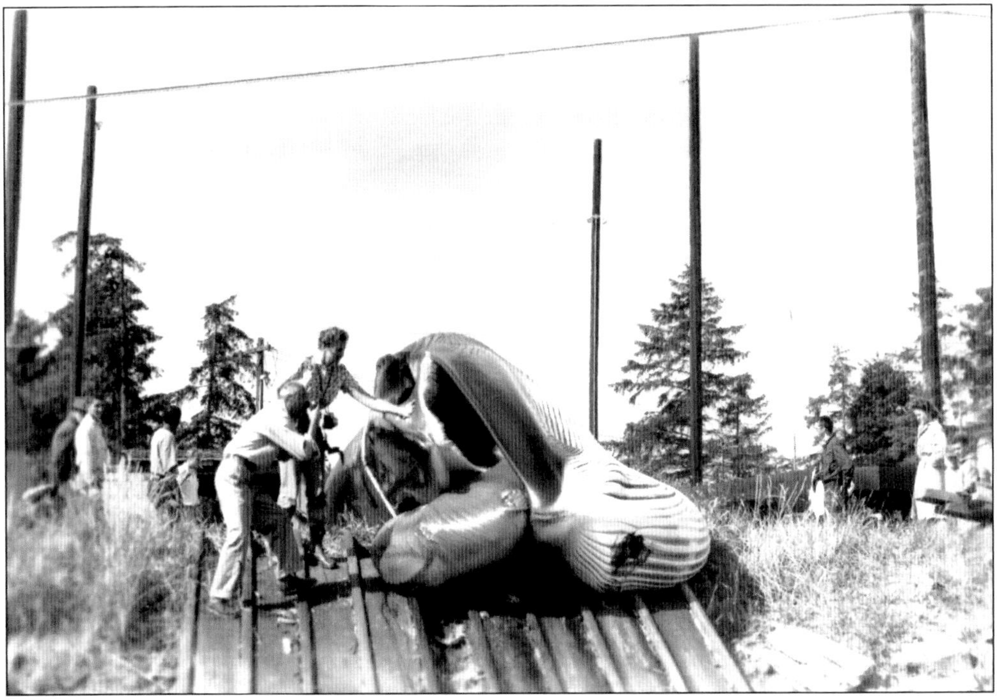

This humpback whale, identified by its long, winglike side fins, is being brought to the top of the ramp for flensing. Water was used to keep the surface wet and facilitate the flensing process.

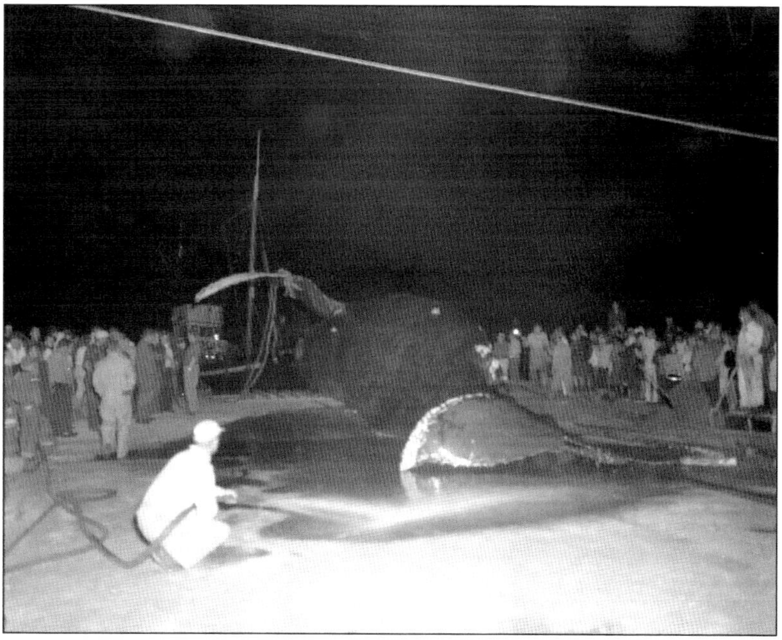

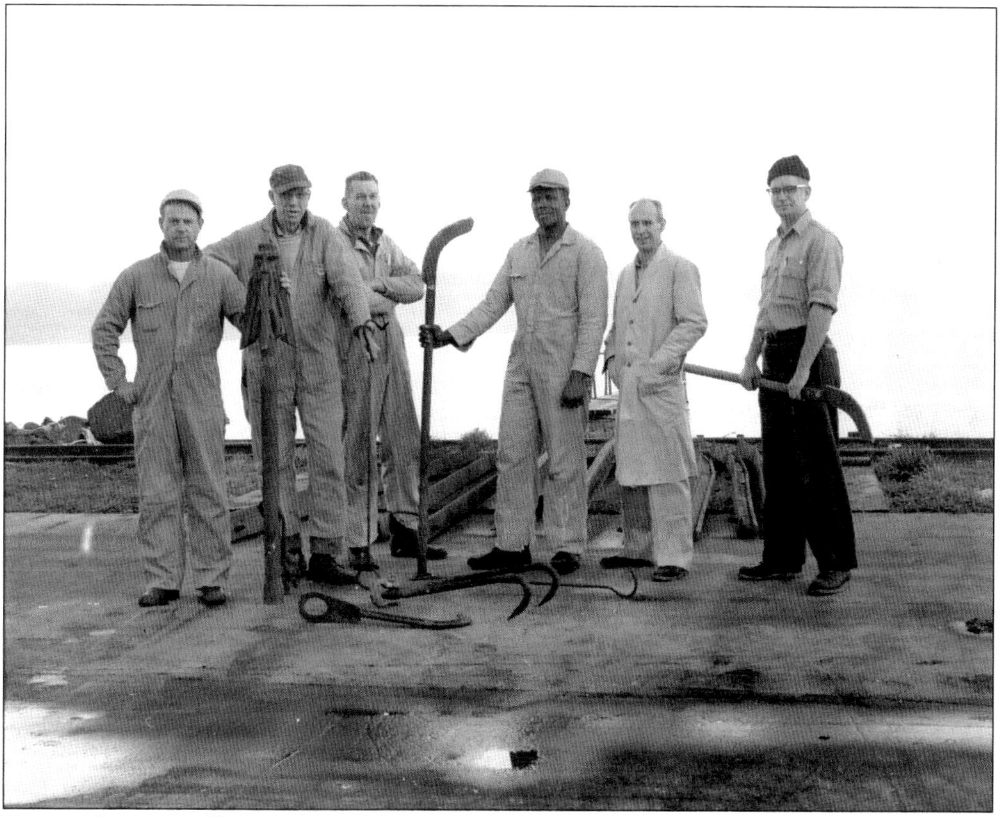

Pictured here is the flensing crew of the Bioproducts Inc. plant. Standing at far left is Alva Elliott, who was a gunner. The others are, from left to right, Harold Cunningham, Orvo Puppo, Mark Dozier, Lyle Anderson, and Richard Carruthers.

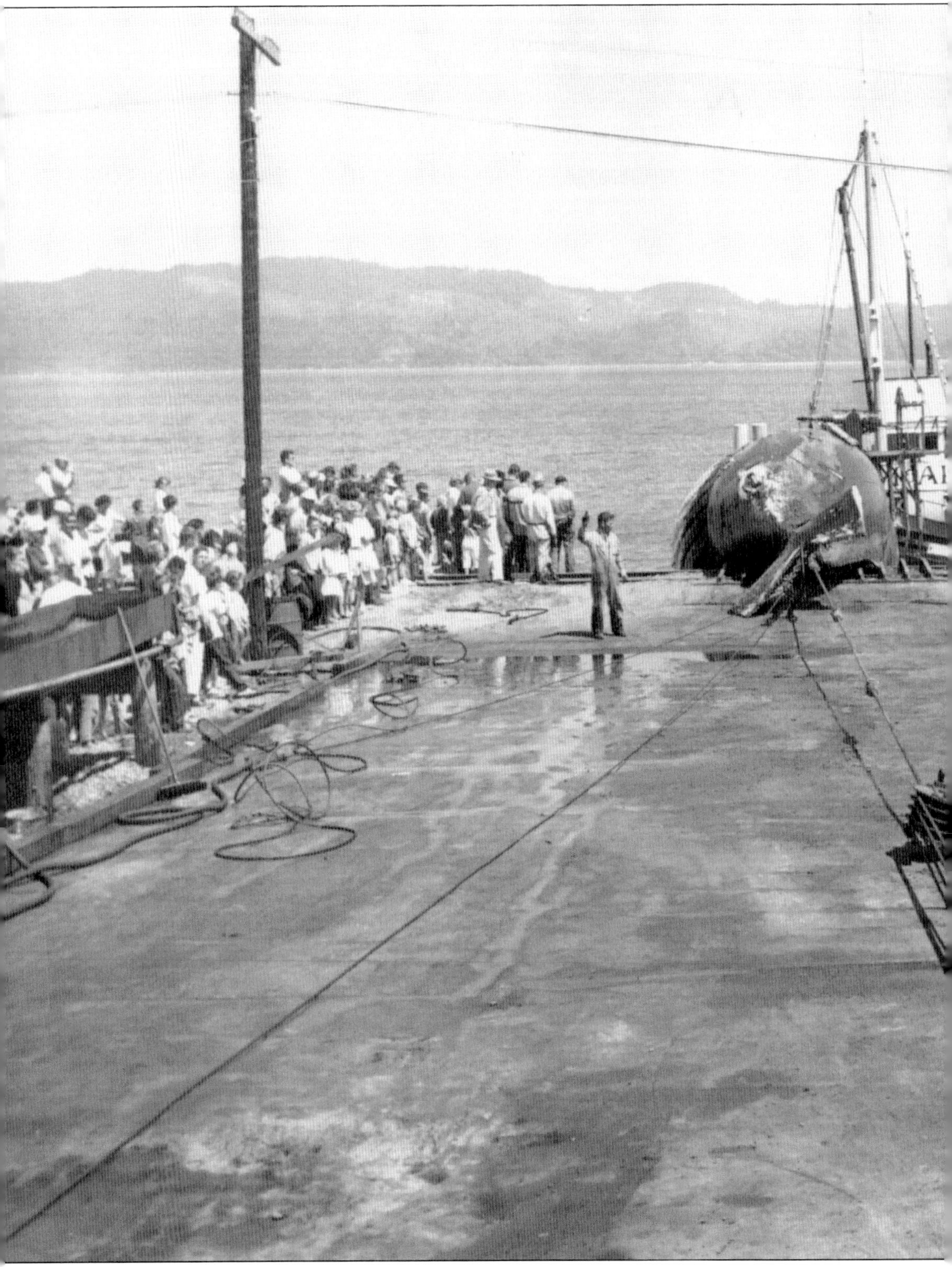

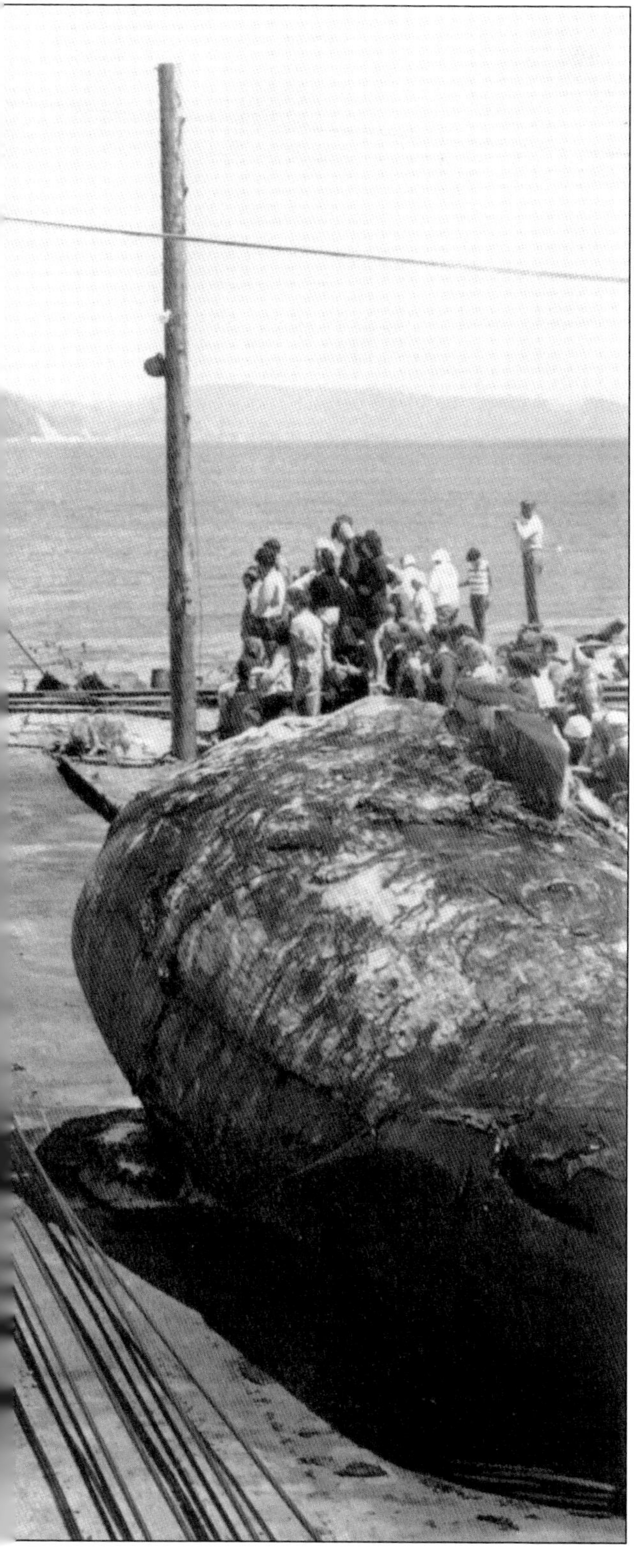

This photograph appears to show two sperm whales on the deck at Bioproducts Inc.—with one ready for flensing and the other still being brought up the ramp. The *Tom & Al*, which just brought the whales in, is in the background. When a whale was brought in, a bell was rung and crowds would gather to watch the process.

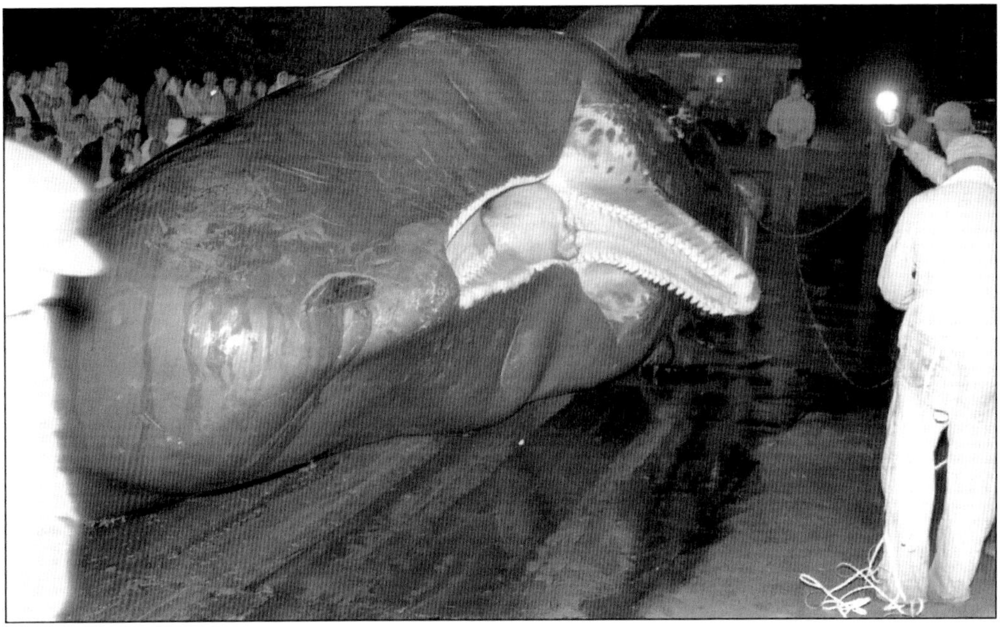

The mouth of a sperm whale, with its lower jaw full of teeth, is shown here. The swelling of the tongue is visible. The sperm whale was an especially important catch for the oil in its head. It was used to make what was probably the best machine oil available. It was also sold as sewing machine oil.

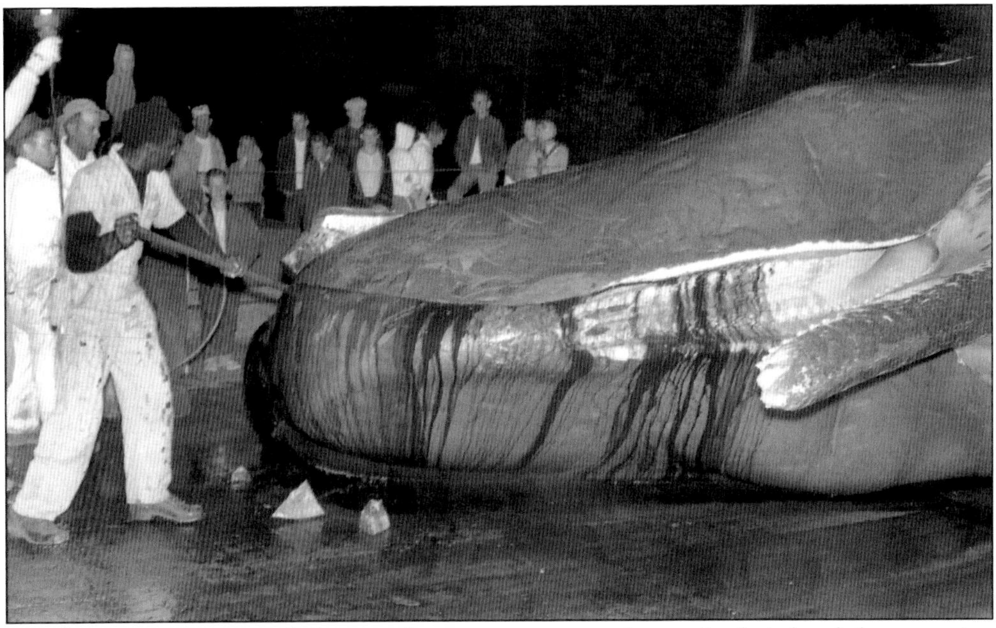

The first cut on a sperm whale is made to gain access to the sac in their head that contains the spermaceti. It was kept separate from other oils rendered from whales, as it brought in the most money.

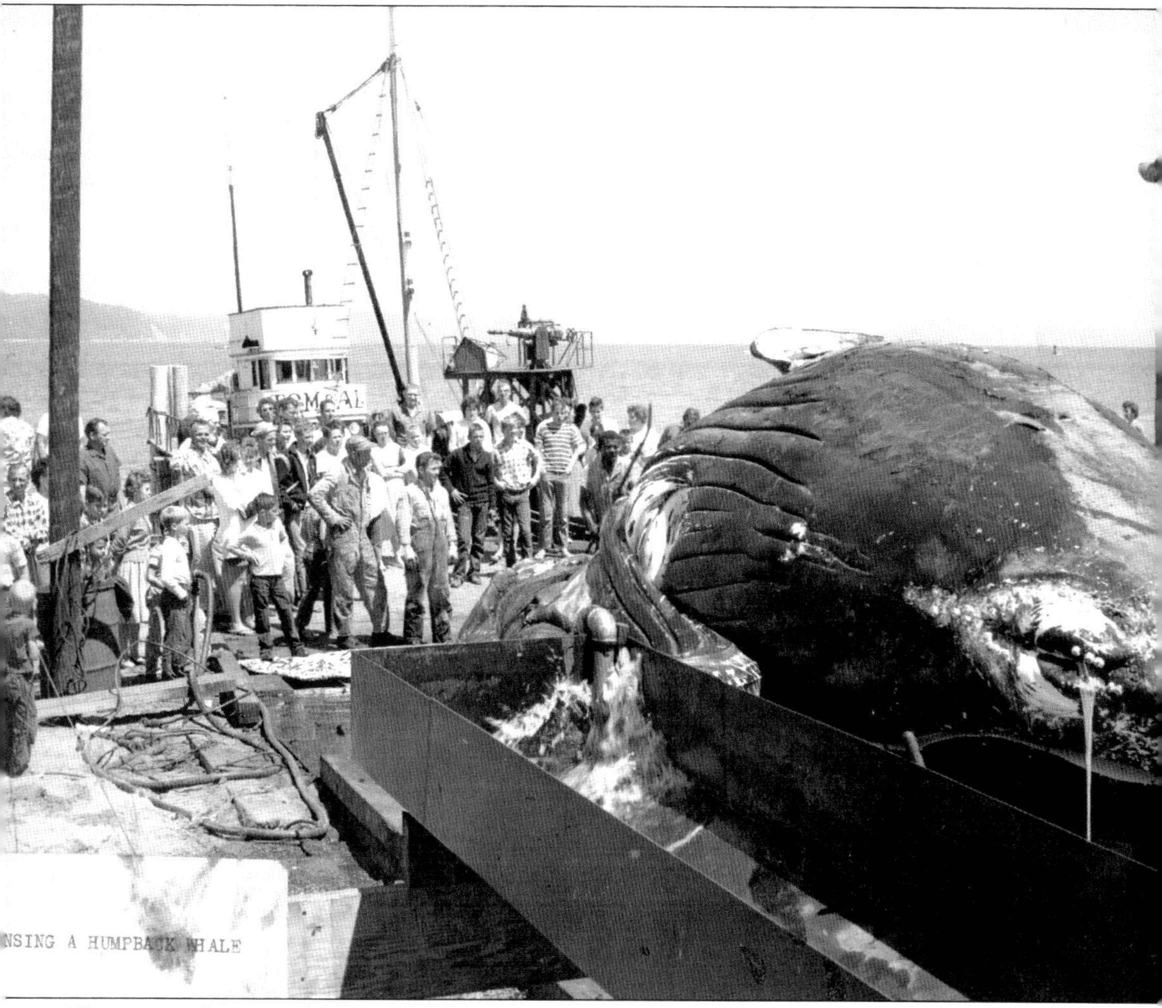

The crew is flensing a humpback whale in this photograph, while many people from the small town look on. The *Tom & Al* is visible in the background.

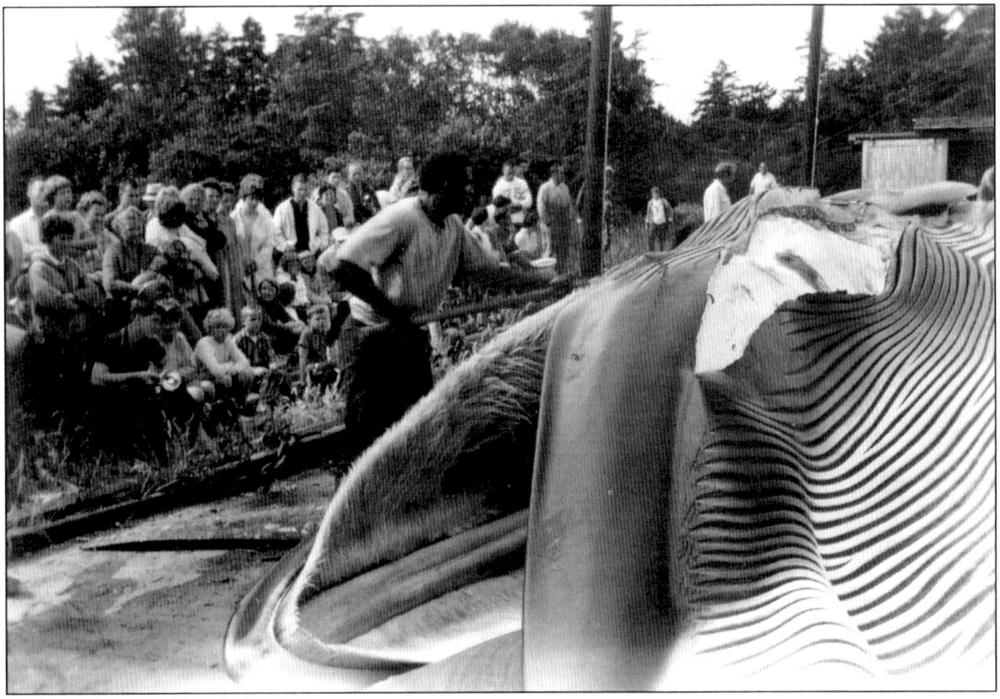

The first cuts on a baleen whale are to remove the fat, or blubber, and skin from the whale in long sheets, which can easily be cut up into smaller pieces. After the blubber and skin have been removed, the whalers have to get to the meat and bones. The whale will be disarticulated in the process and cut down for processing.

Jim Carruthers, president of Bioproducts, is pictured here—sitting in the mouth of a whale that has had its lower jaw removed. The white, feathery material to his right is baleen. The whale is probably a finback or a humpback.

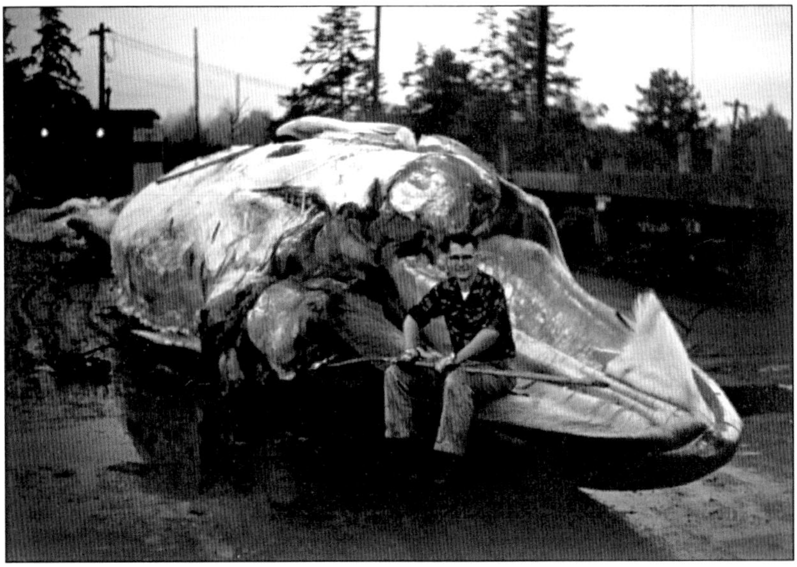

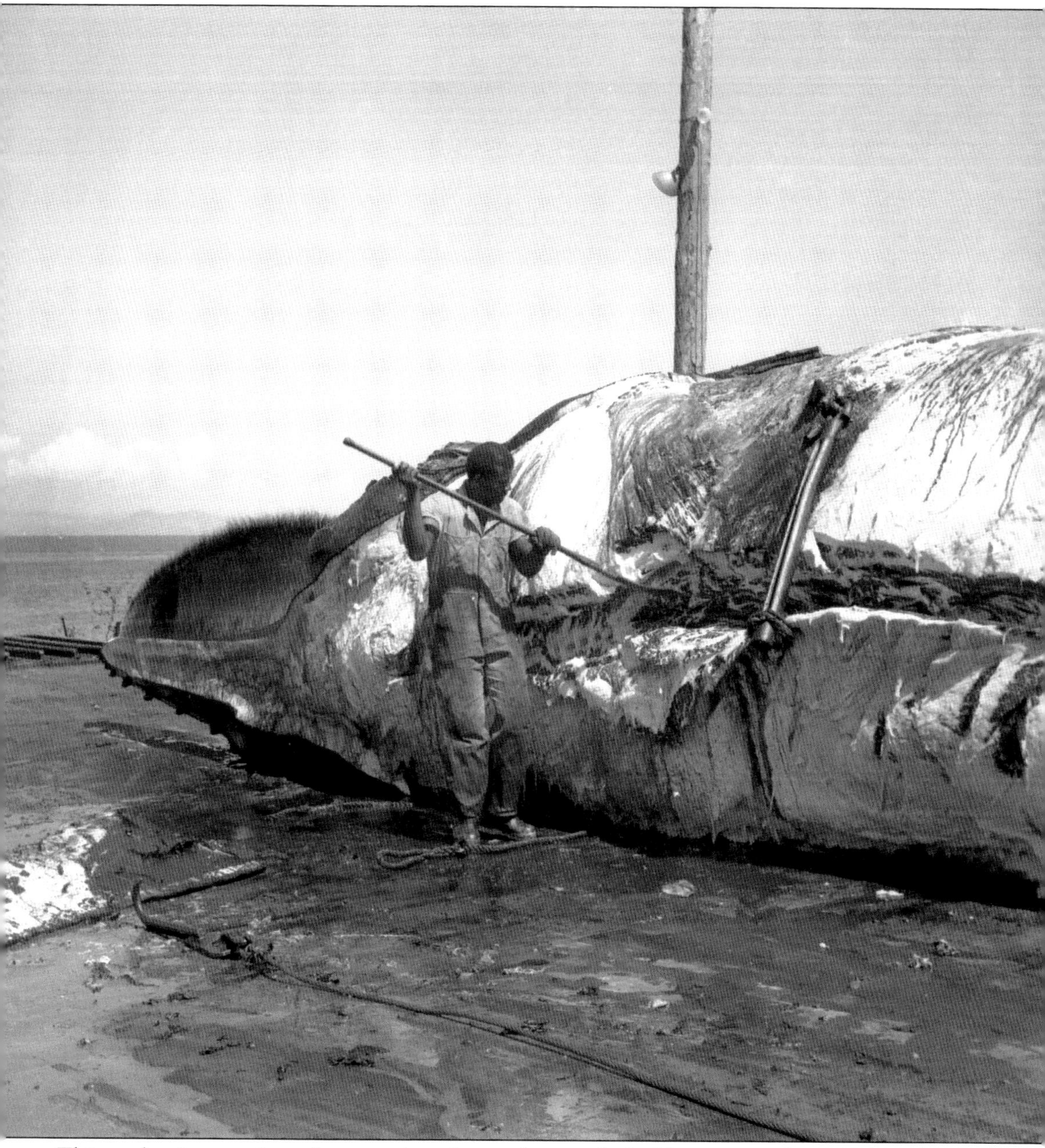

This worker is removing a large section of meat from a whale. He is using a long spade with a very sharp end.

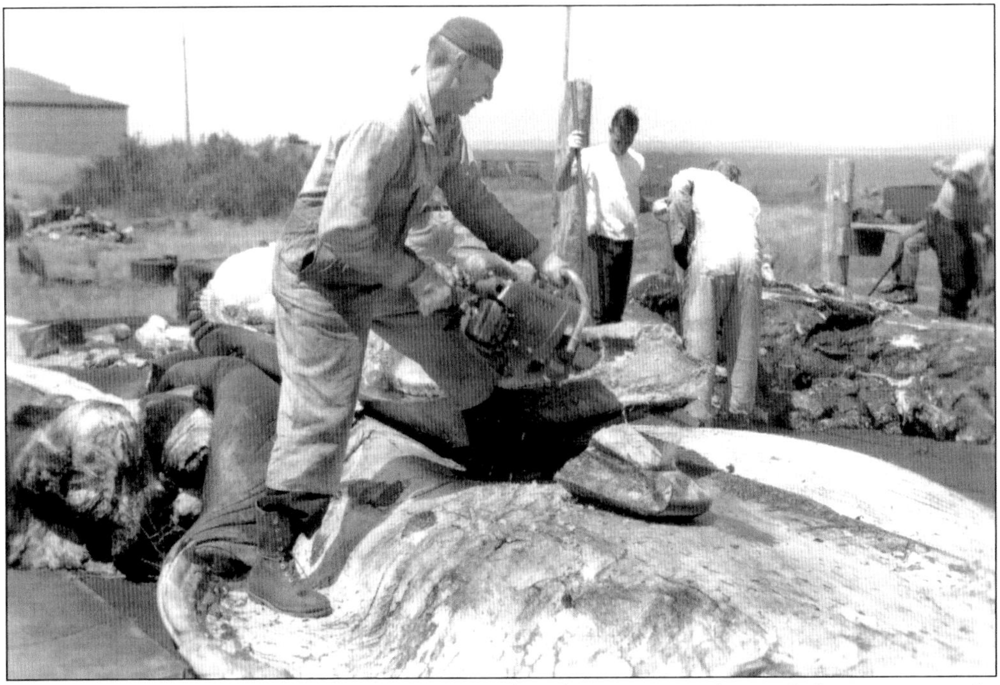

The company did not have a lot of money to spend on the equipment that a whaling station might traditionally have. Here, a chain saw is being used in place of a bone saw.

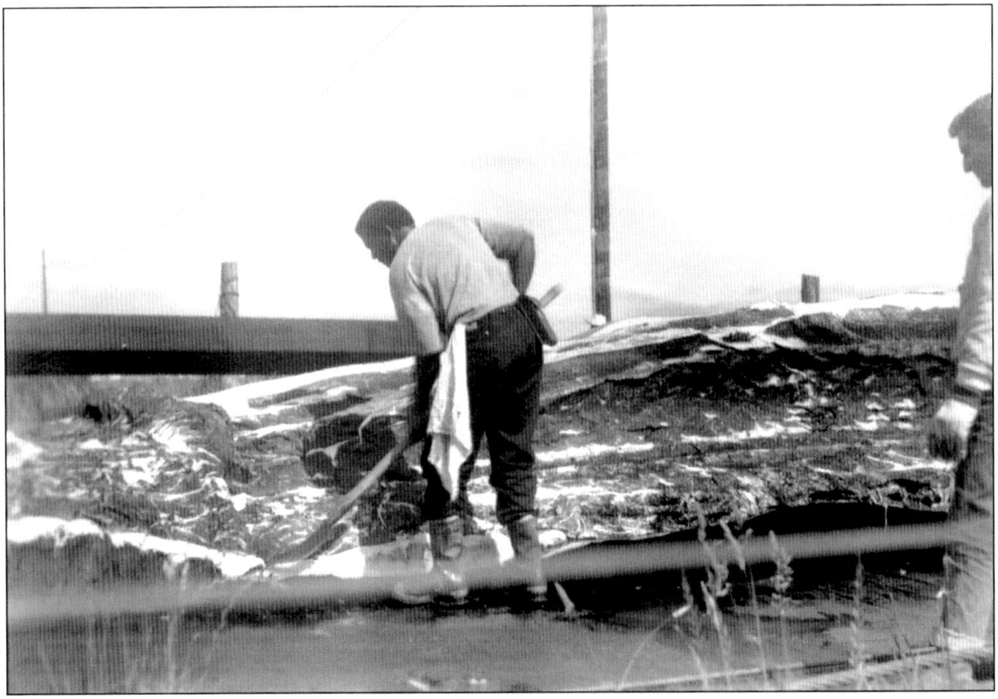

This section of meat has been removed from the whale and is being cut in smaller pieces. The best meat of the finback whale was sold for human consumption. This meat was popular during wartime rationing, but people went back to beef once it was available again.

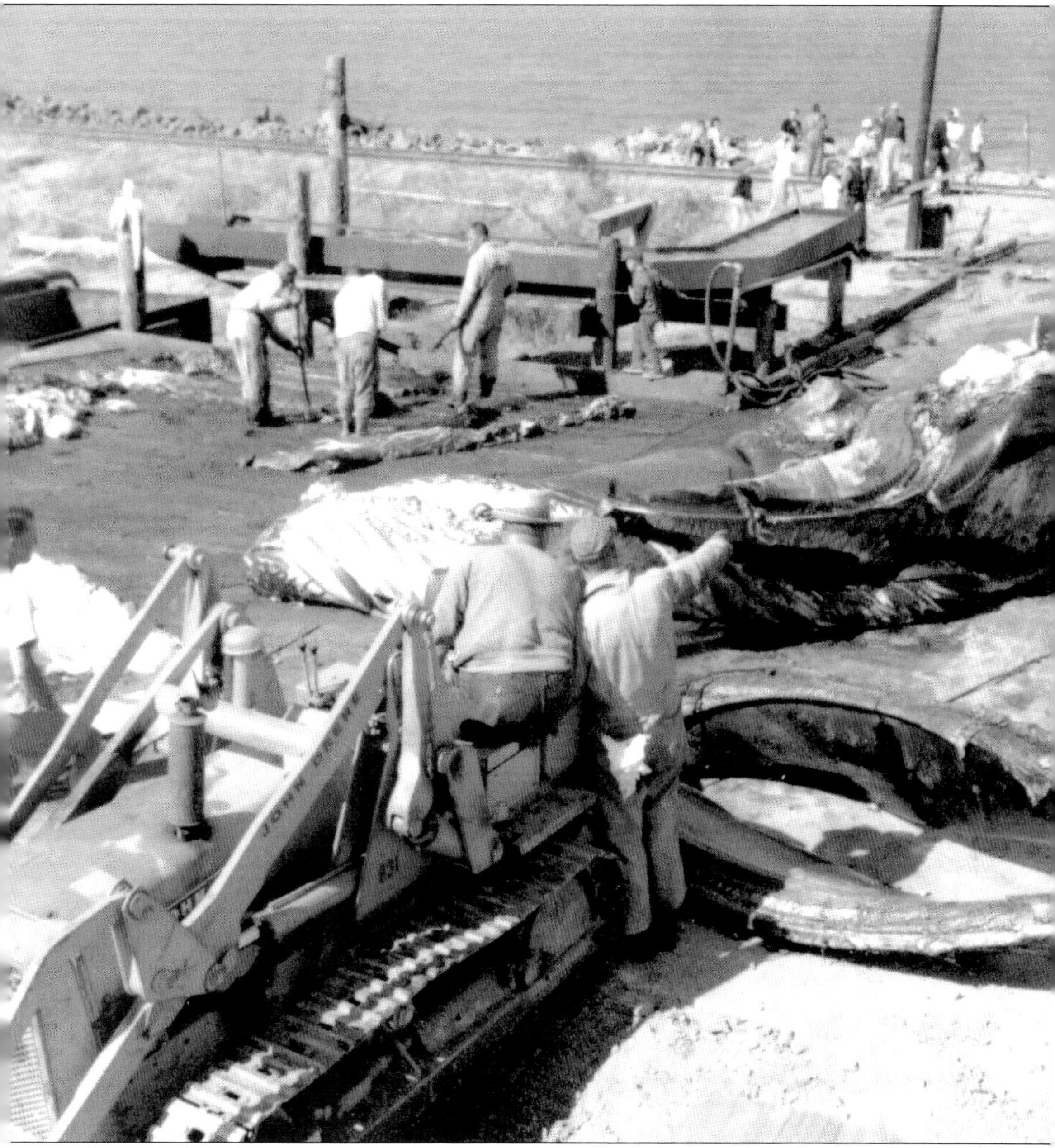

After a whale had been dissected, the company used a John Deere tractor to move the large pieces around the station.

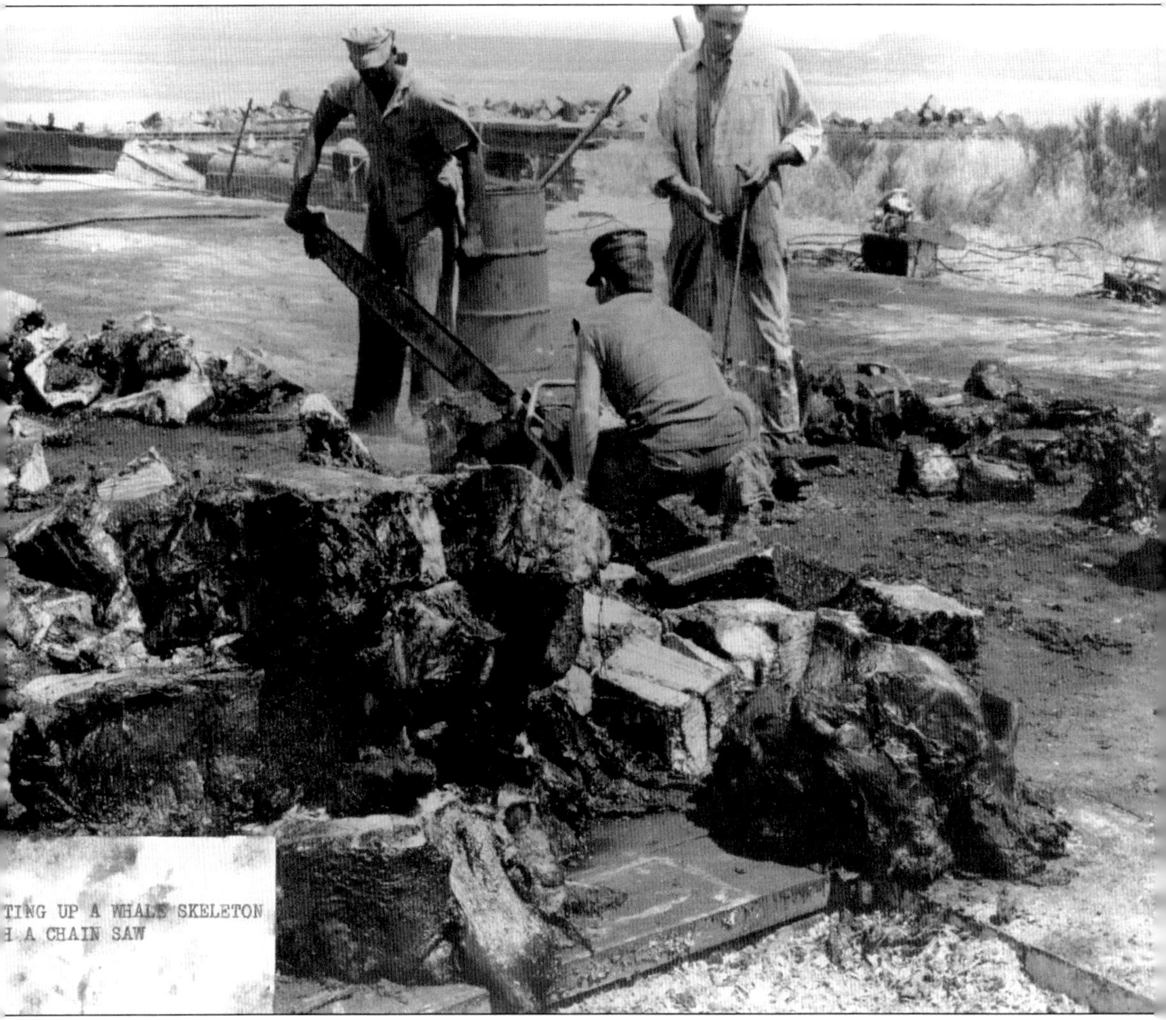

The note on this photograph says, "Cutting up a whale skeleton with a chainsaw." The bones and remaining meat would be ground up and made into fertilizer.

The president of the company, Richard Carruthers, is seen here—using a spade to cut sections of the meat up. Note that whale meat does not have marbled fat like beef or other common meats. This makes the meat very lean, and it needs some oil in the pan to fry it.

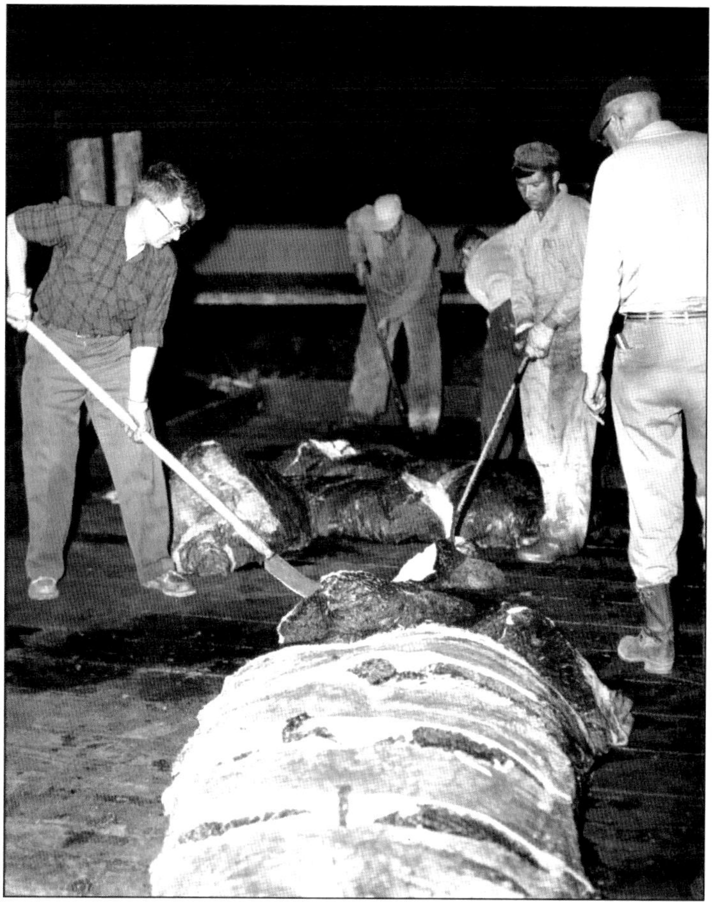

The carcass of this large humpback whale has had all of the blubber removed. The process of removing the meat would begin next.

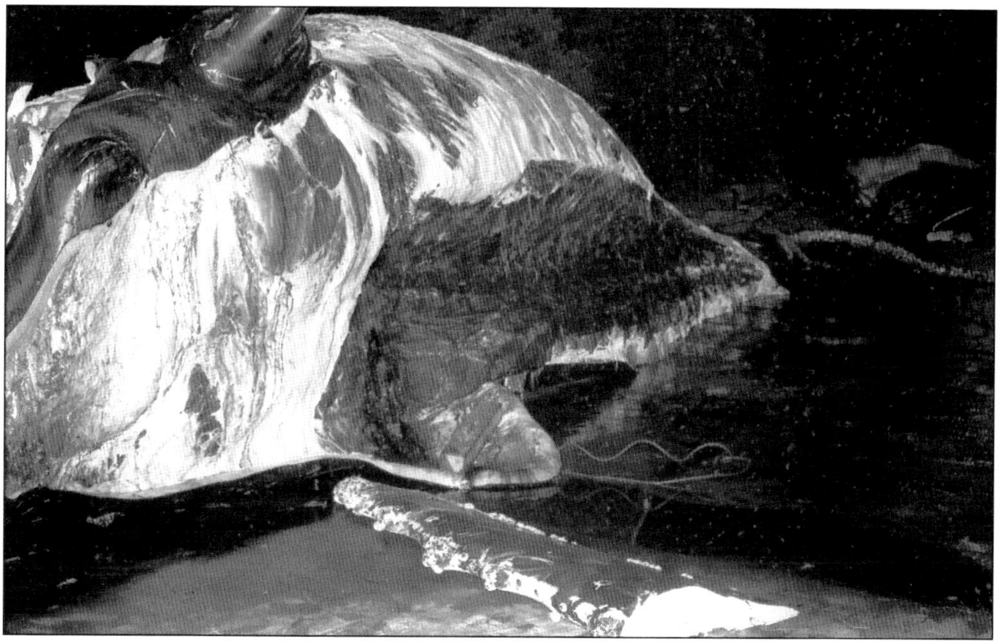

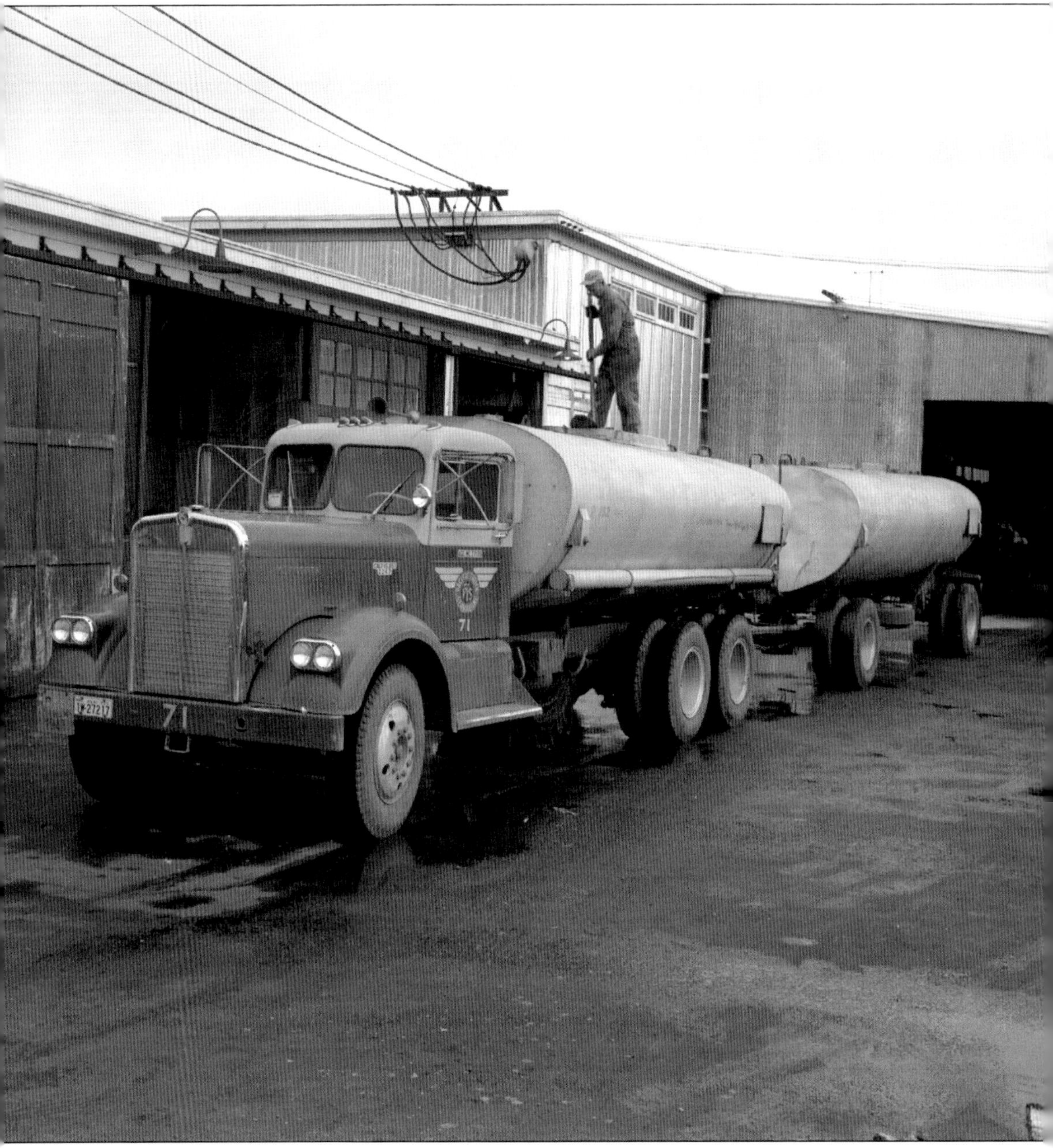

The meat was taken away in trucks and sent to the Oregon Fur Farmers Association, where it was cut into smaller pieces and frozen for sale to fur farmers. The oil was sold to the Mt. Hood Soap Company, which processed the oil into soap. At the time, the company was making bar soap for personal use, and it is likely that the whale oil was used in this soap.

Four

Early British Columbia Whaling

Starting in the 1880s, there were several developments in whaleboats, guns, and processing methods. Sven Foyn developed a steam-powered catcher boat that could keep up with the greater speeds of some whales—particularly the fin and blue whales. He also developed a larger harpoon gun that was mounted to the front of the whaleboat. This cannon fired a projectile with an explosive head, which improved the whale catch and kill statistics. Dr. Rismuller came from Newfoundland, where he had participated in the design of whale stations. In British Columbia, he continued to install these stations while improving his processes for utilizing the whole whale. Newfoundland had been a good testing ground for Foyn, Rismuller, and others' processes. With this new equipment, whalers and investors were anxious to start whaling in British Columbia again.

It was well known that a fast moving school of finback whales were available off the west coast of Vancouver Island. The sealers in this area were well acquainted with them. These men were also aware of Sven Foyn's advances in whaling technology. It was a couple of these sealers who first began planning to establish a whaling operation off of Vancouver Island. Capt. Sprott Balcom and William Grant, sealers from the area, created the Pacific Whaling Company in 1904.

The first whaling company on Vancouver Island, the Pacific Whaling Company (in the book *Whalers No More*, William Hagelund refers to it as the Canadian Pacific Whaling Company), was made up of two partners from the Victoria Sealing Company. Capt. Sprott Balcom and Capt. William Grant started their venture from the Victoria Sealing Company's dock in Victoria, British Columbia. Another man, Reuben Balcom, was sent to Norway to supervise the construction of a new whaling vessel. At Victoria, plans were underway to build a whaling plant similar to those in Newfoundland. The plant was built in Barclay Sound and became known as Sechart. Sechart began operations in 1905, with a new steamer named the *Orion*. Reuben's son Willis was the captain of the vessel and returned with 300 whales in 1905.

Balcom and Grant also opened stations at Kyuquot and Pages Lagoon. Balcom and Grant were looking to expand their business and were working to combine with the Prince Rupert Whaling Company and the Queen Charlotte Whaling Company. These two companies had acquired whaling licenses, and while Sprott Balcom controlled most licenses, he wanted these also. When stock offerings on these companies became available, Balcom purchased a major interest in each company. By these means, Balcom could acquire these companies. It has been speculated that Balcom had friends or acquaintances apply for the whaling licenses for these companies, in which Balcom quickly bought a controlling interest. To supply the stations with whales, a number of older steamers were purchased from Newfoundland—where the catch of whales had been declining. They acquired the *St. Lawrence*, and the oldest whalers *Germania* and *San Sebastian*. After this, Balcom and Grant started making plans to build four more whaling stations and purchase six more steam whalers.

By 1910, there had been changes in the sealing industry—in which Balcom and Grant were heavily invested. They started looking for investors and finally sold out their whaling assets to McKenzie and Mann when investors could not be found. McKenzie and Mann were building the Canadian Railway and were planning to ship coal east for further investment. They continued to operate the Canadian North Pacific Fisheries in 1910 and also operated the stations at Sechart, Kyuquot, Rose, and Naden Harbors under this parent company. They also incorporated the American Pacific Whaling Company and its associated whaling station in Bay City, Washington.

In 1911, Mackenzie and Brown went to Europe to raise capital, and—in the spring—began accepting their remaining "killer" ships, the *Blue* and *Brown*, as they arrived at Victoria. The company continued to do very well until the end of 1913, when over 4,000 whales had been landed and there was a glut of whale products on the market. Petroleum products were also well established by then, and were beginning to decrease in price. Mackenzie and Mann were also experiencing trouble in their railroad and coal businesses. The country was slipping toward depression as land prices had fallen, and Mackenzie and Mann's whaling companies were confronting race issues due to their practice of hiring Chinese and East Indian workers when angry white workers could not find work. In 1914, World War I began and—due to all of these reasons—the whaling industry was beginning to falter.

By 1915, the whaling company and its sources of financing had failed completely, and one man stepped up to try to buy it. William Schupp had been in the whaling business for only a couple of years when he stepped in to buy the Alaska Whaling Company—with its station at Akutan—from its Norwegian owners and renamed it the North Pacific Sea Products Company. Schupp had done well during the war, securing licenses to sell whale products in Canada and the United States.

Schupp was able to buy Mackenzie and Mann's whaling business and start whaling operations at the Kyuquot and Naden Harbor stations before the end of the 1915 season. He even managed to pay off the company's debt by year's end, thanks to a vibrant wartime market. In *Whalers No More*, Hagelund says that, "In the last two years of the war, Schupp's whaling venture annually grossed over a million dollars, more than five times the price he paid Yorkshire Securities."

After the wartime economy had receded, the whaling business settled into a very tight economy. Schupp was a frugal owner, not spending money unless absolutely necessary. This helped the business continue for many years, and though it was not always profitable, it provided employment to many in a time when many companies could not say the same.

Schupp eventually put all of his companies together under the umbrella of the Consolidated Whaling Corporation of Seattle. These companies included the North Pacific Sea Products, with the Akutan, Alaska station and Port Hobron; The American Pacific Whaling Company, with its station at Bay City; and the Victoria Whaling Company, with the stations at Sechart, Kyuquot, Rose, and Naden Harbor. A few years later, Schupp reorganized the companies again, naming them The Consolidated Whaling Company of Victoria, and the American Pacific Whaling Company.

Leading into World War II, Akutan was strafed and bombed, and naval restrictions were put in place west of Vancouver Island. Japanese workers were interned, and naval vessels were placed at strategic points near the entrances to the inland waterways. Rose Harbor operated for a little while in 1942, and then all operations ceased. Vessels and equipment rotted away during the long war years, and there was no attempt at upkeep. In 1947, attempts were made to go whaling, but none of the ships could pass inspection and loans from the 1930s were called in. As a result, the vessels were seized and auctioned off in order to pay the debts. Schupp died in 1948, a few months after his empire crumbled.

This is the harpoon gun on a Canadian whaler. Note the strap that binds the barbs together until the harpoon enters the whale. The heavy rope coiled on the deck allows the whale to run, but tethers it to the boat with a long line. Eventually, the whale tires and a winch will start to bring him in—much like in traditional fishing.

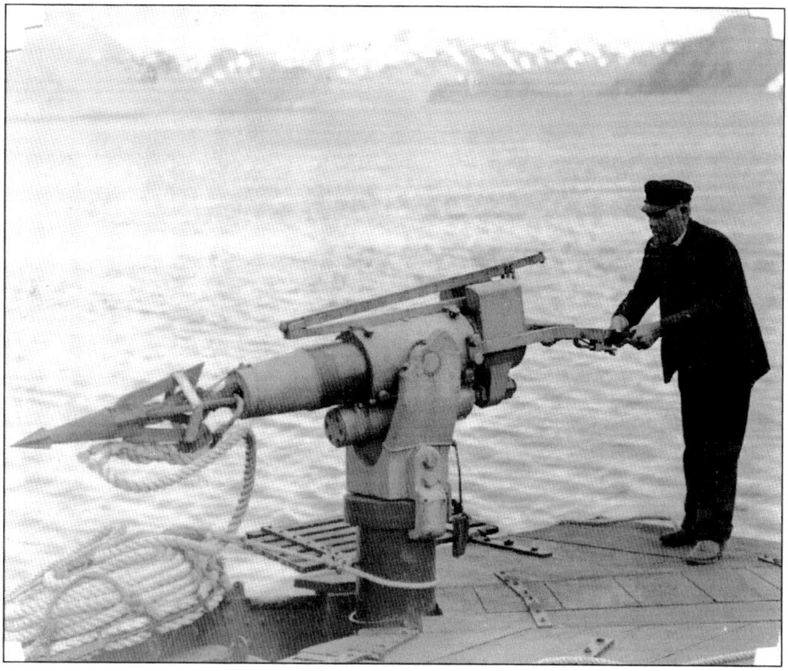

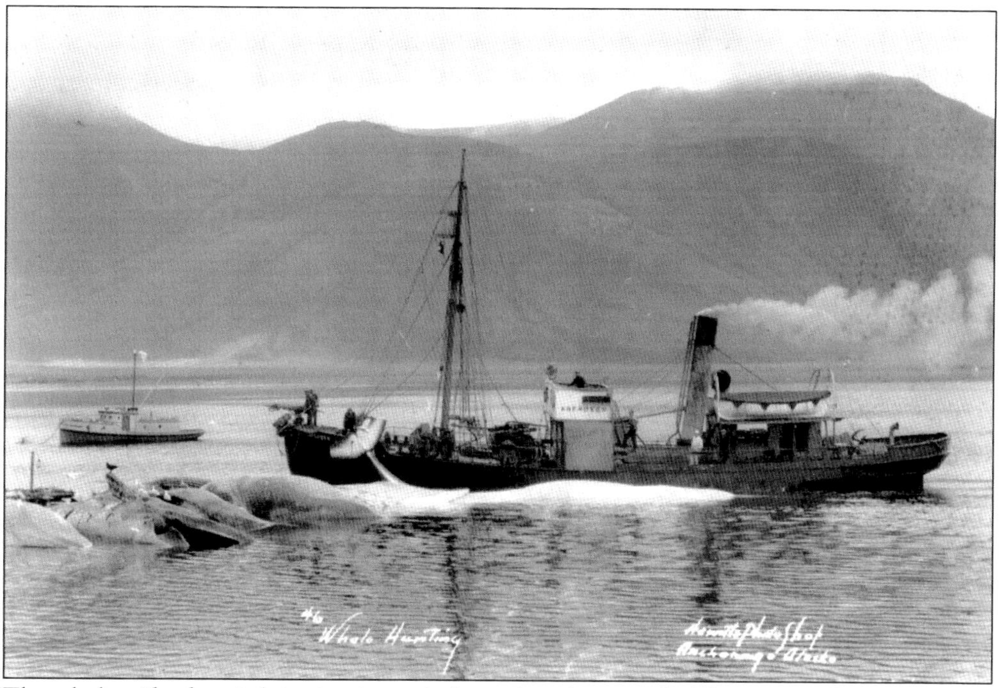

The whaler *Aberdeen* is bringing in a whale in this photograph. There are at least six whales already waiting to be processed. The *Aberdeen* was built and entered service in 1912. She was 88 feet long and 19 feet wide.

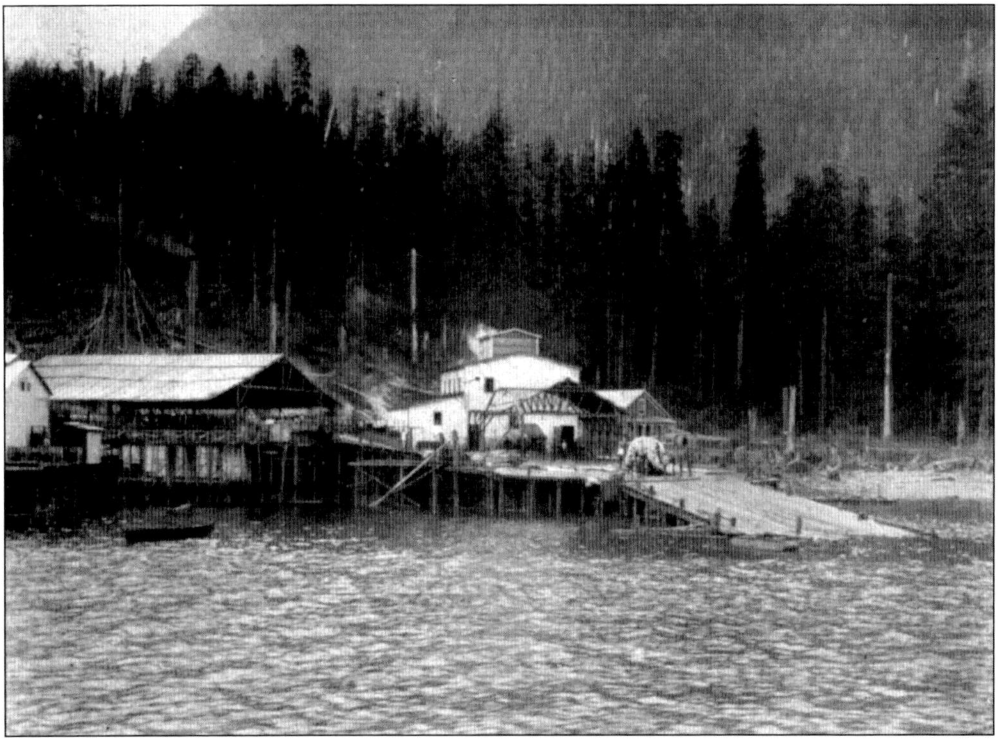

The whaling station on Page's Lagoon was five miles north of Nanaimo. The station was used in shore whaling as a place to flense whales, and a tryworks could be built there for boiling oil. The Nanaimo whaling station was built in 1907 by Sprott Balcolm. The station was not very successful and was abandoned. It was sold to a land speculator in 1912.

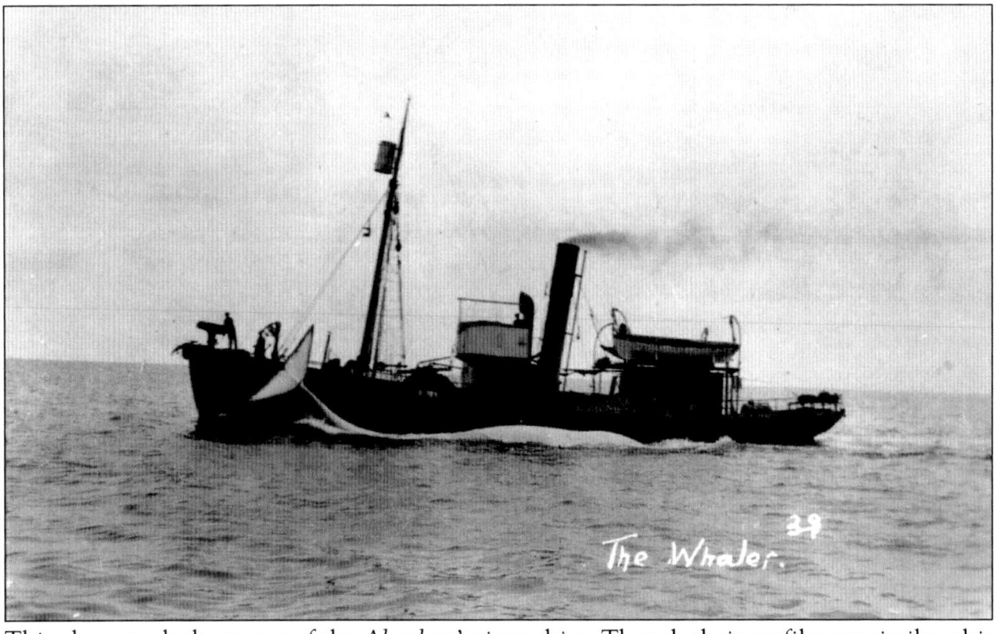

This photograph shows one of the *Aberdeen*'s sister ships. Though their profiles are similar, this ship does not have some of the *Aberdeen*'s distinctive markings.

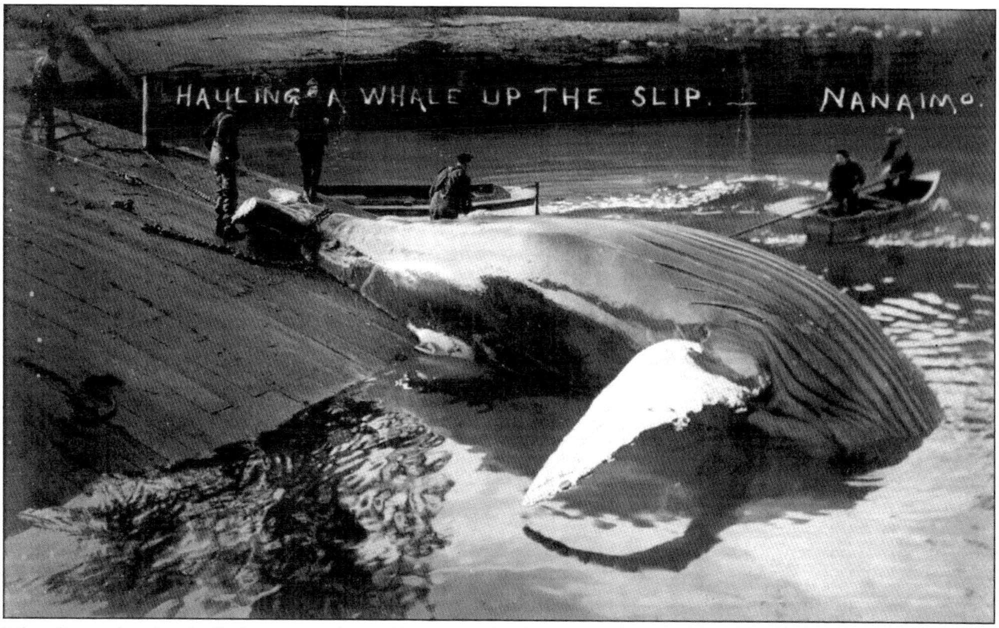

This humpback whale has been brought in to the Nanaimo station, and it lies at the foot of the ramp. This is an early photograph, from between 1907 and 1911.

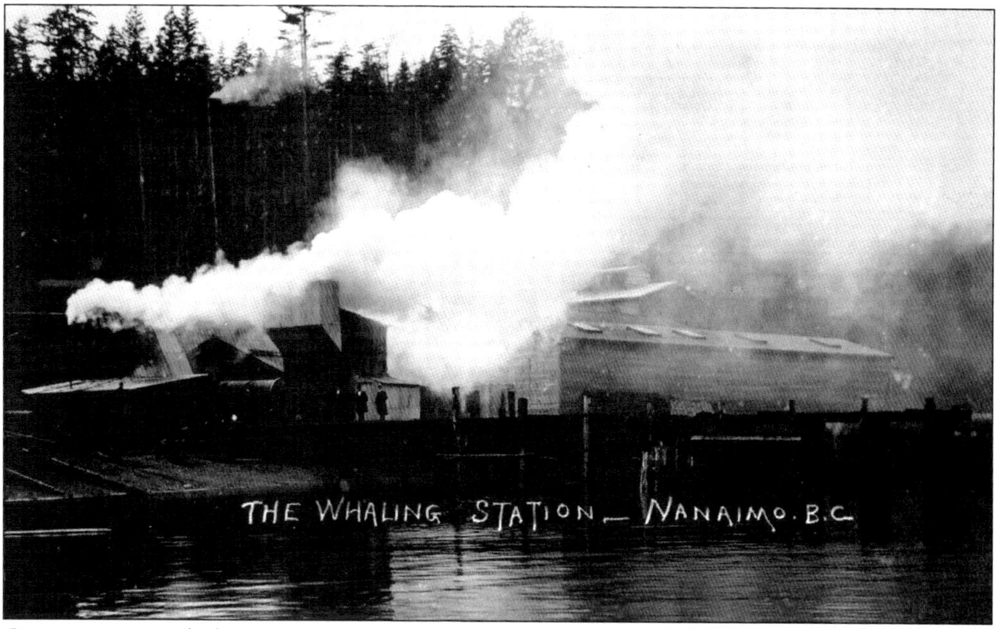

Cutting into a whale at one of the early stations in British Columbia was hard work—and messy too!

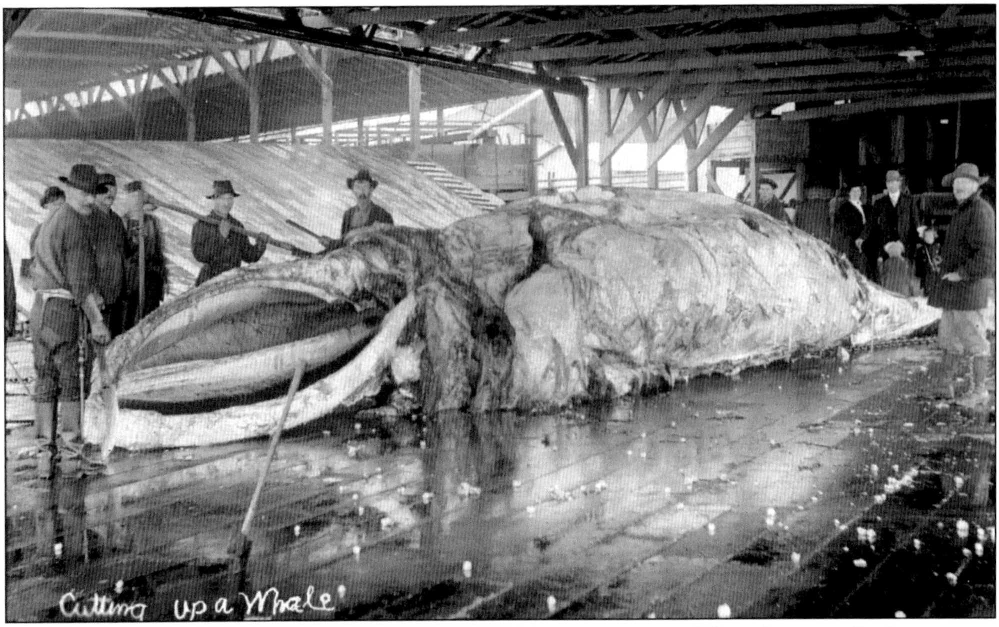

This photograph shows a California gray whale, and the crew that is flensing it. The blubber has been removed, and the crew will soon remove the meat and break up the bones.

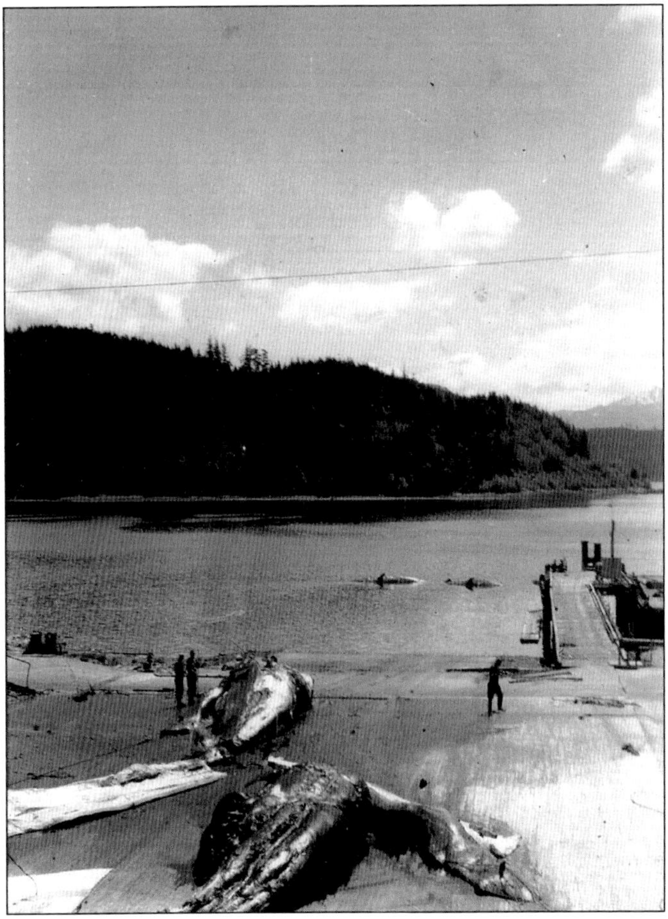

A Vancouver Island whaling station is seen here. There are two whales on the ramp, and two more in the water. One of the whales has had about half of its blubber removed in a single piece.

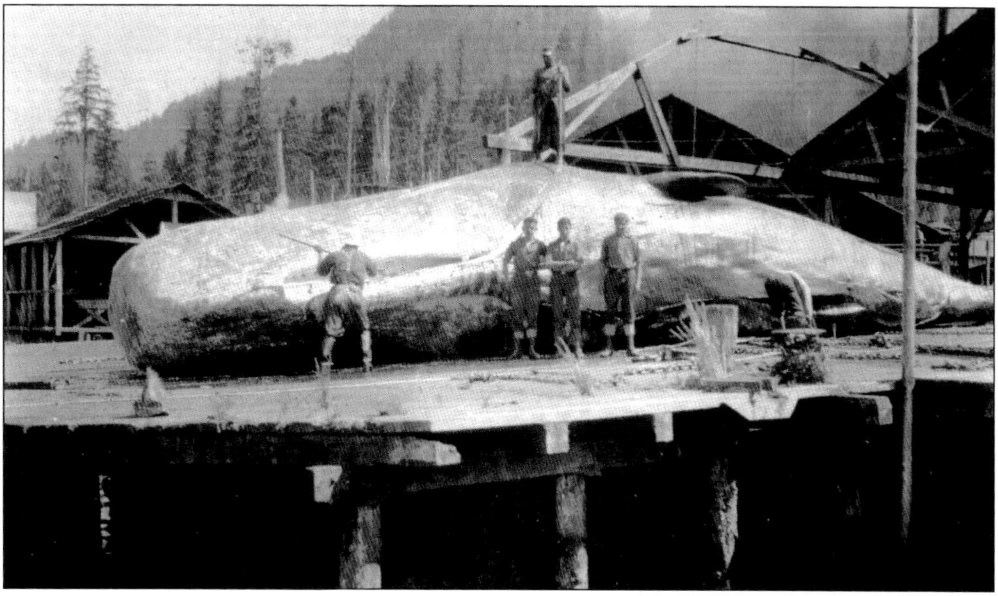

The sperm whale on this platform is ready to be flensed. In photographs like this, the head flenser normally poses on top of the whale in the center with his flensing tool—as seen here. It is his responsibility to make the first major cuts into the whale, which will allow the blubber to come off in several very large pieces.

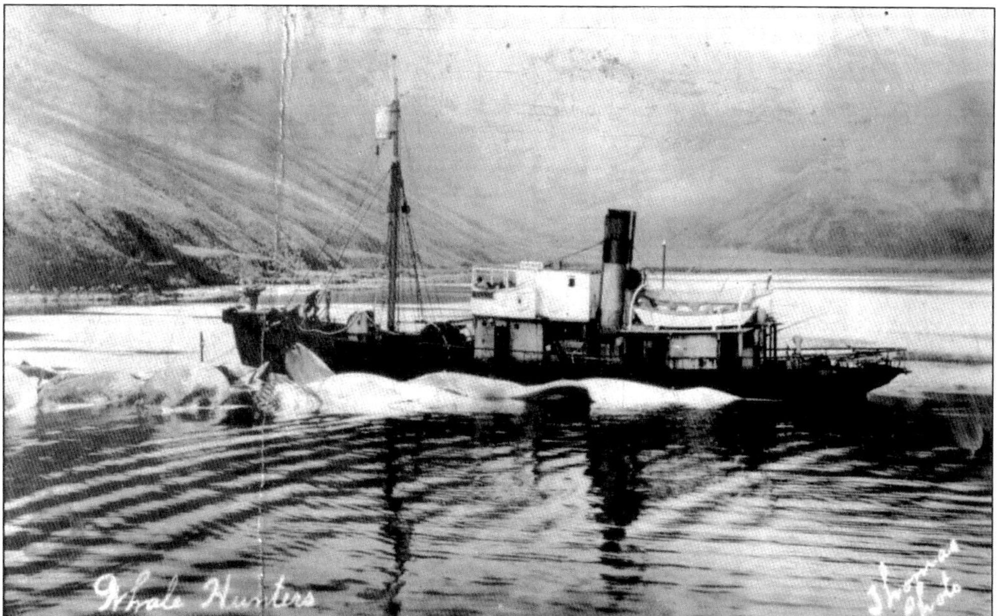

The whaler in this photograph is unidentified, but features a large secondary cabin to the aft of the main cabin. This may be unique among Pacific Northwest whalers.

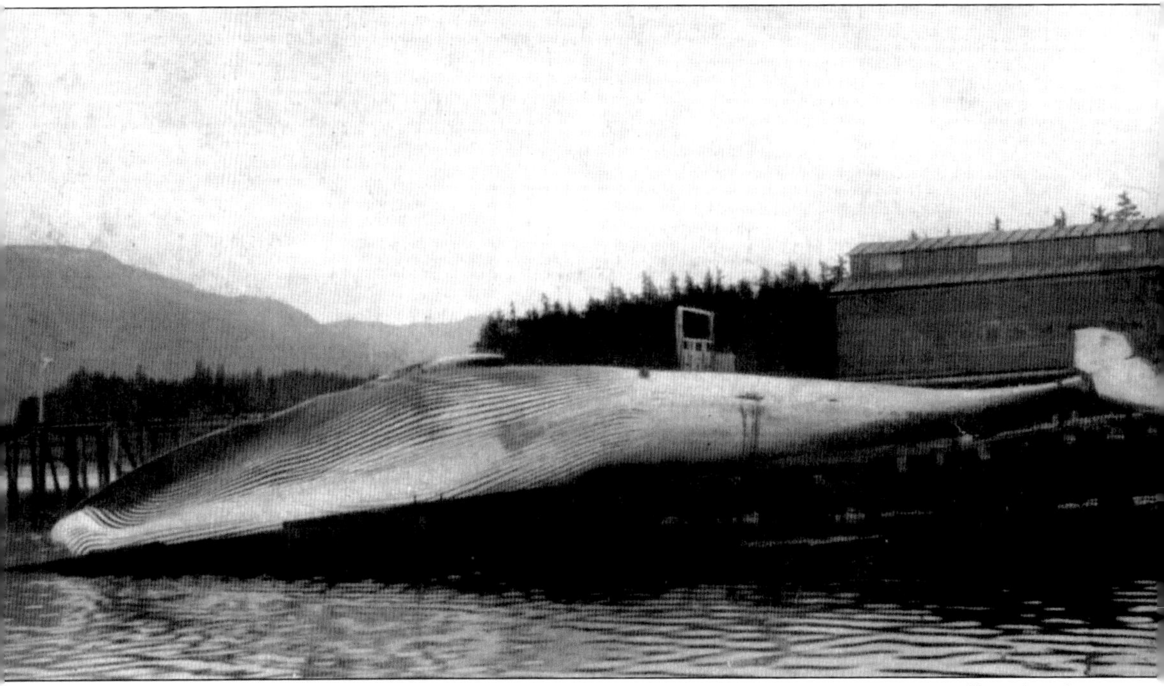

This photograph shows a humpback whale on the platform. The picture was originally taken by Roy Chapman Andrews of the American Museum when he visited the area around 1920.

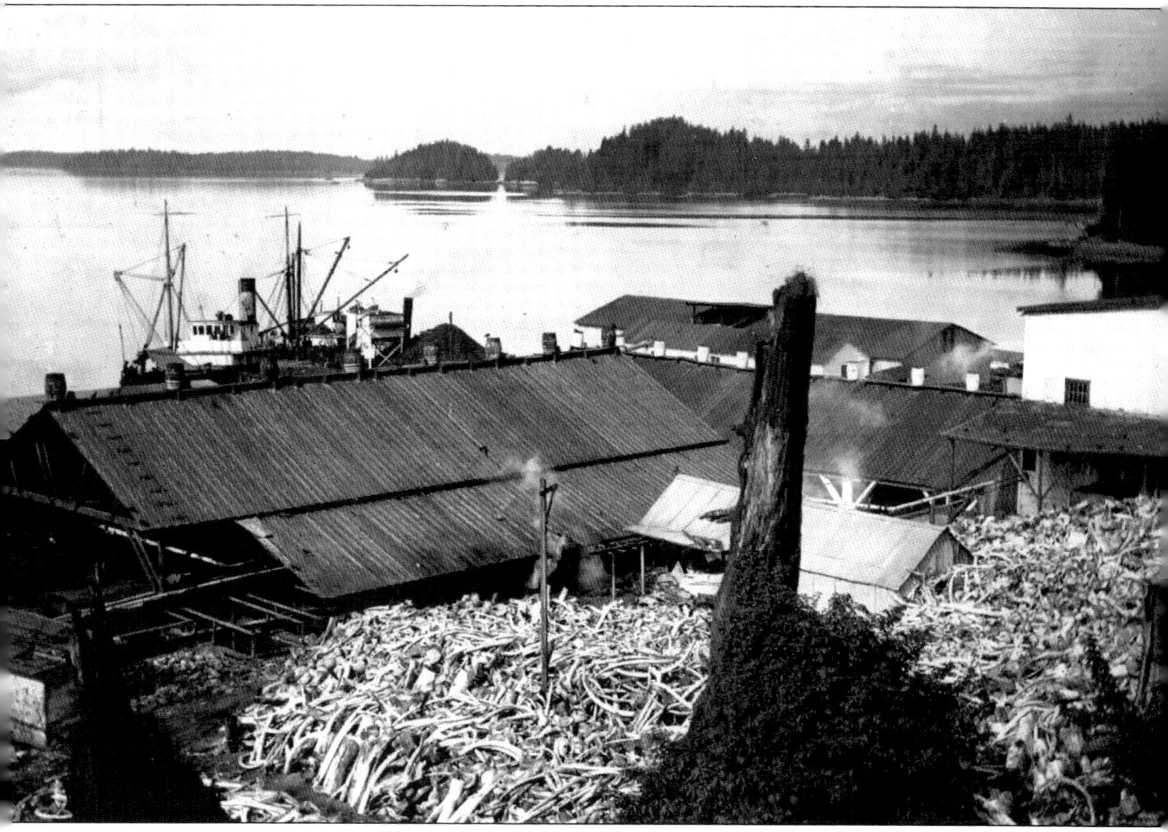

This photograph of Ucluelet station from the end of the season shows the large pile of whalebones that will be ground up for use in fertilizer.

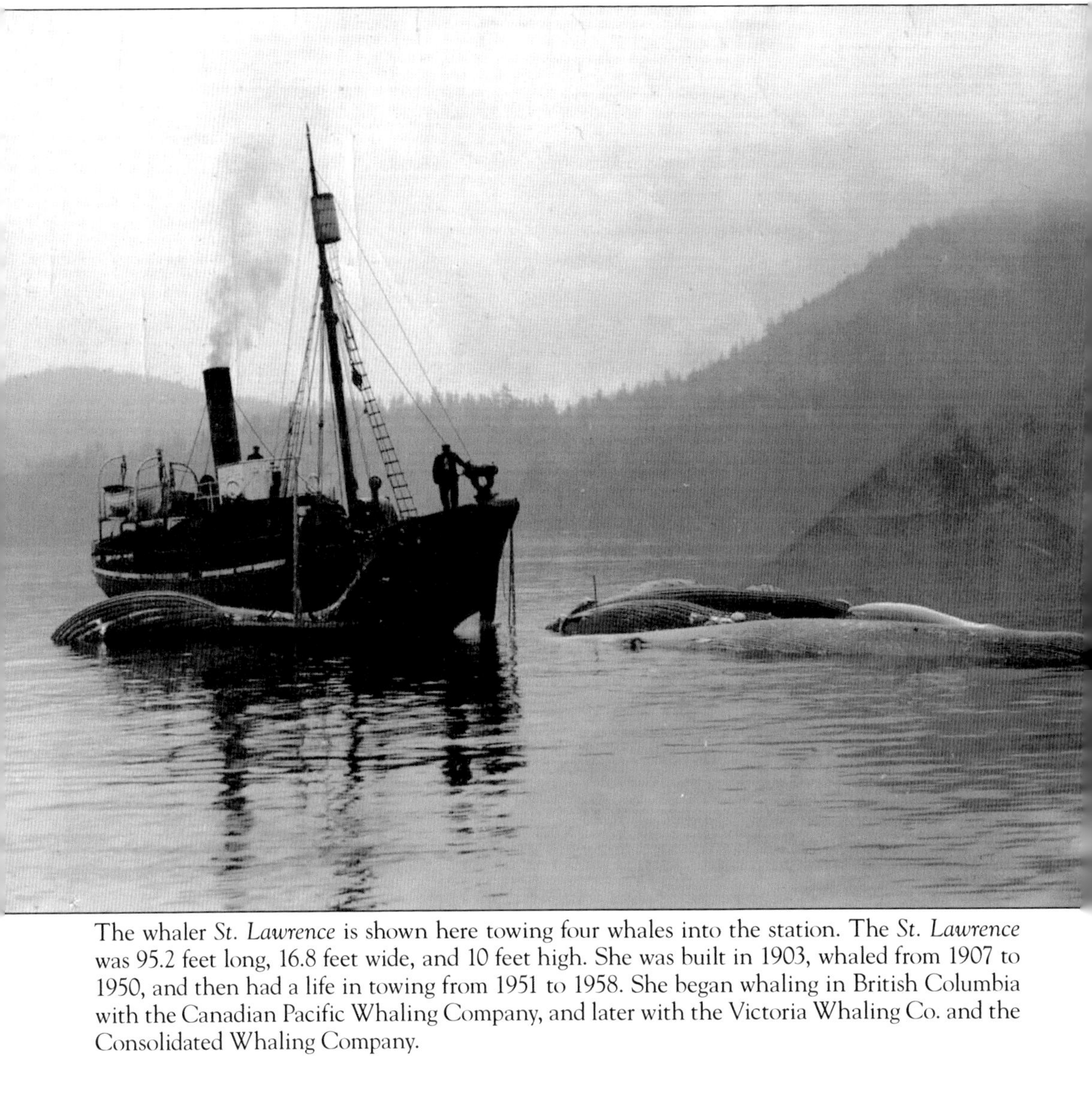

The whaler *St. Lawrence* is shown here towing four whales into the station. The *St. Lawrence* was 95.2 feet long, 16.8 feet wide, and 10 feet high. She was built in 1903, whaled from 1907 to 1950, and then had a life in towing from 1951 to 1958. She began whaling in British Columbia with the Canadian Pacific Whaling Company, and later with the Victoria Whaling Co. and the Consolidated Whaling Company.

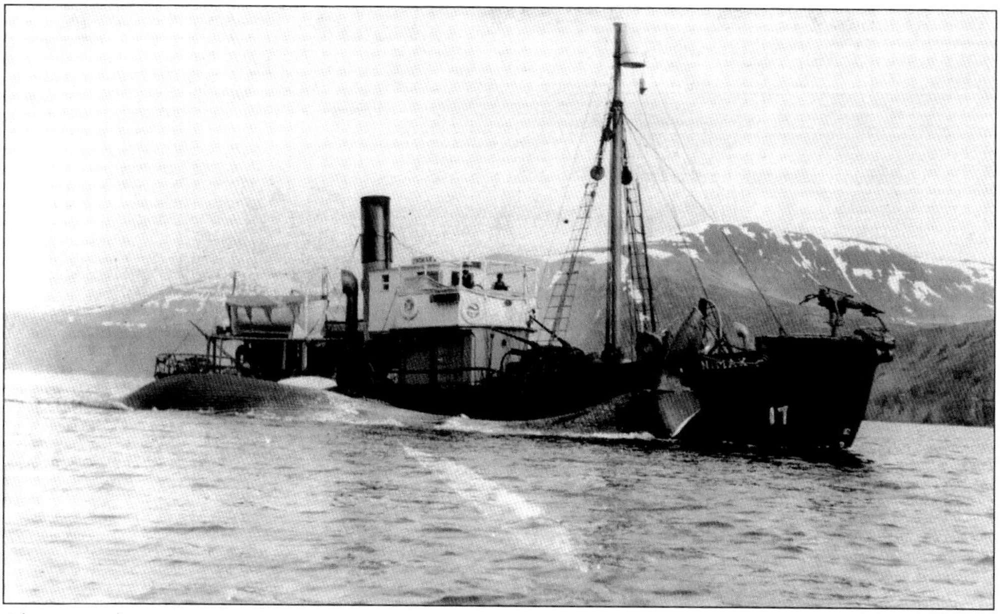

This is a photograph of the whaler *Unimak*, which was built in 1912 by J.F. Duthie of Seattle. The *Unimak* was 100 feet long and weighed 99 tons.

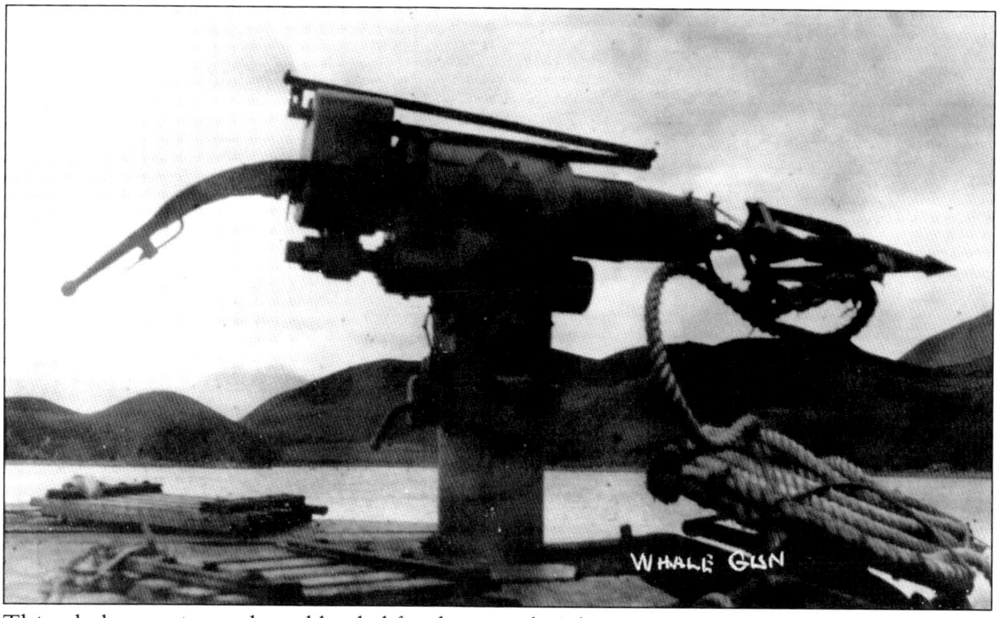

This whale gun sits ready and loaded for the next day's hunting.

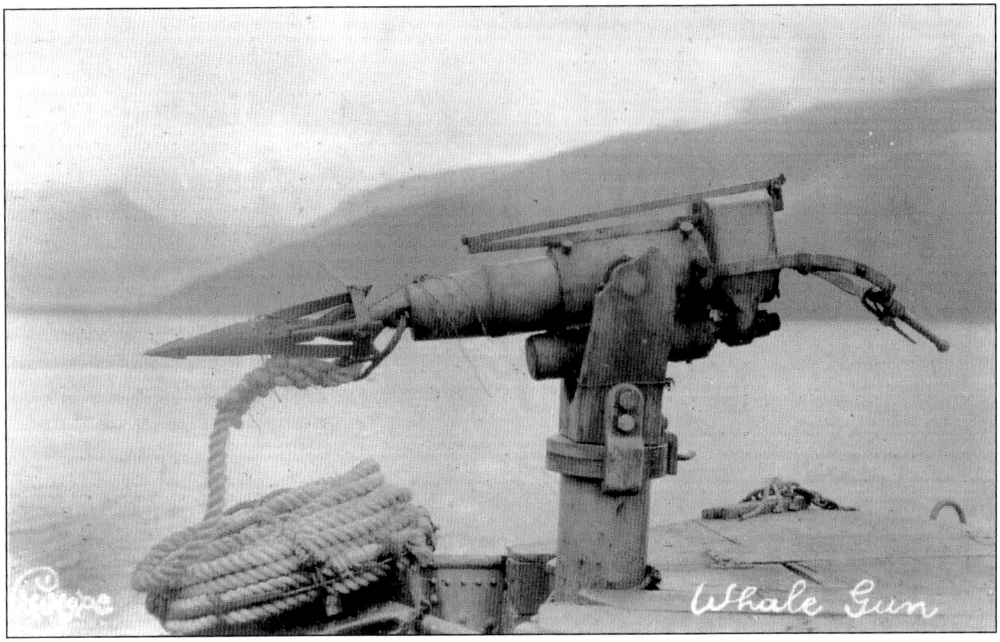

This whale gun is similar to the one on the previous page.

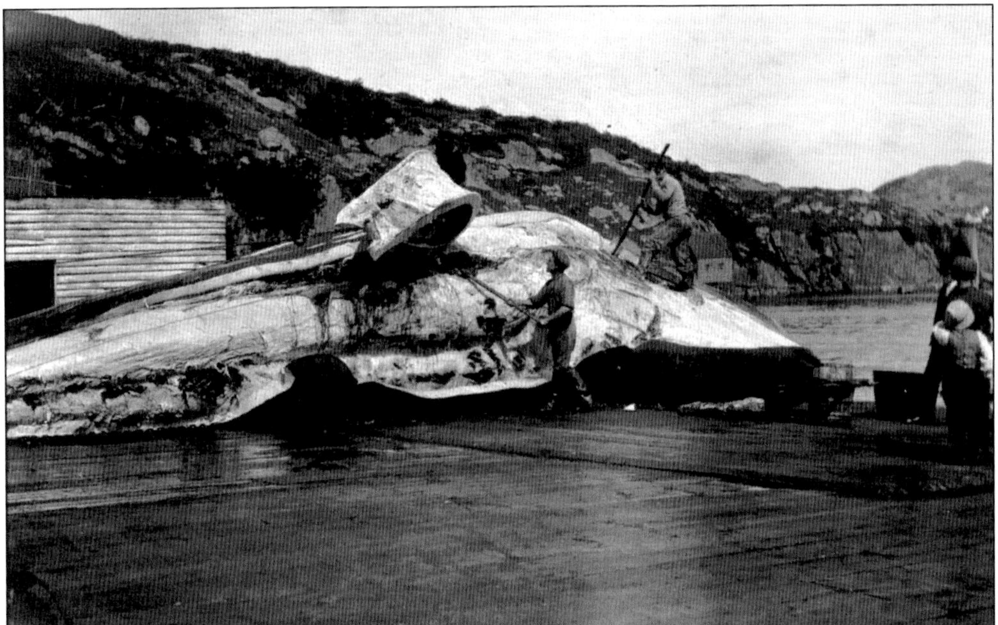
In this photograph, blubber is being pulled off of a whale with the help of a winch. It is also being cut by the flenser as it is peeled back.

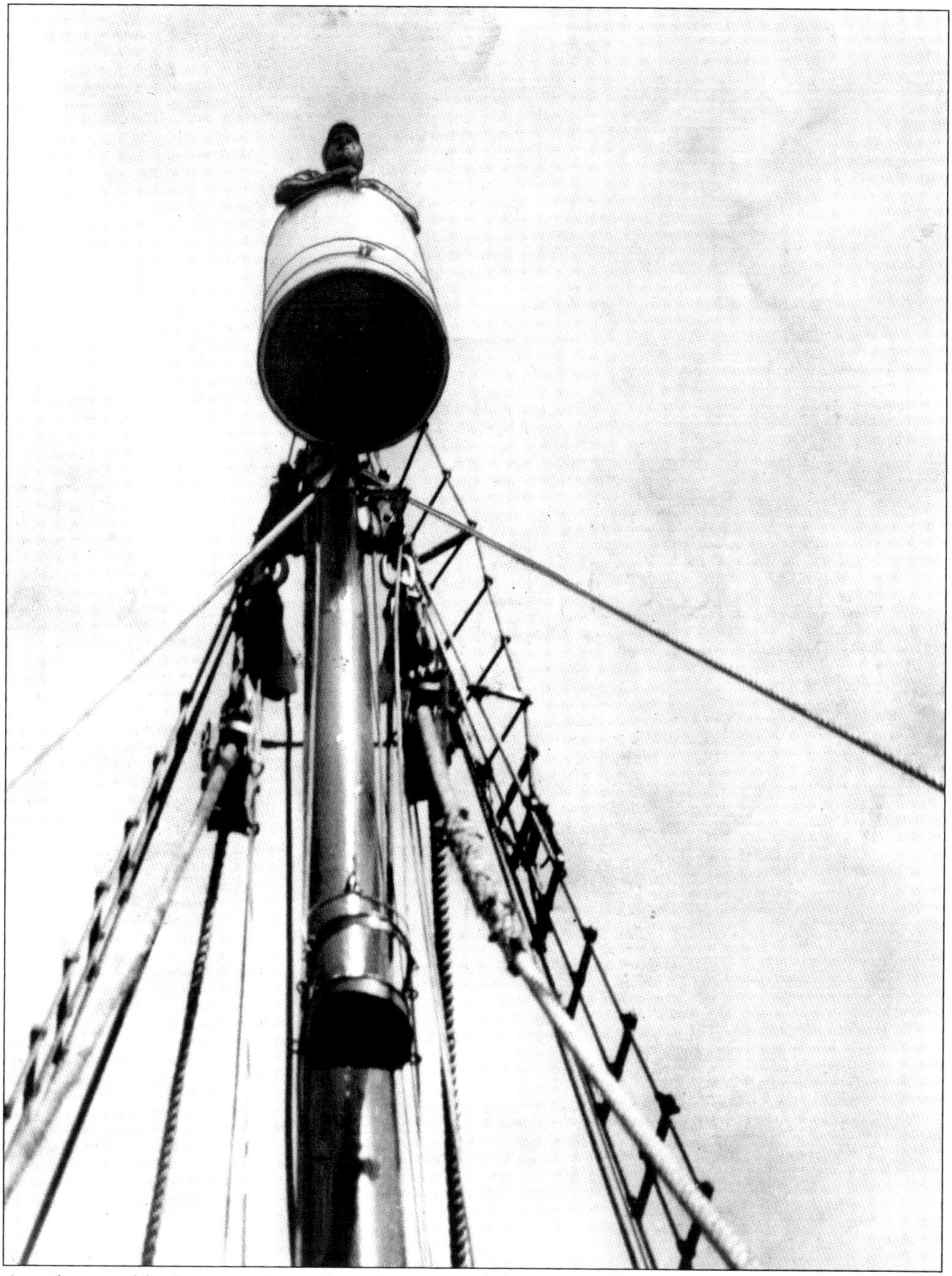

A sailor would often stand in a barrel on top of the mast, which was one distinctive mark of a whaling vessel. This photograph looks up to the lookout station, where whalers took turns watching for whales. They would alert the crew when whales were spotted.

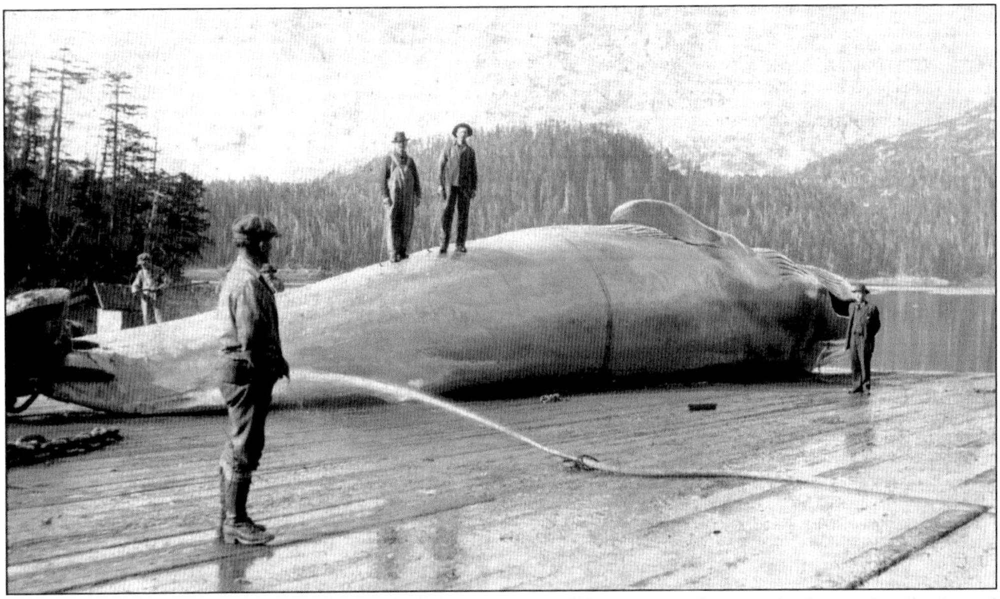

A finback is being brought up the deck for processing. Water is used to wash down the deck and the whale, and to provide a lubricant so that the whale slides more easily.

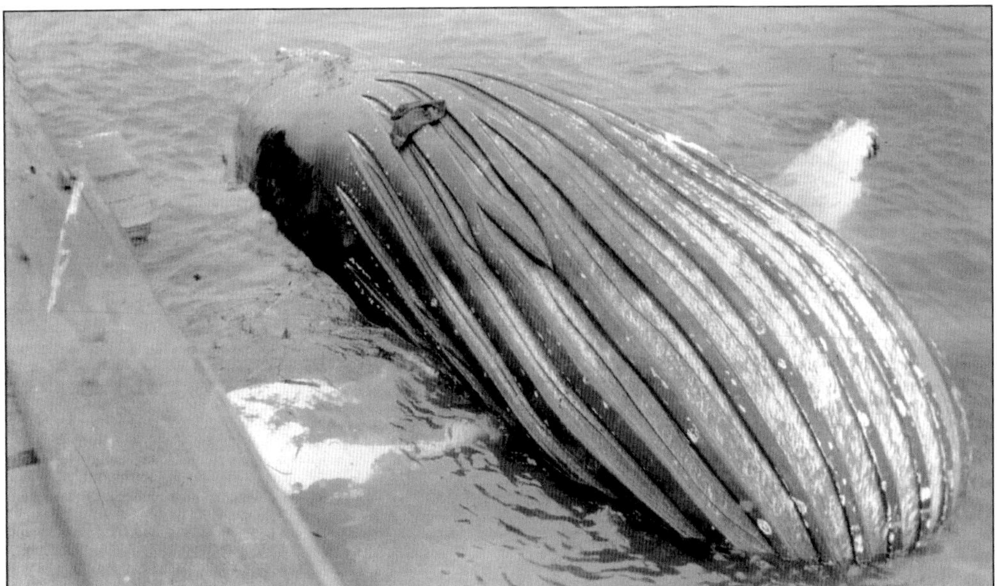

Here, the body of a humpback whale lies in the water off the dock, showing its "wings" and ventral grooves.

Five

Washington Whaling

Commercial whaling in Washington state consisted of one whaling station, which became operational before the end of 1911. The location for the whaling site was initially acquired by Frank Hall and Cereno Jones Kelley, both of whom had previously been associated with a whaling concern on Big Dundas Island. In 1910, Hall and Kelley had the only active license for an unbuilt station, and Balcom wanted it. He applied for the license on behalf of Frank Hall, Alexander McCrimmon, and himself, which would apply to Milbank Sound, Estevan Sound, Nepean Sound, and the north end of Nootka Sound. The license to build the station was valuable for several reasons—initially it was one of only three licenses for stations on American soil, it was the only license out of about 10 that was not held by Sprott Balcolm, and Balcolm clearly wanted it. Before construction began, Hall had the name of the company changed to the American Pacific Whaling Company. The location for the whaling station was in Grays Harbor, Washington, which has also been called Westport and Bay City.

William Schupp acquired Sprott Balcolm's Pacific Whaling Company in 1909–1910. He also acquired the American Pacific Whaling Company and its shore station at Westport, in Grays Harbor. According to Robert Webb in *On the Northwest*, "In an affidavit taken in 1921 Sprott Balcolm affirmed that he and Rissmuller had acquired the property, built the station, and arranged for the construction of two steam whaling vessels at a Seattle shipyard, all of which we afterwards turned over to the American Pacific Whaling Company as payment on account of its stock." Dr. Rismuller was involved in most of these whaling companies because he had a patented process for the reduction of whales that was used at most of the whaling stations in the area. He was usually named a stockholder in these companies as payment for his services.

The Bay City station held potential value, as it could have been a point of entry for Canadian oil into the United States. Canadian shipments were duty restricted, but by having stations in both countries, the company created an opportunity for whales caught in Canadian waters to be processed in the Washington station and avoid oil duties. In 1915, however, the Canadian government passed a restriction on shipments of oil out of Canada to foreign countries. The law was intended to restrict shipments of oil getting to Germany, but the law was worded loosely enough to also restrict shipments into the United States. Schupp's intentions were to ship whale oil to Proctor & Gamble's soap plant in Cincinnati, along with other companies. The Canadian government relented, and oil shipments began after a short period of restriction. Wartime production lagged about 25 percent from previous years, but the wartime revenue more than made up for the loss of production.

The two whale killer boats, the *Moran* and the *Paterson*, were built in Seattle by the Moran shipbuilding company and were delivered in 1911. Another two whalers, the *Aberdeen* and the *Westport*, were built by the Seattle Construction and Drydock Company and were delivered in 1912. Together, these four boats pursued whales from the Canadian border to Cape Blanco on the southern Oregon coast, near Port Orford—an area extending 135 miles north and south of the Bay City station. During the first, partial season, Bay City processed 102 whales. In 1914, it was determined that it cost $206 for each whale to be caught. Profits were said to be $140 per average humpback whale of 27 tons, while a 50-ton finback brought in $338, and a 60-ton blue whale brought in $572.

In 1919, a film crew was sent to the Bay City station. The purpose of the filming was to show the firing of a harpoon from a whaling vessel, and the entire process of transforming the whale into oil, whalebone, and canned whale meat.

All of Schupp's plants were closed in 1921, but the stations continued to operate in 1922. The final station was closed after the 1925 season, when only 21 whales had been taken since the previous April. In previous seasons, there would have been 200 to 300 whales caught each season. Possible reasons were that the whales' feeding grounds could have changed due to radical changes in ocean currents. In late August 1922, Bay City hosted a large station which, according to Robert Webb in *On the Northwest*, "was not processing enough whales to pay its way" in the 1924 season. William Schupp then closed the large and costly plant, and it was sold and converted into a facility to process pilchards, or California sardines, which had suddenly appeared in large numbers on the west coast.

This freed men, equipment, and chaser boats for other stations. Schupp's American Pacific Whaling Company was building a new station, to be called Port Hobron, for service in 1926. It was located on Sitkalidek Island in the vicinity of Kodiak in southern Alaska. The Bay City equipment was shipped on a barge to the new station, but unfortunately, it was lost overboard in heavy seas.

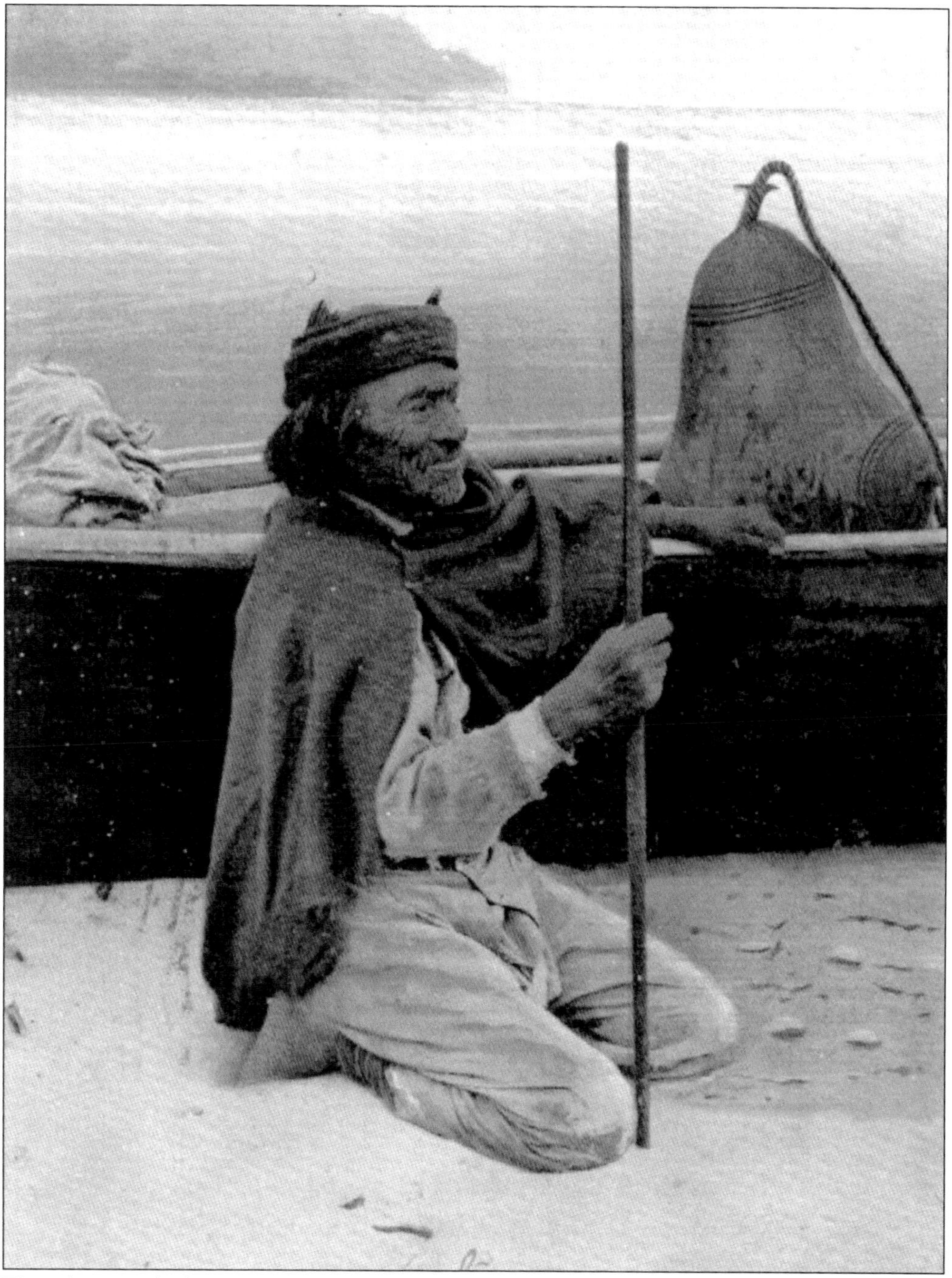

This photograph shows an elderly Indian whale hunter at Puget Sound, praying and preparing his equipment.

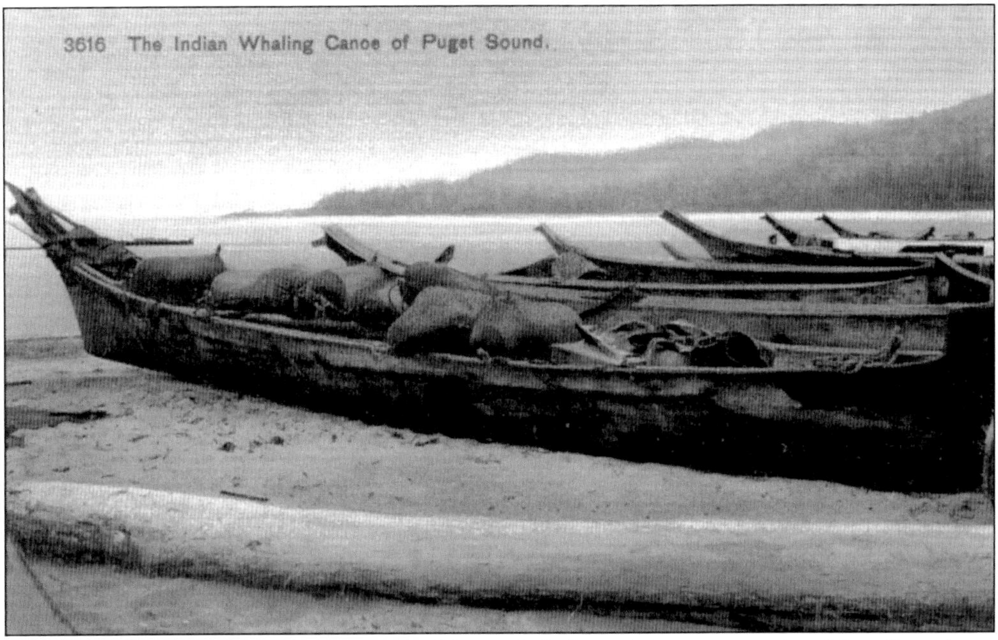

Several Makah Indian canoes are prepared for a whale hunt. The spears and sealskin floats have already been loaded.

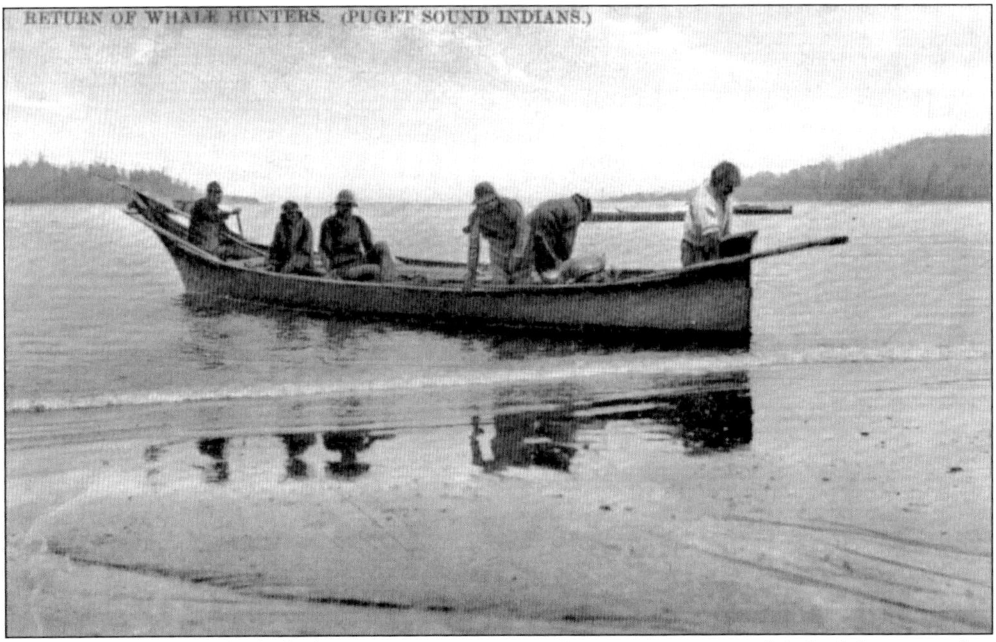

Several Puget Sound whale hunters are returning from an unsuccessful day's hunt in this photograph. The days are long and exhausting. More days the men return without a whale than with their quarry.

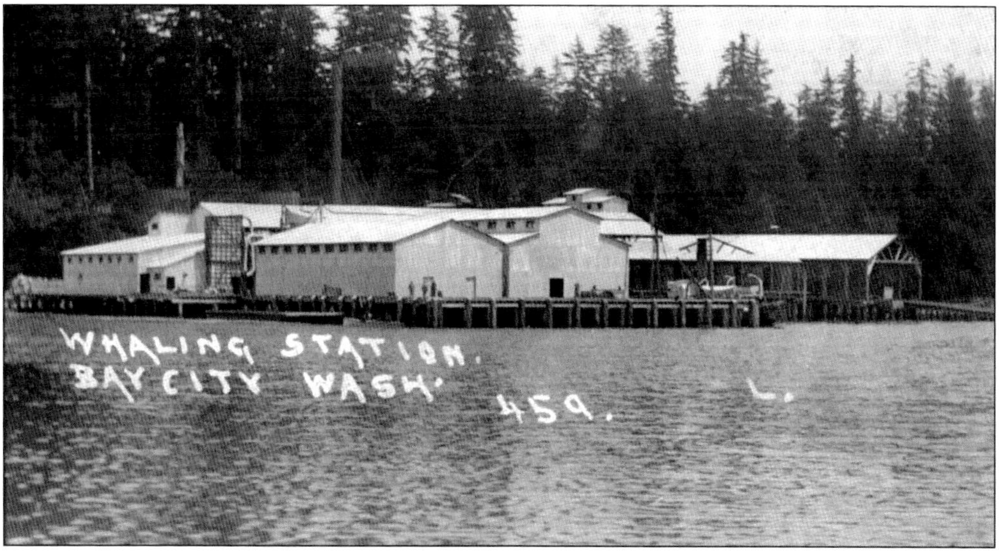

This photograph shows the Bay City whaling station from the sea.

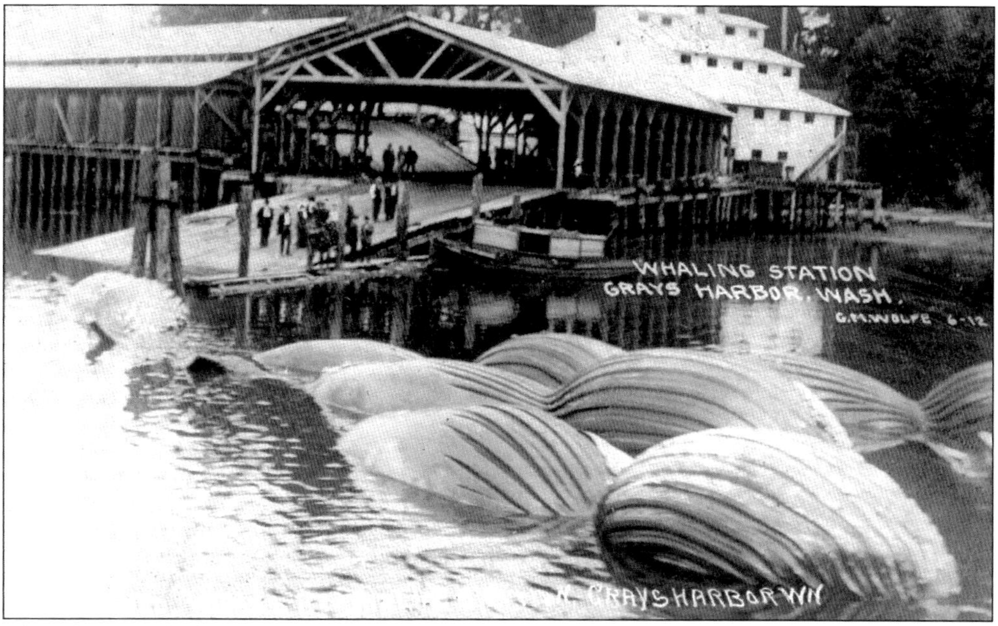

This photograph shows the Grays Harbor whaling station, from the direction of the ramp area where the whales will be winched up and flensed.

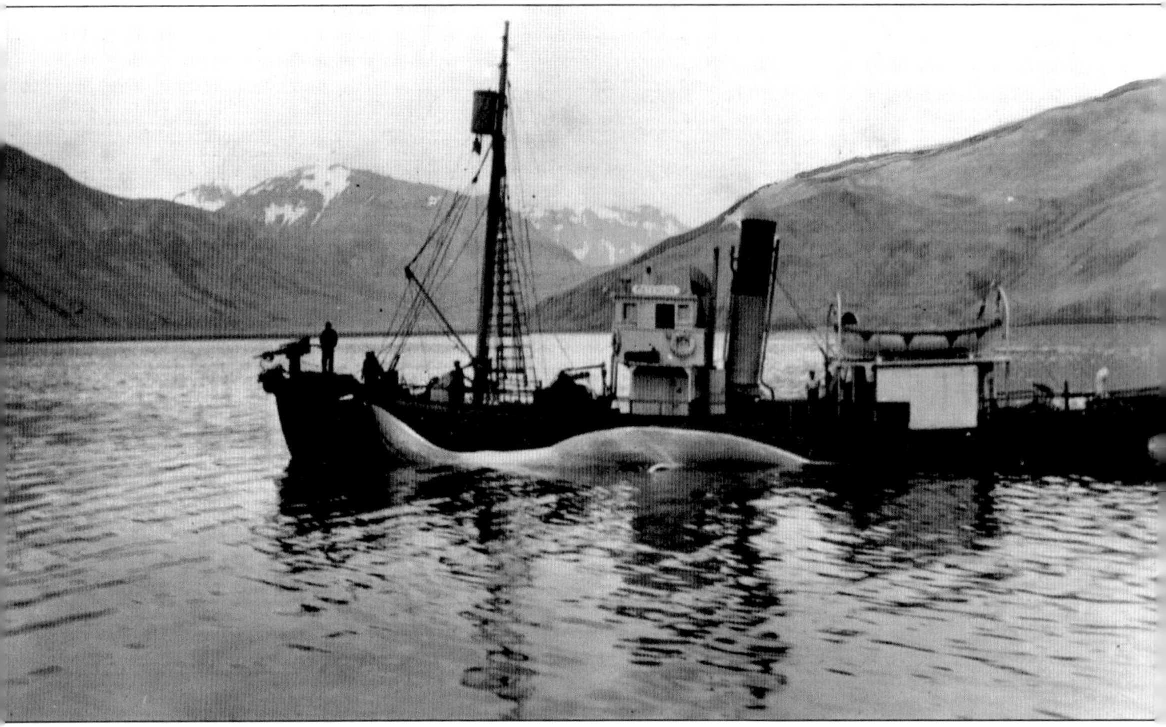

The whaler *Paterson* is seen here with a whale, waiting for its turn to approach the dock and unload.

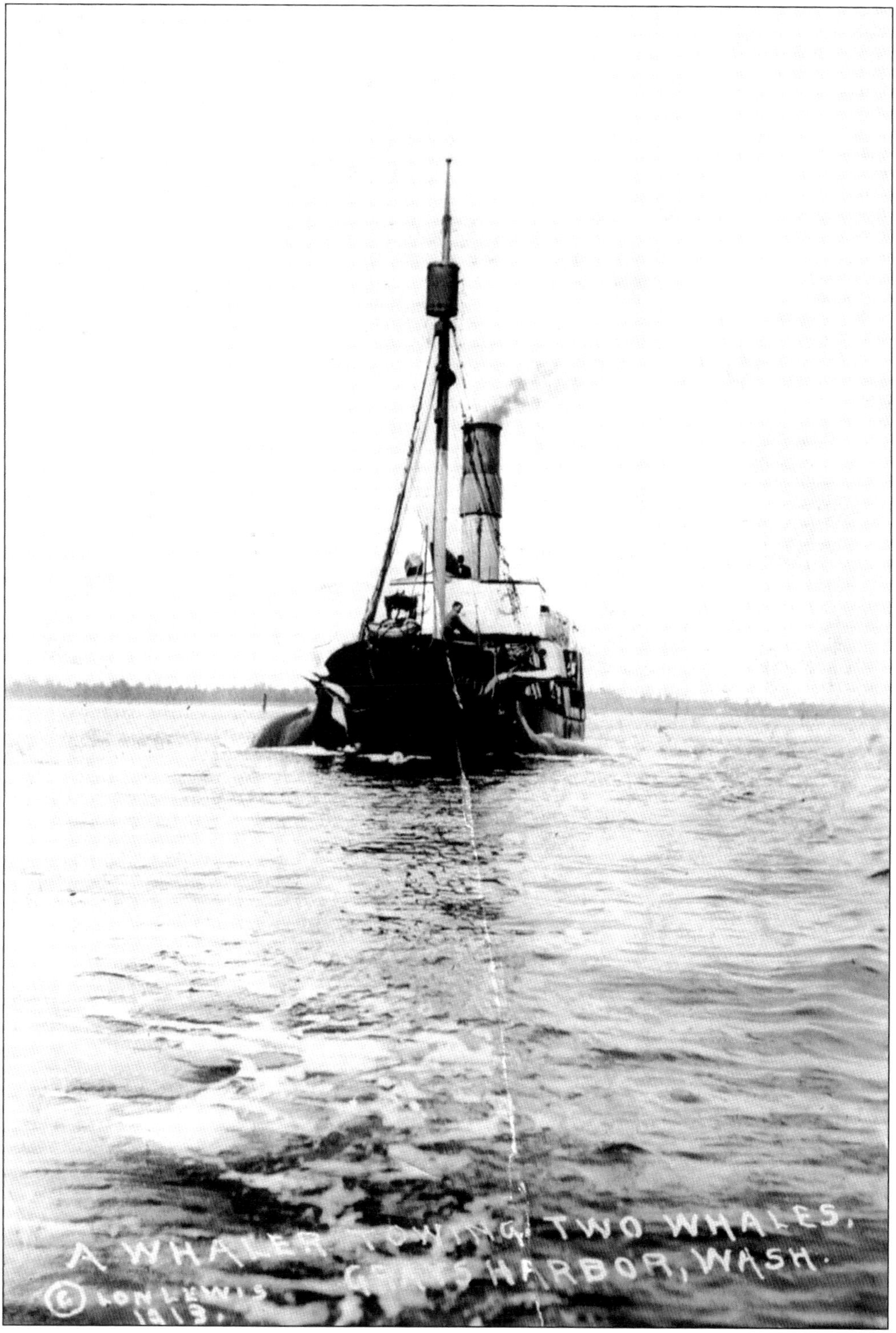

This early photograph shows the steamer *Moran* coming into Grays Harbor, Washington, with two whales—one on each side.

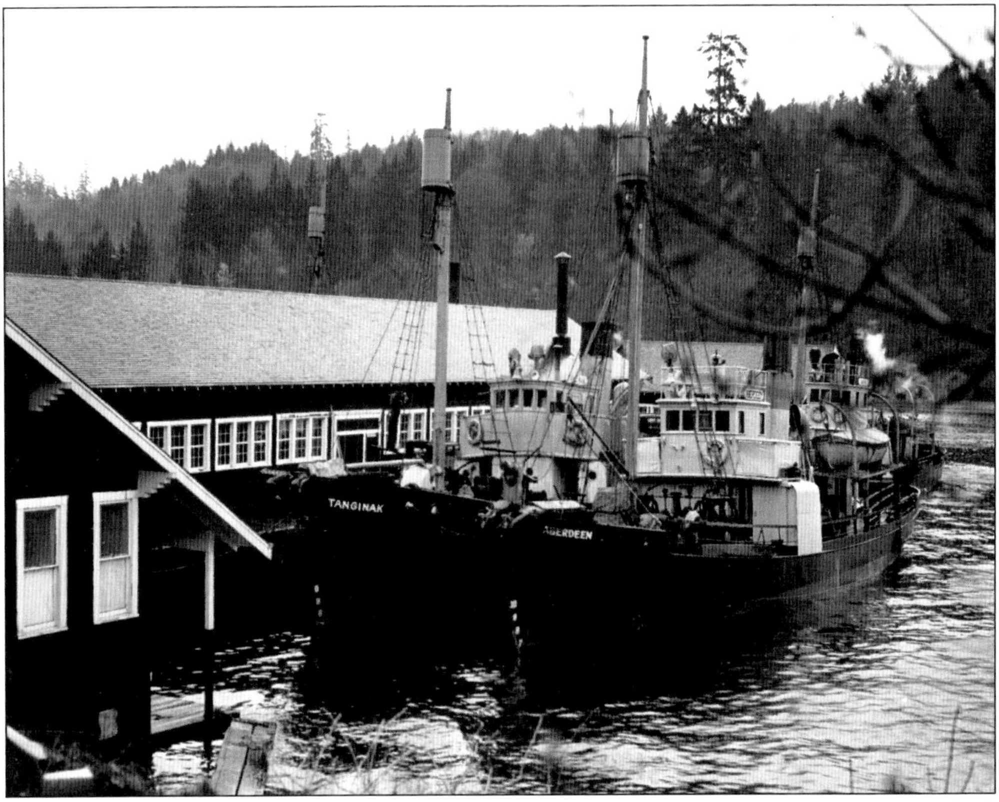

Here are the whalers *Tanginak*—which was once the *Tyee Jr.*—and *Aberdeen* at their winter dock at Lake Washington near Seattle.

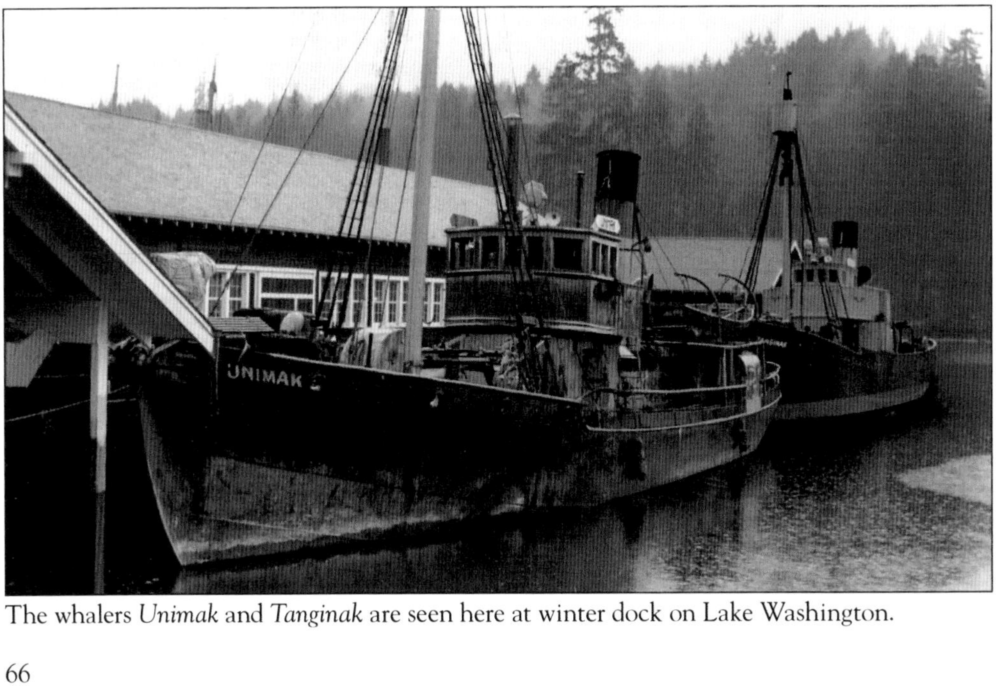

The whalers *Unimak* and *Tanginak* are seen here at winter dock on Lake Washington.

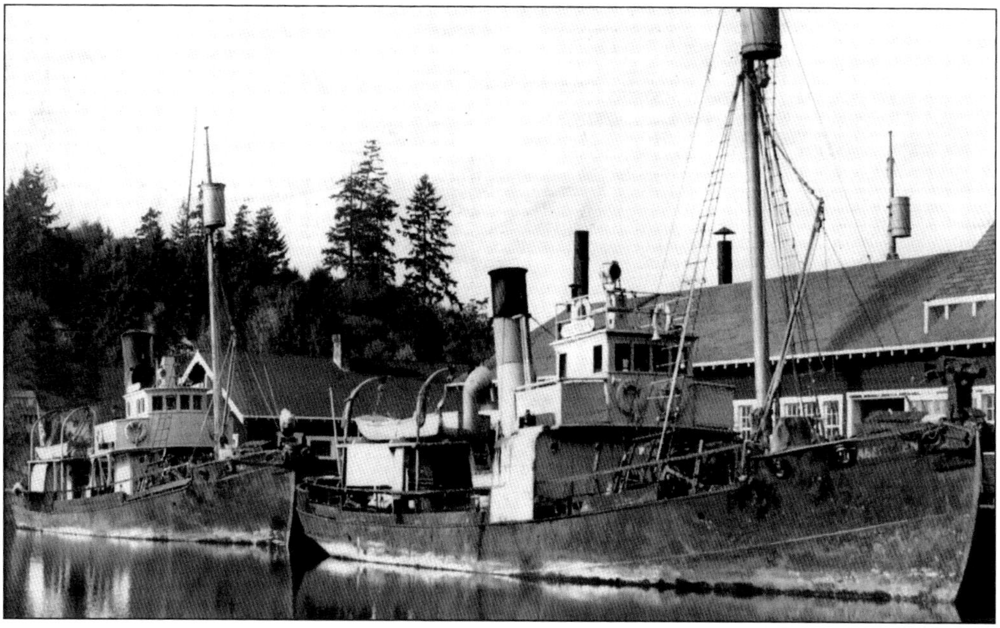

The whalers *Aberdeen* and *Paterson* are pictured here at their wintering location on Lake Washington.

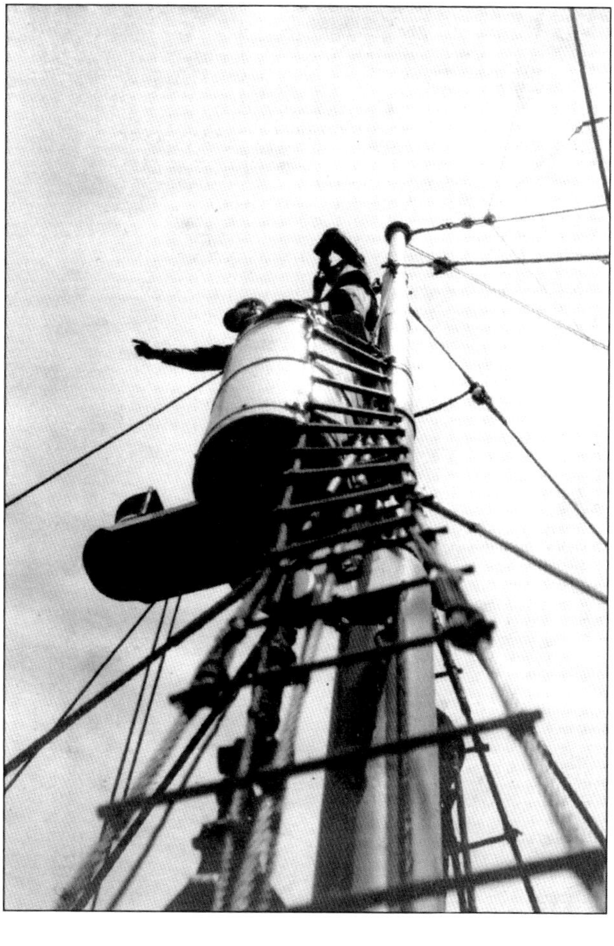

A whaler lookout is seen here, pointing. He is probably indicating the speed and direction of a whale.

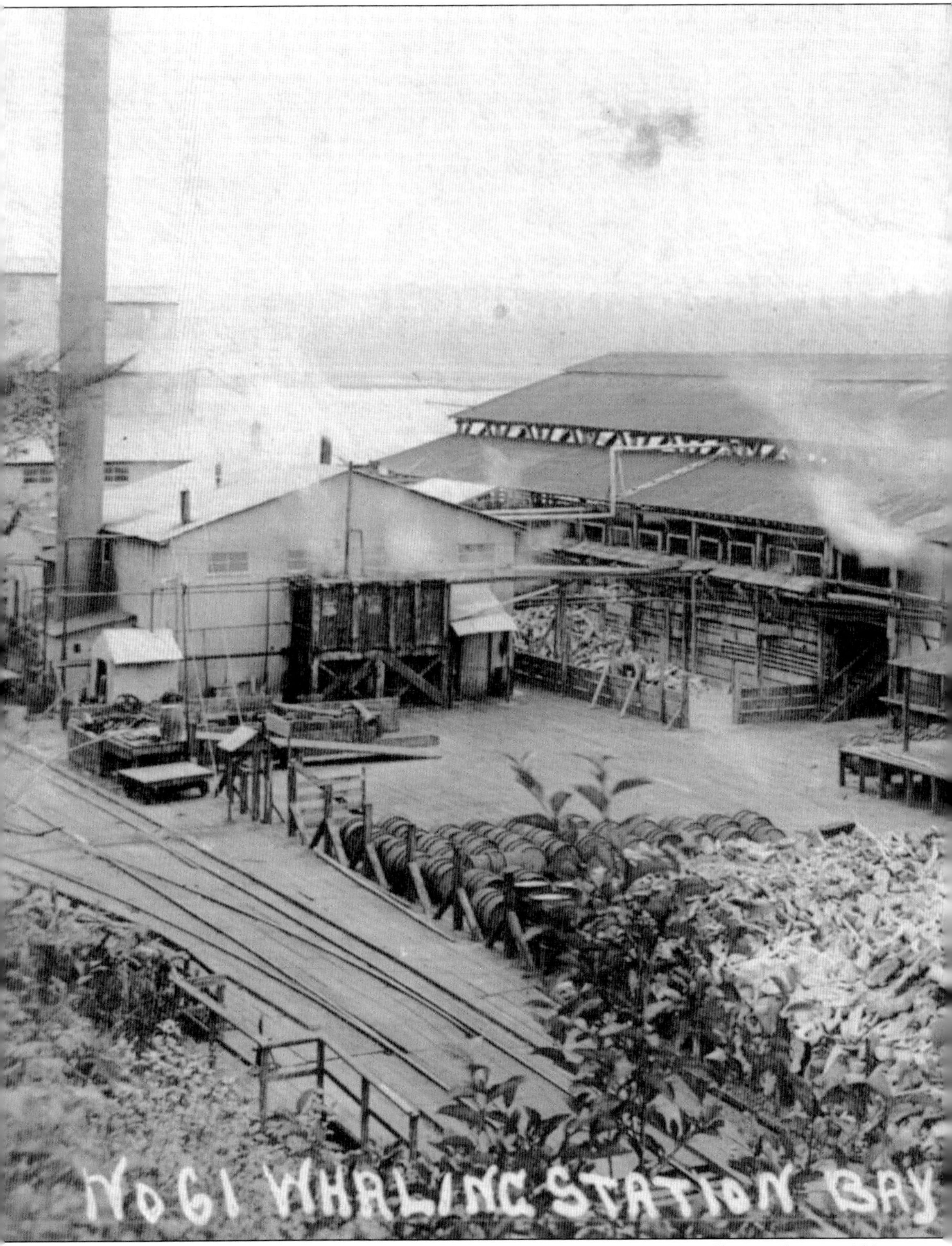

This view of the rear of the Bay City whaling station shows the large pile of bones that would be

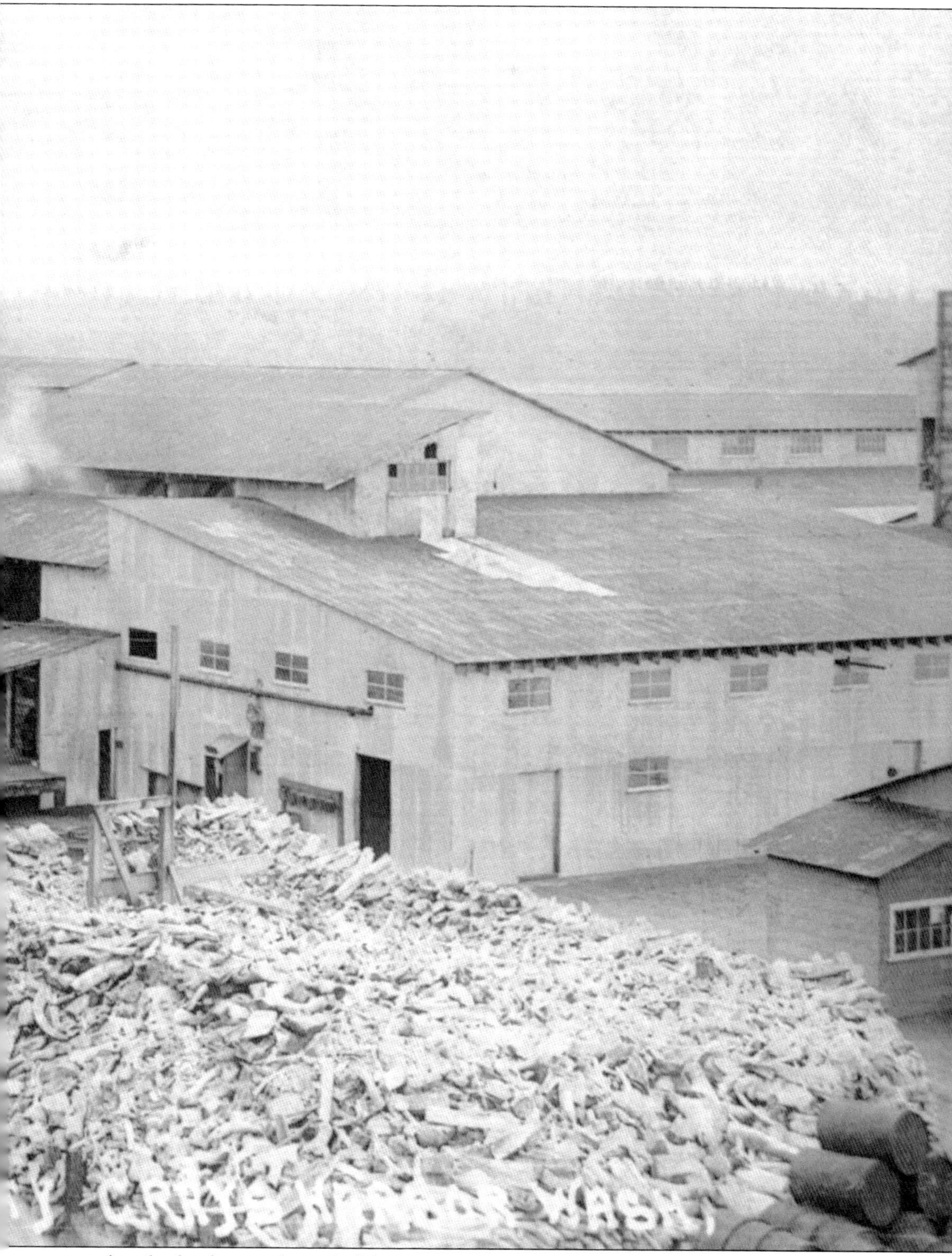

ground up for fertilizer at the end of the season.

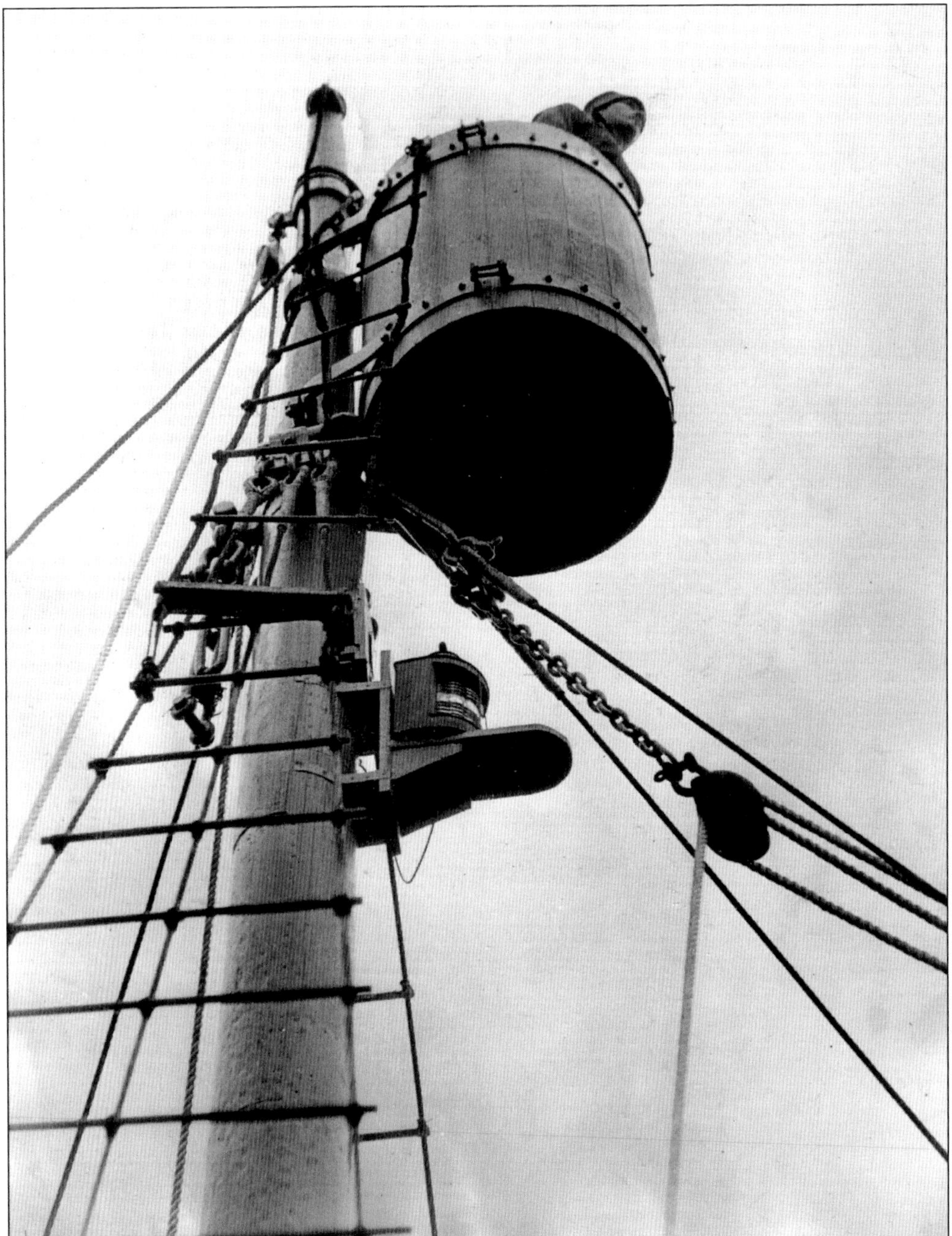

A man is seen here in the crow's nest of the whaler *Tanginak*. His view of the surrounding ocean and any whales swimming or spouting was far superior to that on deck. He would signal the others below when a whale was spotted, and give them the information necessary to intercept the whale.

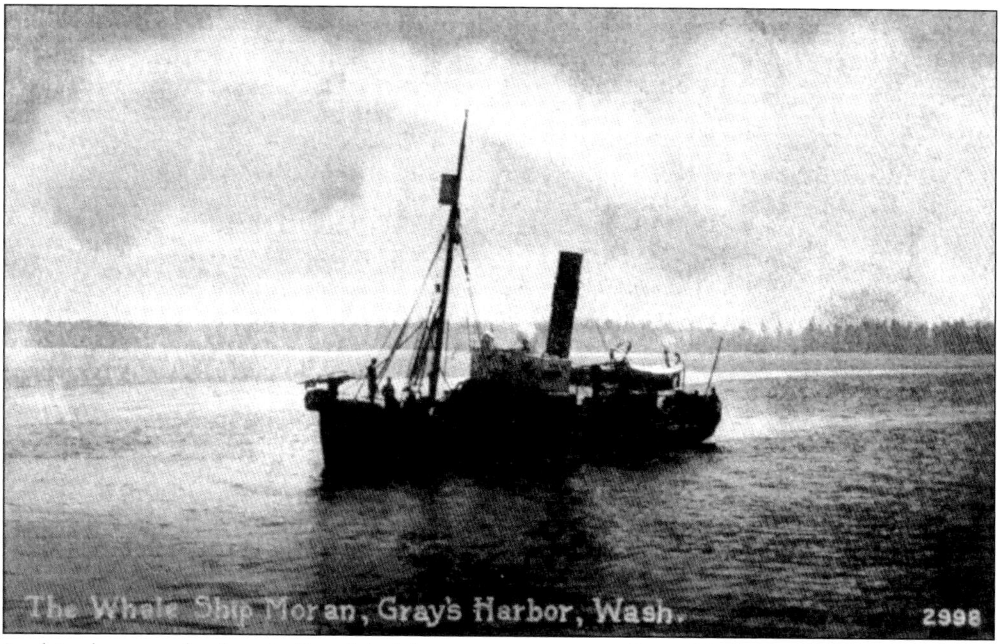

In this photograph, the whaling ship *Moran* is coming into Grays Harbor with a whale.

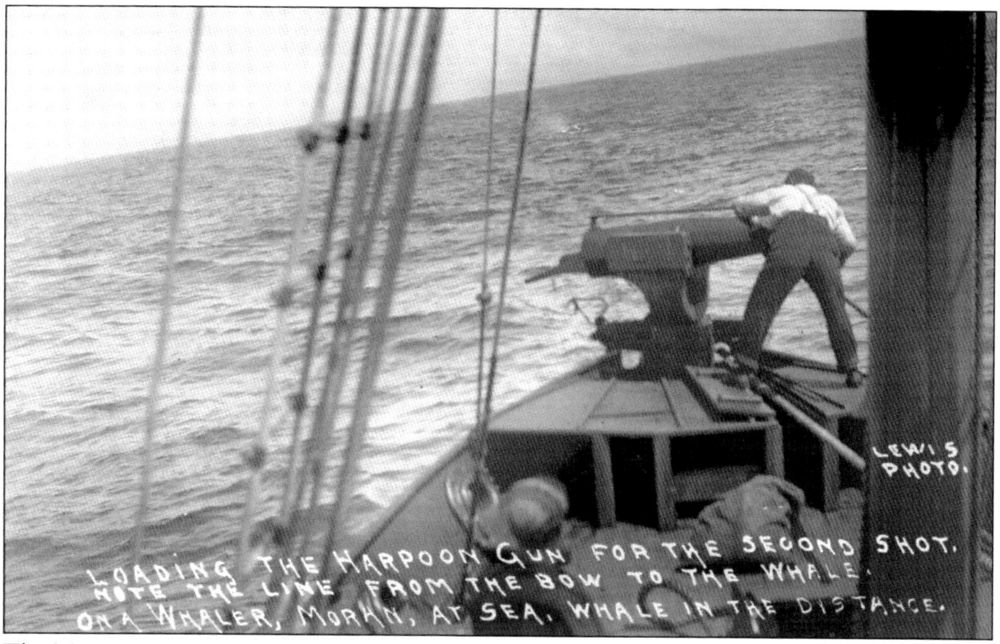

The *Moran* sits at sea in this photograph, while the gunner reloads for a second shot. Note that the line from the first shot is between his feet, running from the ship's bow to the whale.

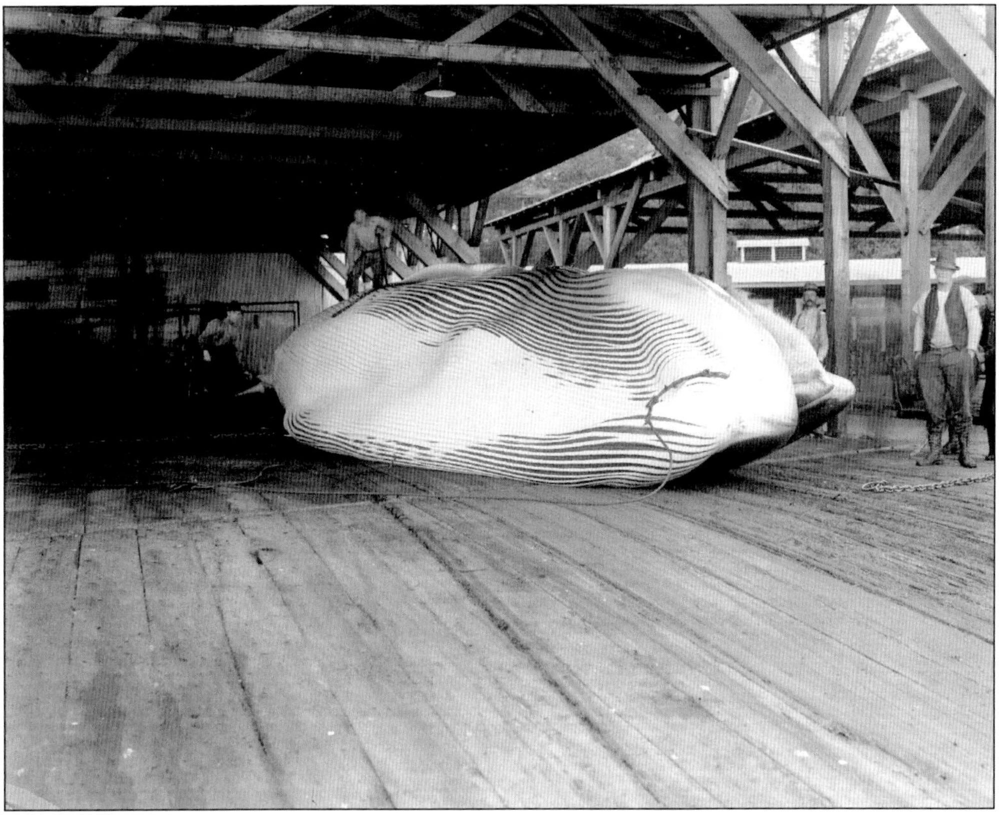

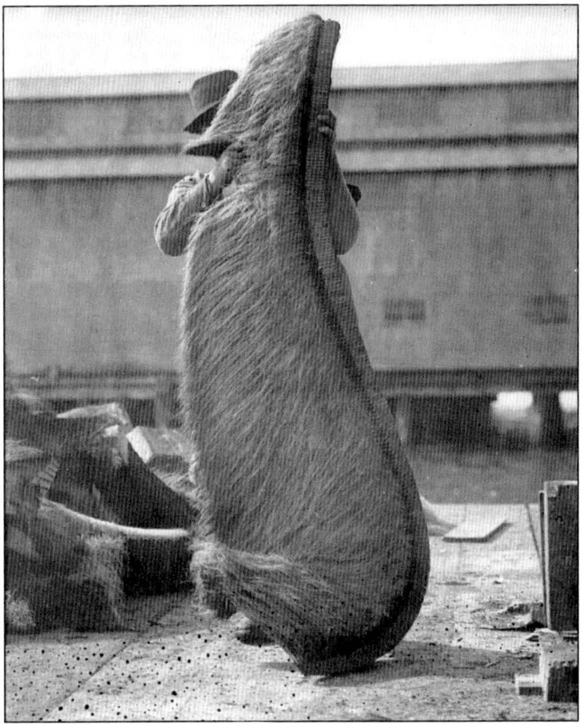

This fin whale is being worked on to remove the baleen. To start the process, a cut is being made along the length of the whale.

This worker is holding a large piece of baleen from a whale. These are not hairs, but rather rows of material that resemble plastic. This material was used for many purposes before the invention of petroleum plastics.

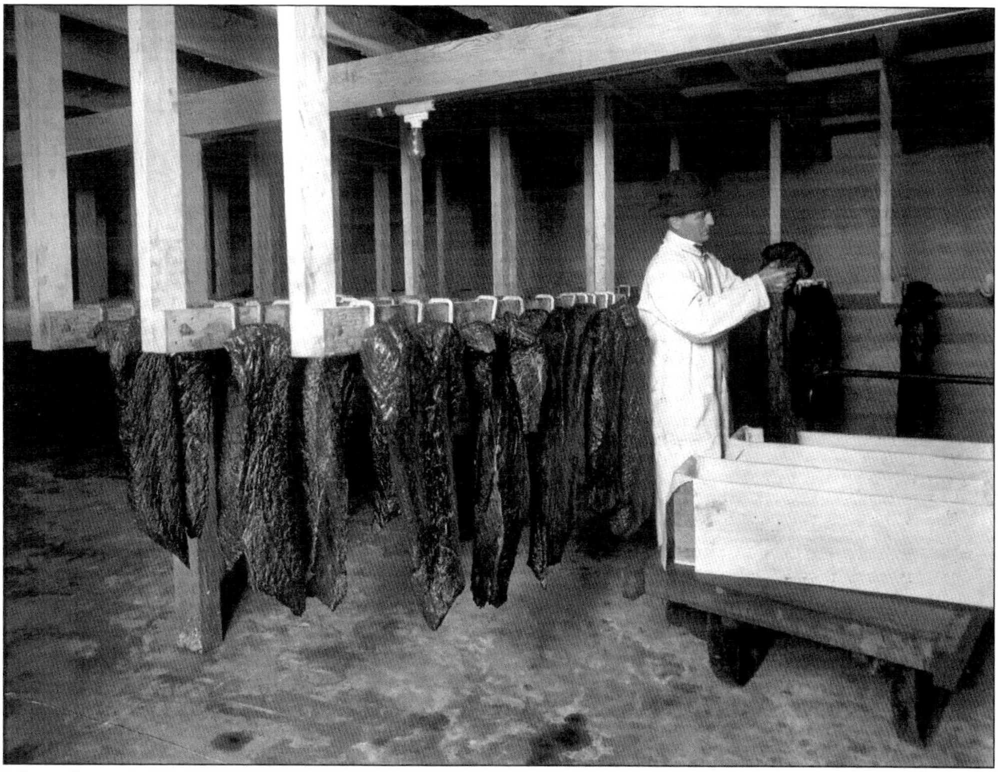

This photograph shows the meat locker at the Grays Harbor whaling station. The meat is being dried to remove blood and improve its quality.

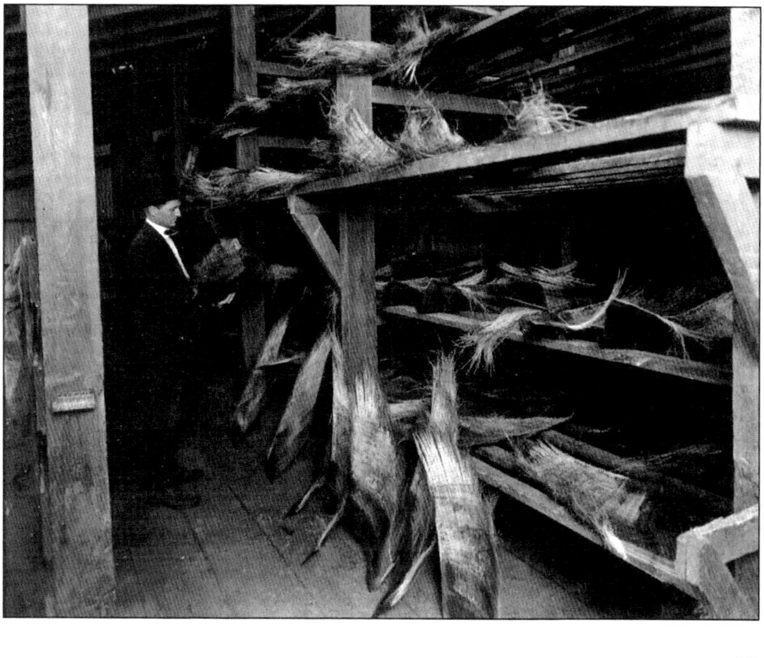

Baleen is being stored out of the elements in this photograph. Companies bought baleen and cut it into pieces for use in manufactured products. Baleen has been replaced by plastic extrusions and machined parts.

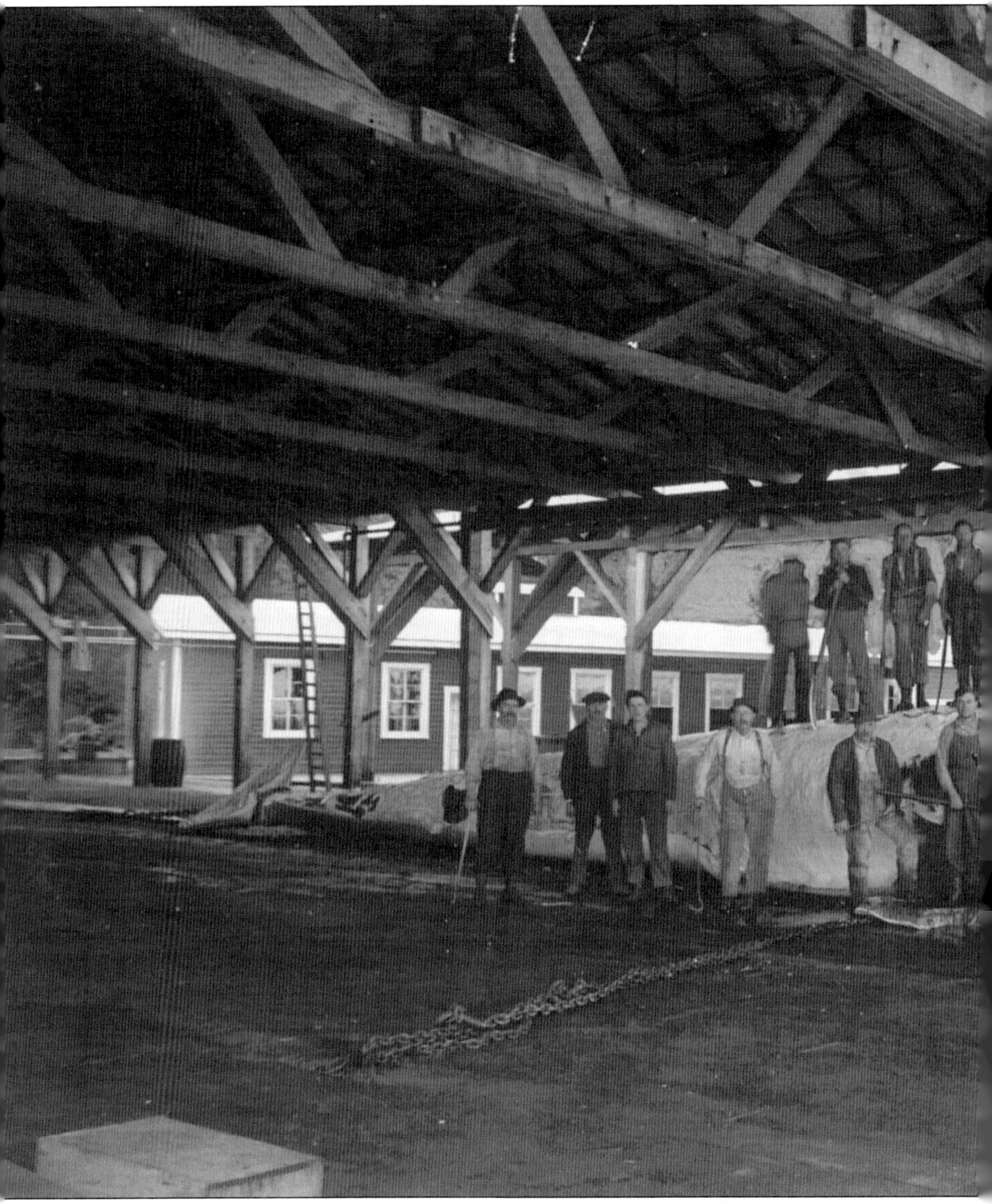

Here, a group of workers pose for a photograph with the whale that they have been working on.

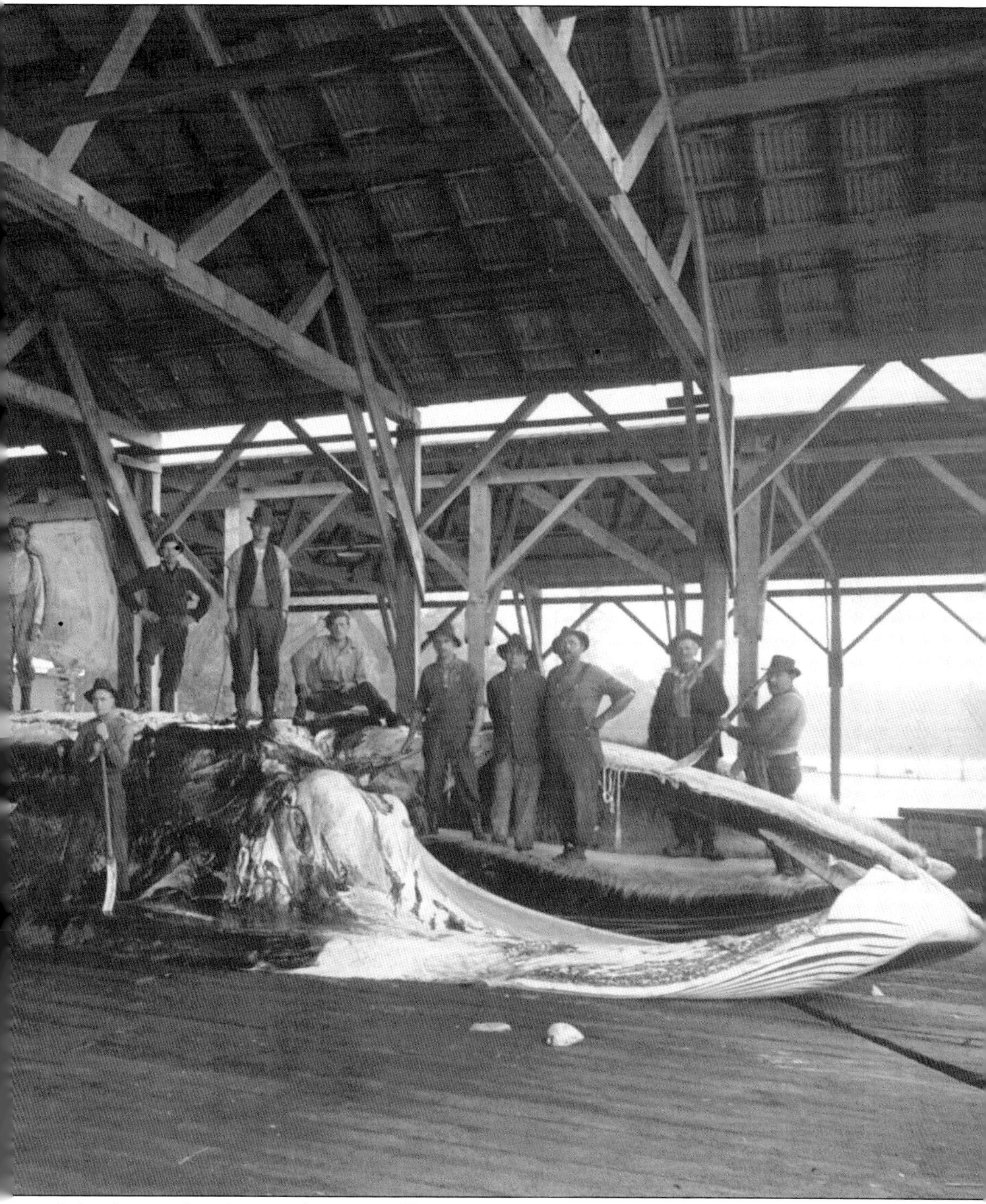

It has been reduced to mostly meat and bones.

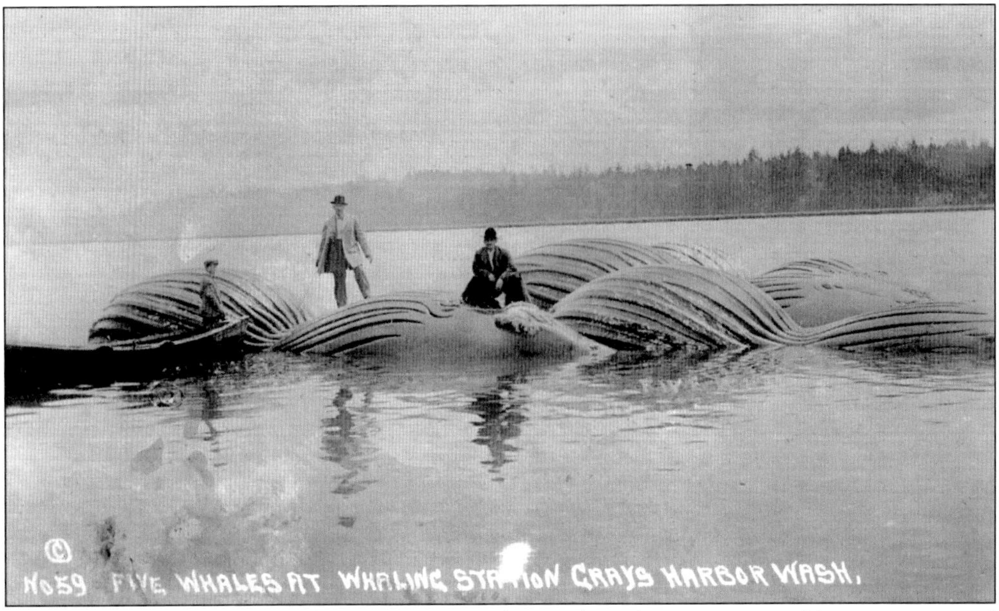

These whales have been tied up at Grays Harbor and are being inspected by a woman and two men.

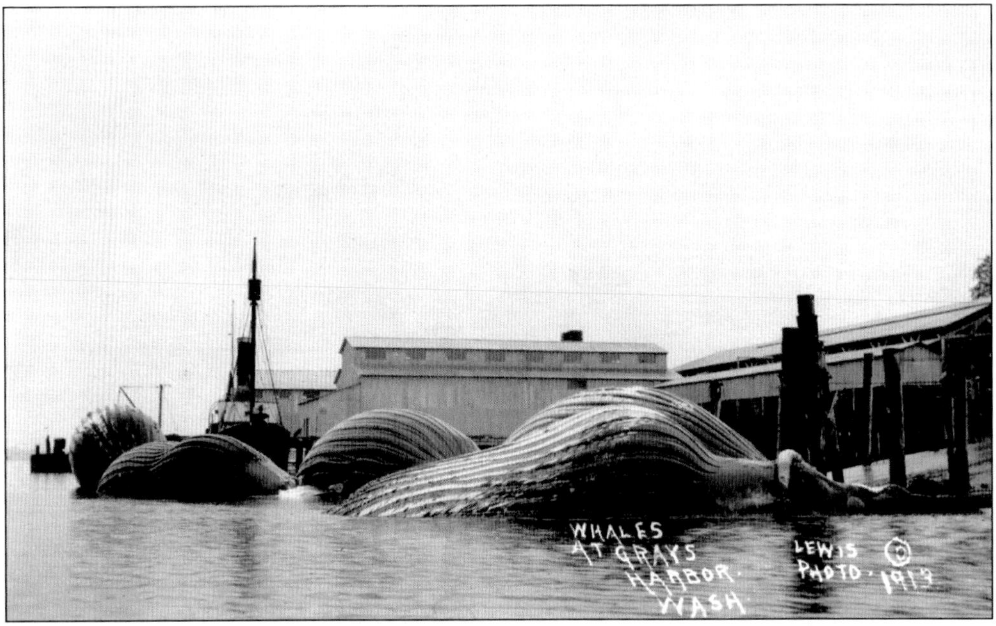

In this photograph, a whaler and at least five whales are present at Grays Harbor.

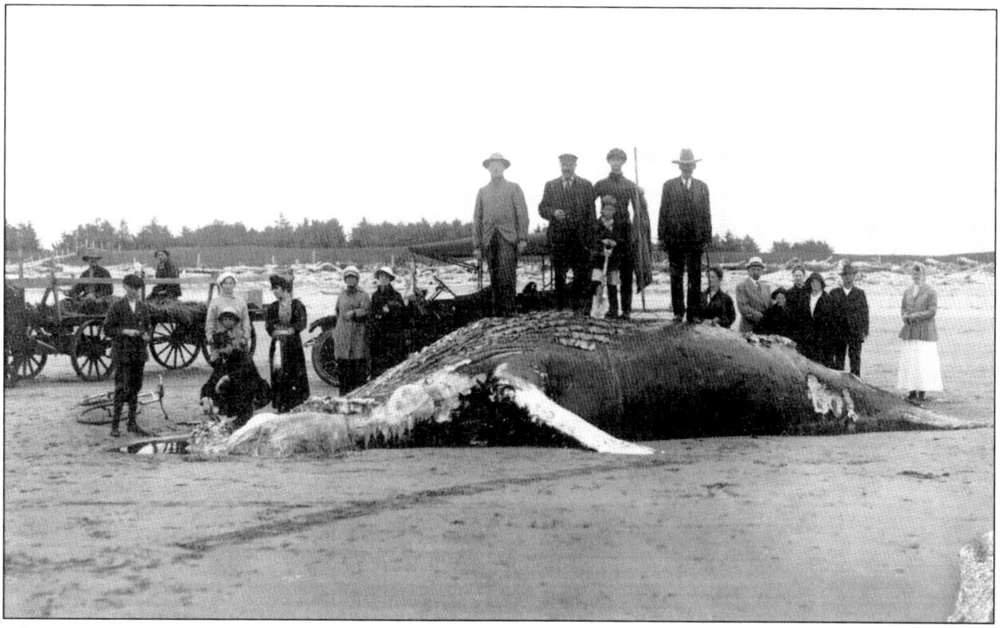

This appears to be a young humpback whale. The first person to find the whale has apparently put his mark on it. Some people are on the beach visiting the whale.

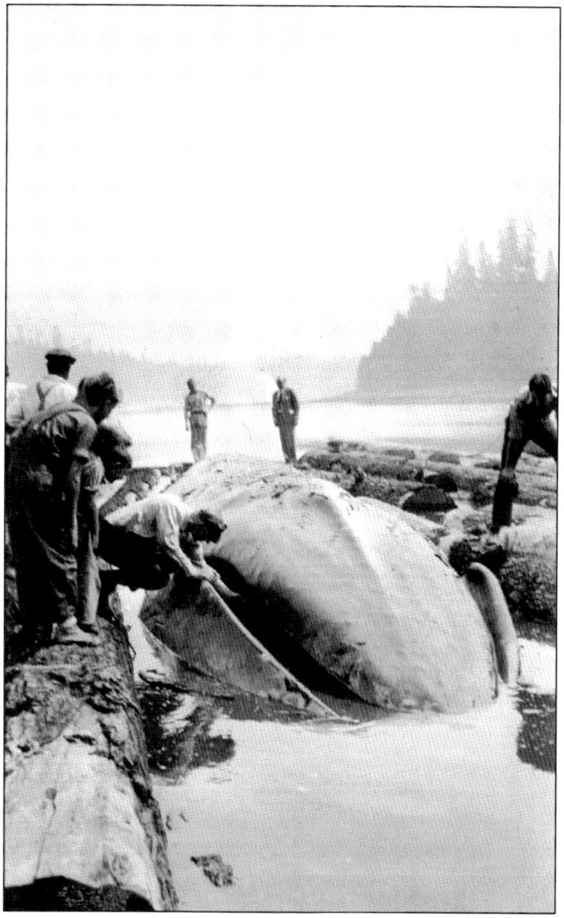

This whale died and ended up in a log boom. Or it was caught in a log boom and then died. In either case, these men have some work ahead of them to extricate the body.

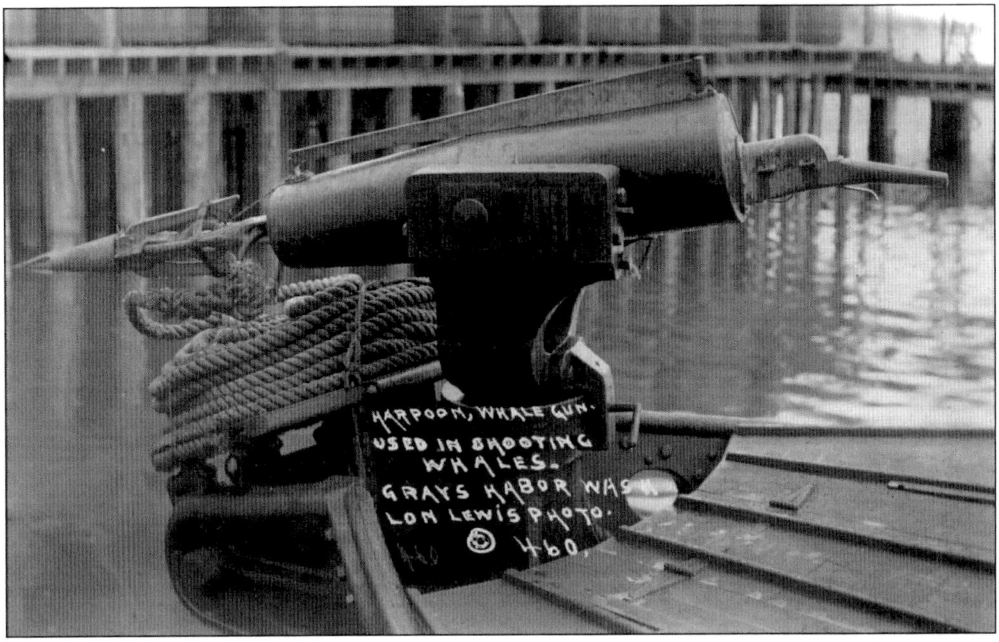

This photograph was used on postcards, and saw several printings. It was originally taken by Lon Lewis. The image shows that the harpoon gun is ready to go, which indicates that the ship is ready to begin whaling.

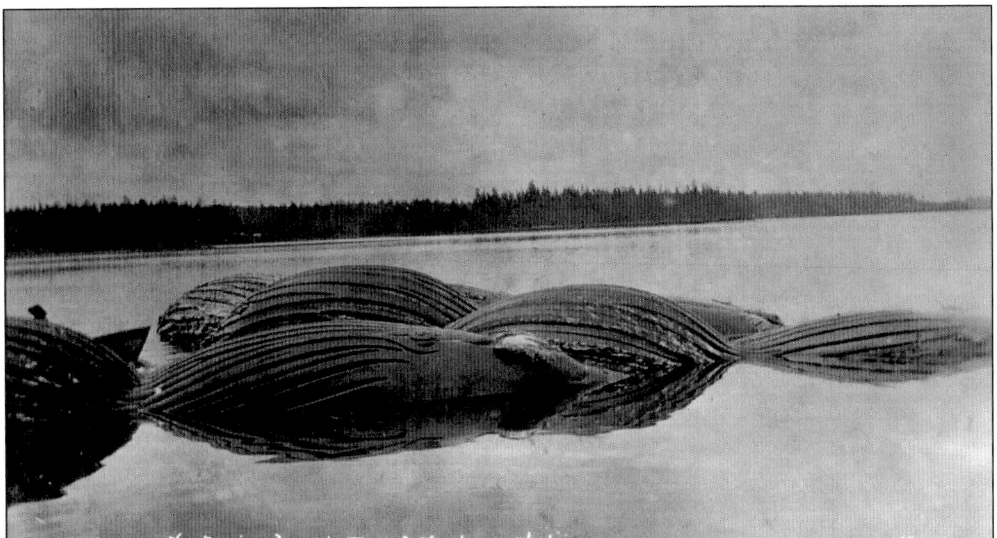

In this photograph, a group of five or six whales has been brought in to the Grays Harbor station. In some years, whales were brought up from Oregon and arrived in groups of four or more.

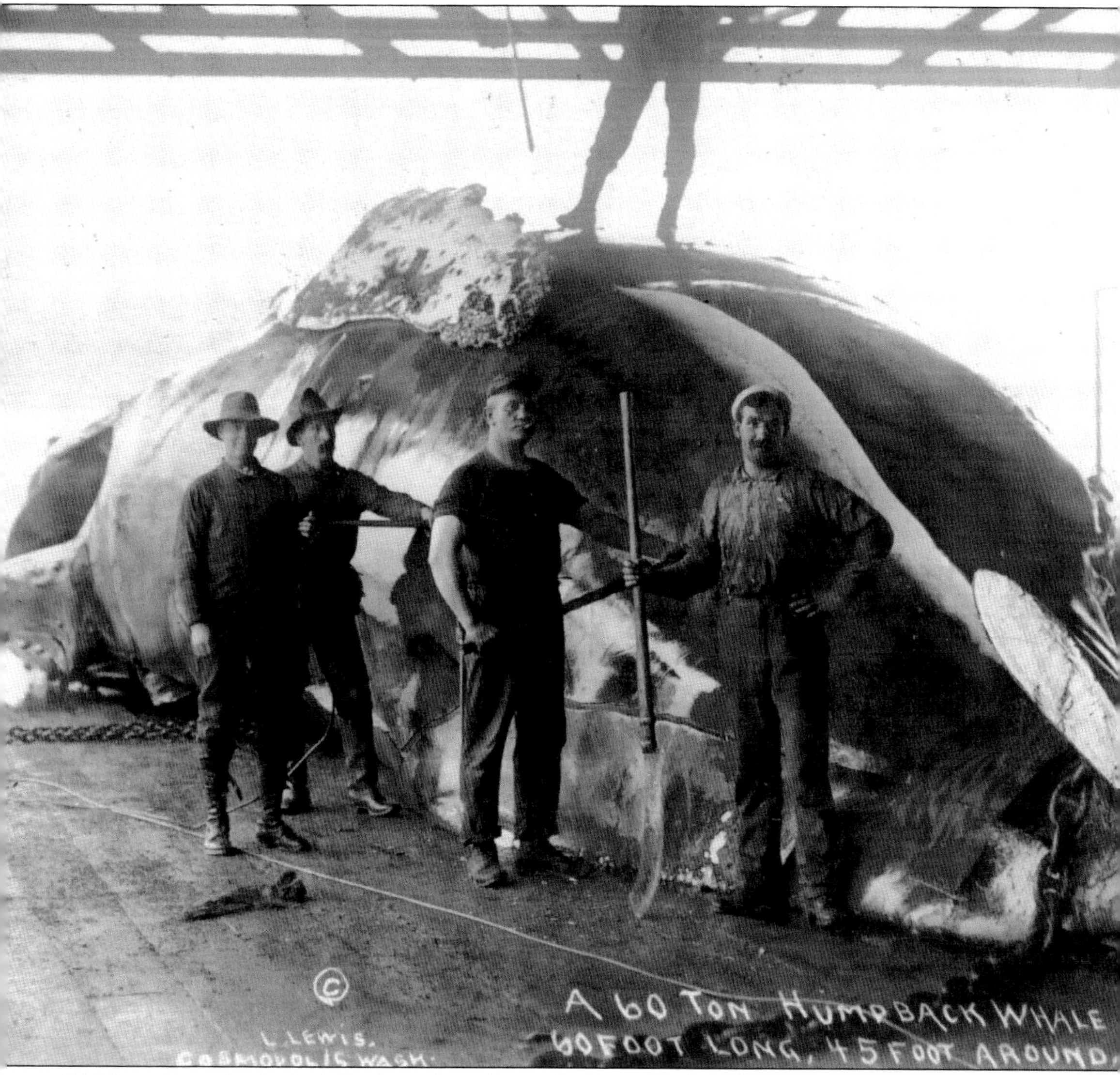

This large humpback whale has been brought up the Grays Harbor platform and into the flensing area. The head flenser has made the first cut, and the crew is posing for pictures before the remainder of the flensing occurs.

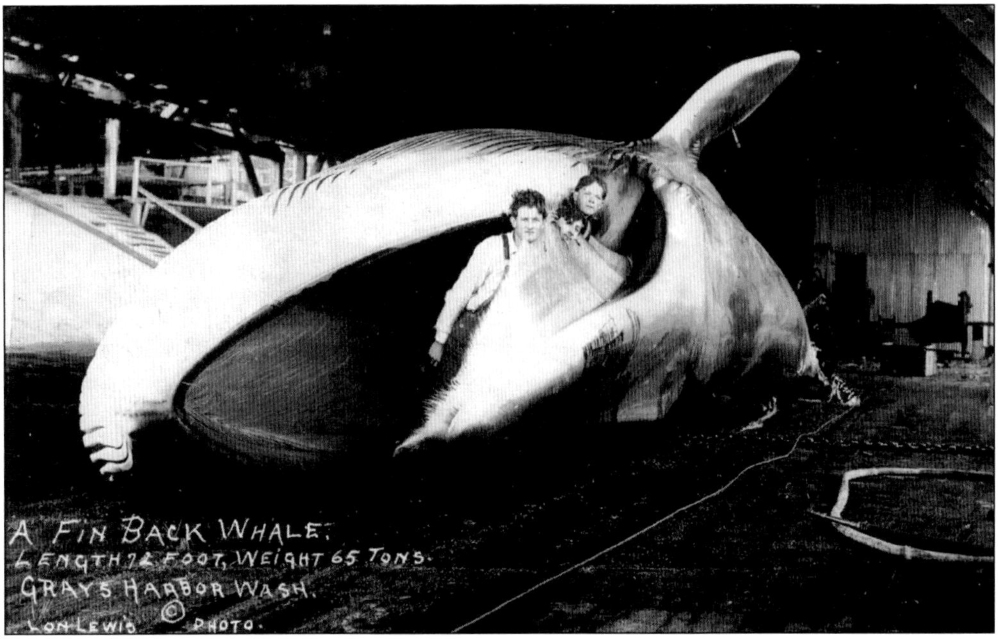

A man and two boys pose in the mouth of a 65-ton finback whale at Grays Harbor.

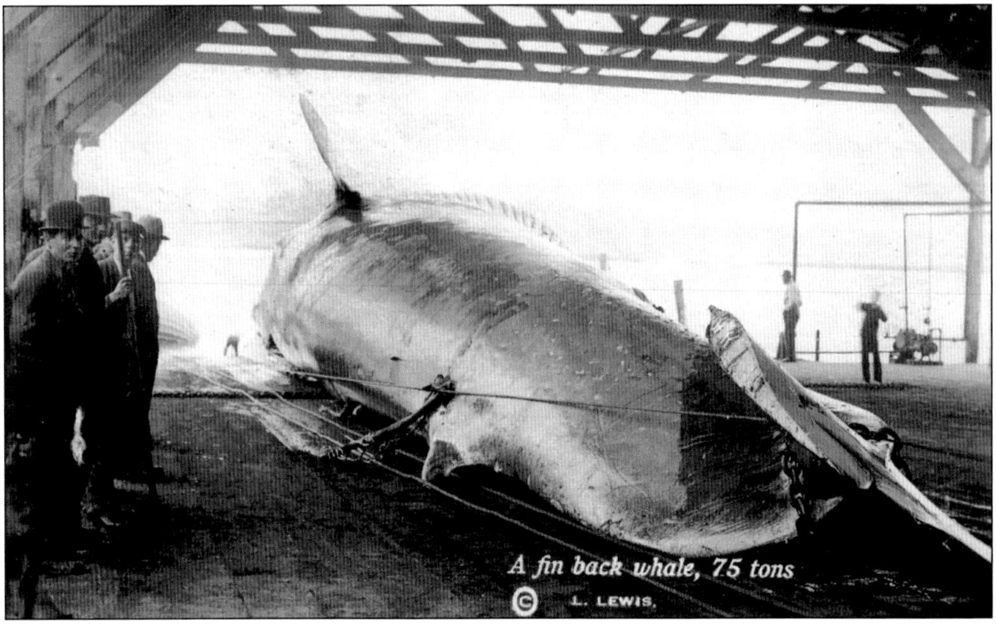

In this photograph, a finback whale has just been brought in for flensing at Grays Harbor.

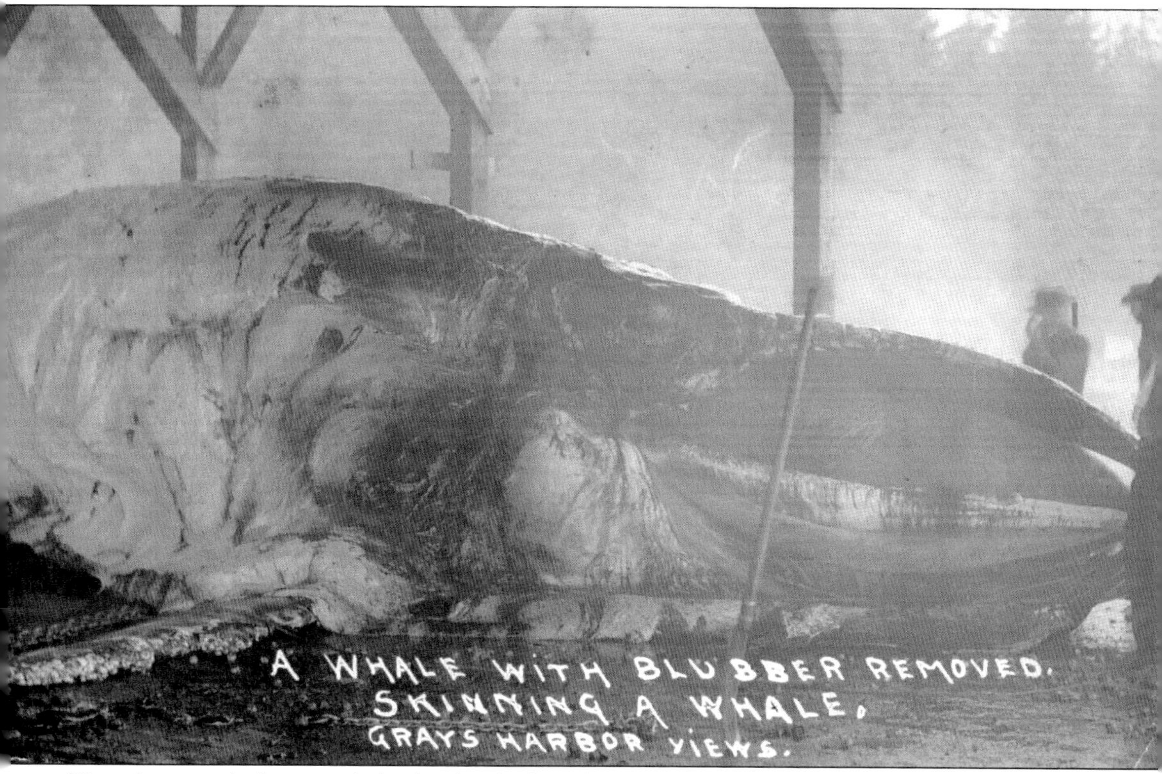

This photograph shows a whale that has had its skin and blubber removed.

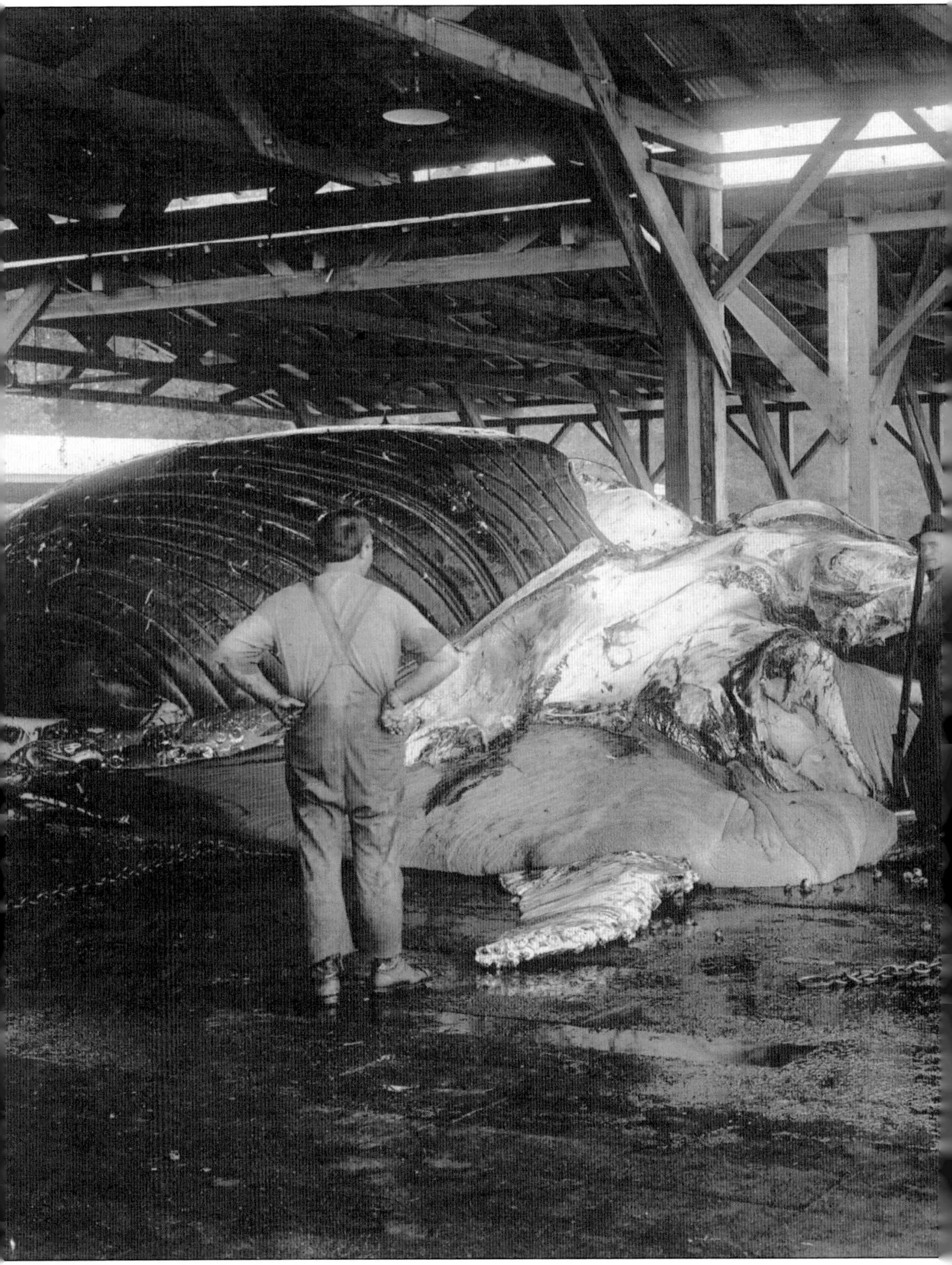

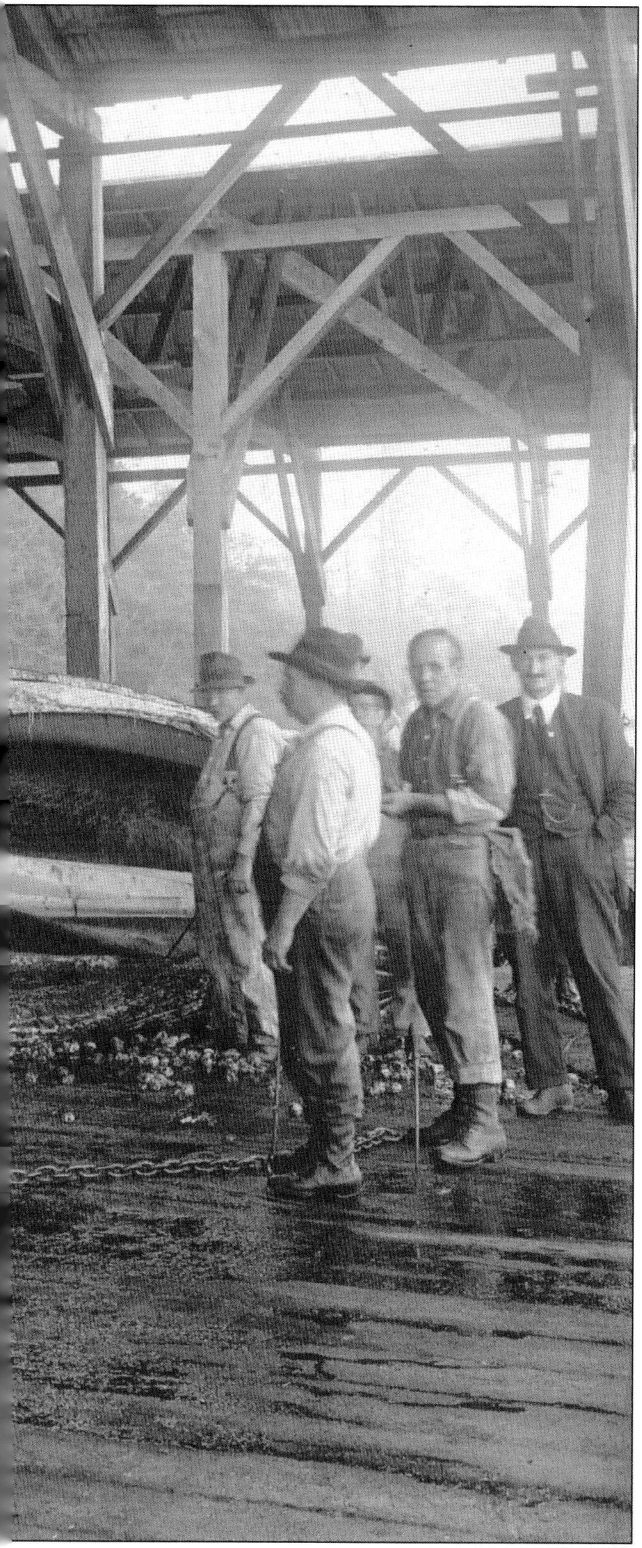

Workers pose during the flensing of a humpback whale at Grays Harbor. Someone from management appears to be looking on from the right.

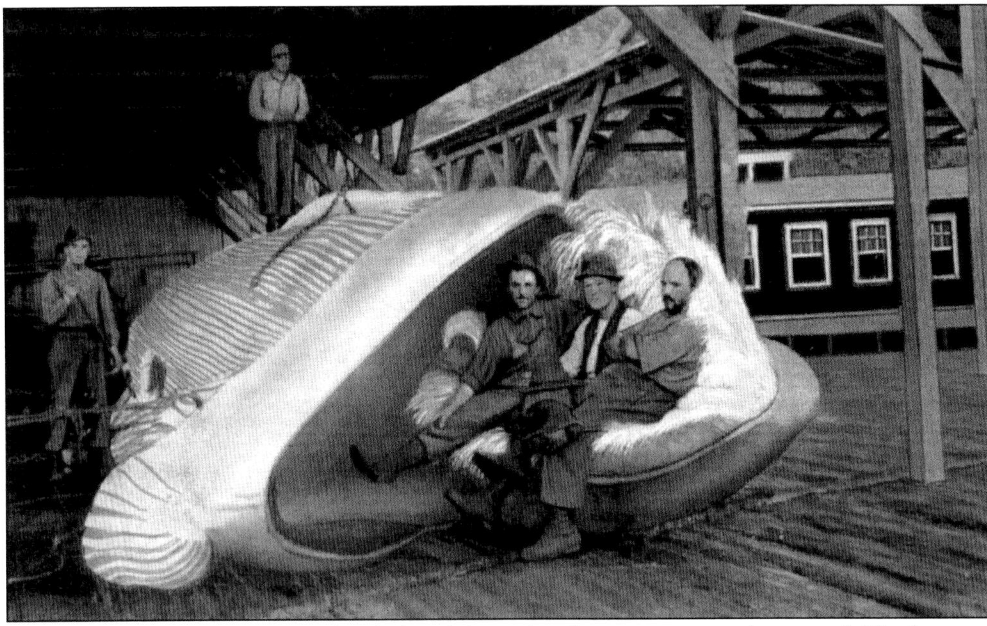

Three men relax in the mouth of a whale, while workers begin to process the animal. The harpoon is still in the whale, as shown by the chain that drapes down the animal's side.

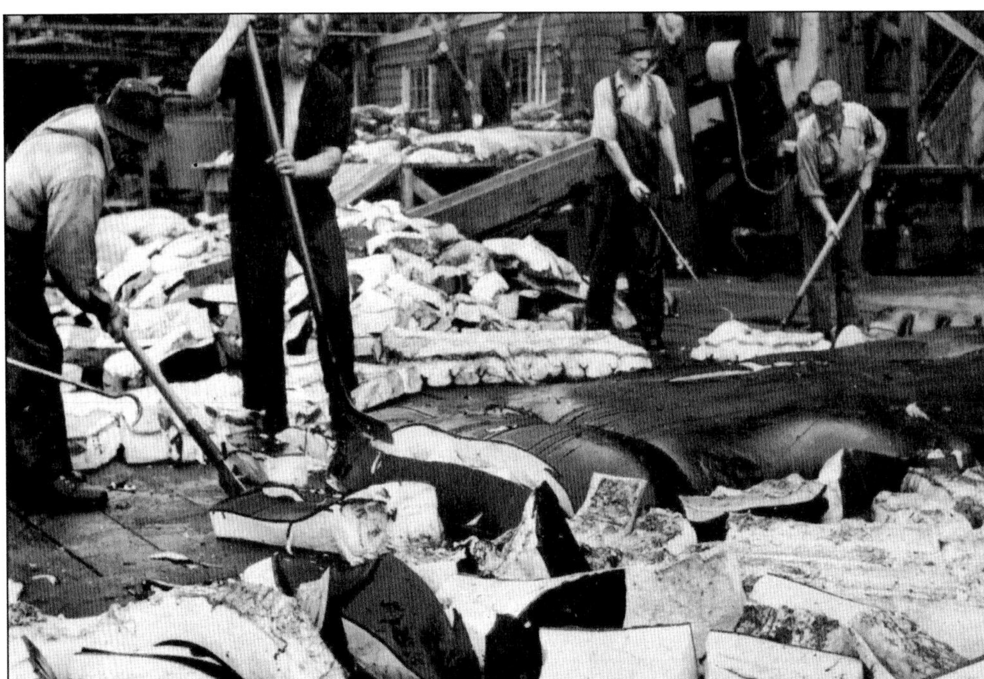

These workers are using spades to cut blubber into smaller pieces. These pieces will be put into cookers to remove as much of the oil as possible.

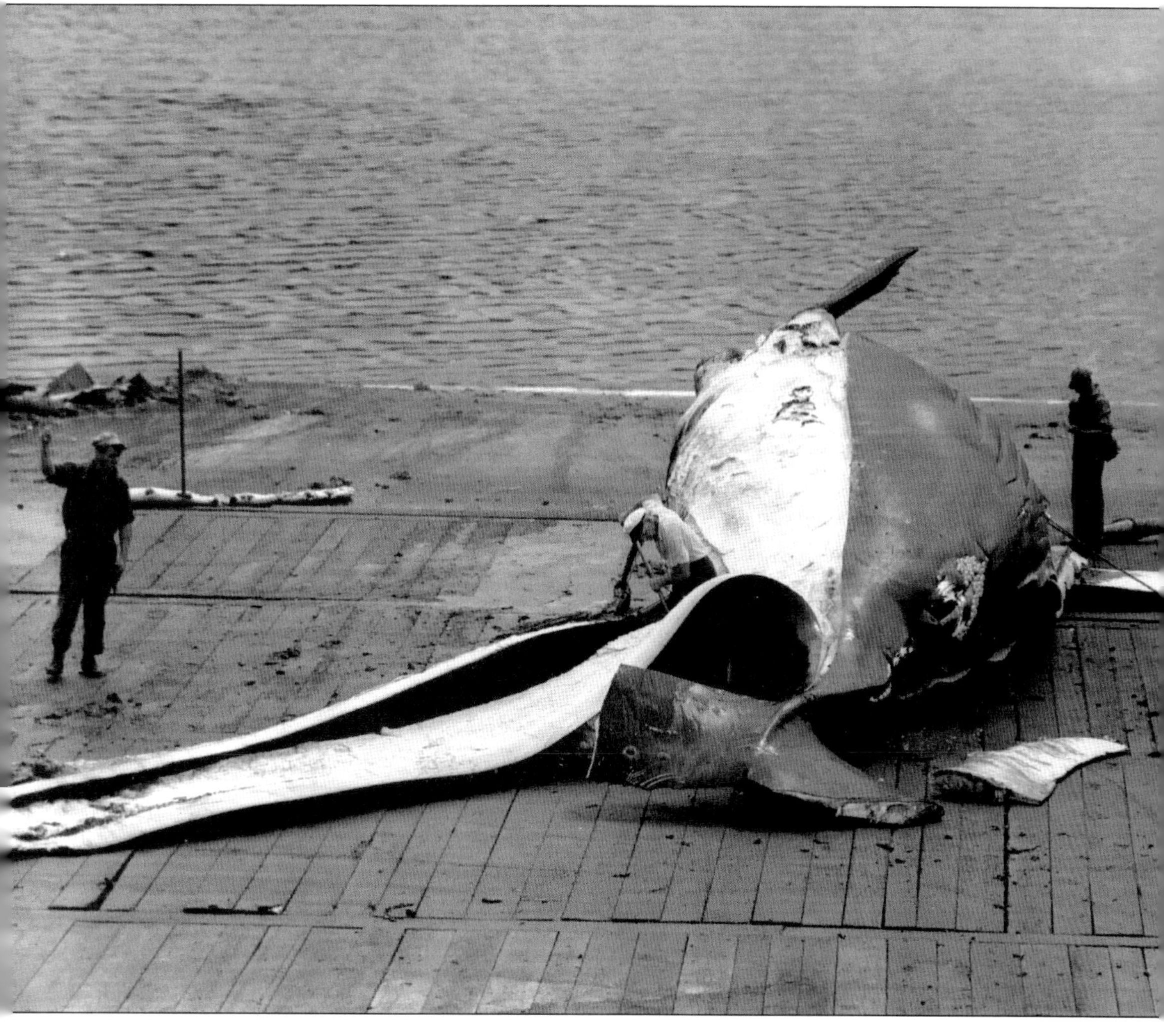

The crew of the *Nahmint* killed this humpback whale, which is now on the flensing platform.

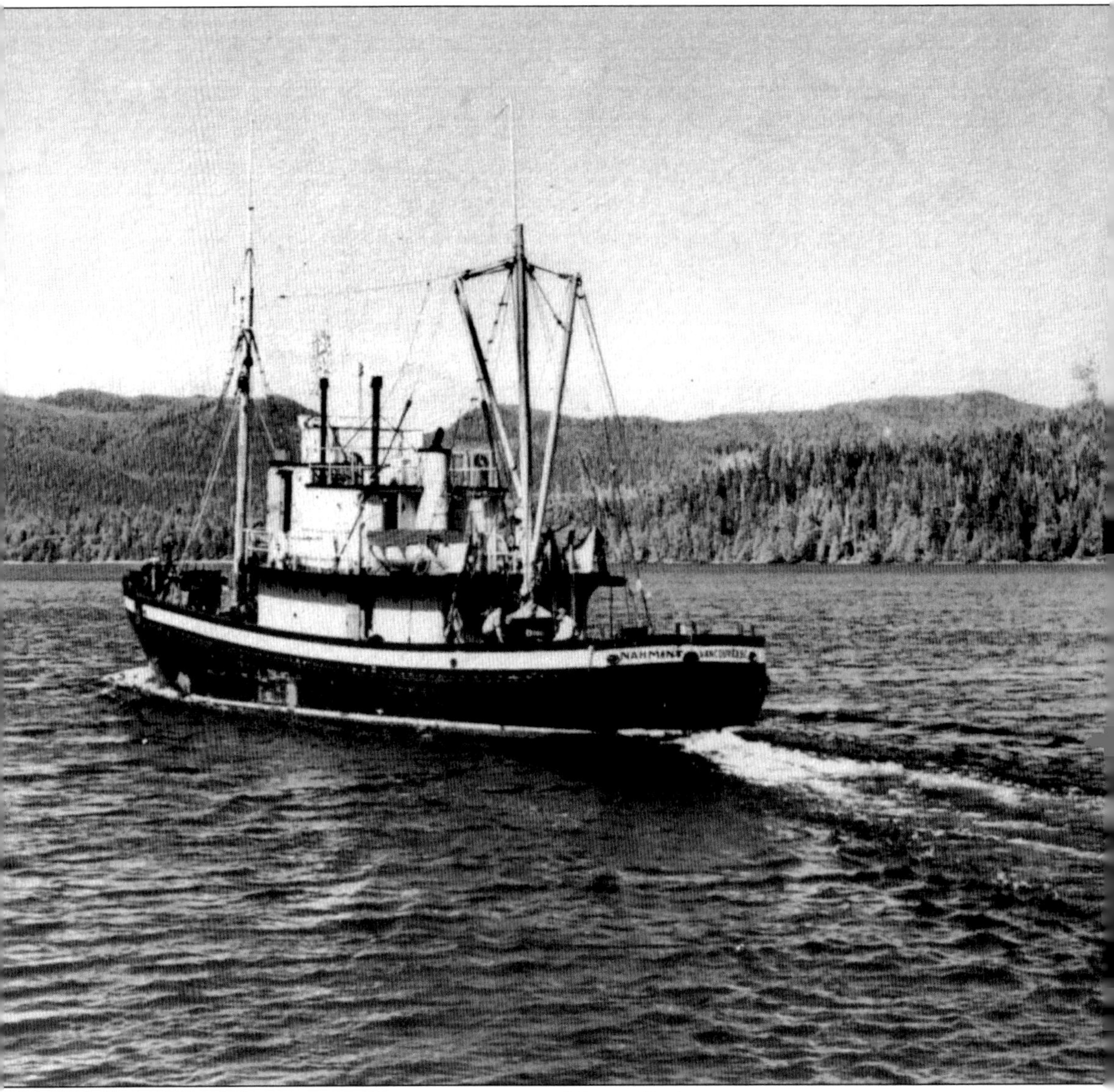

The whaler *Nahmint* is seen here cruising out of Grays Harbor.

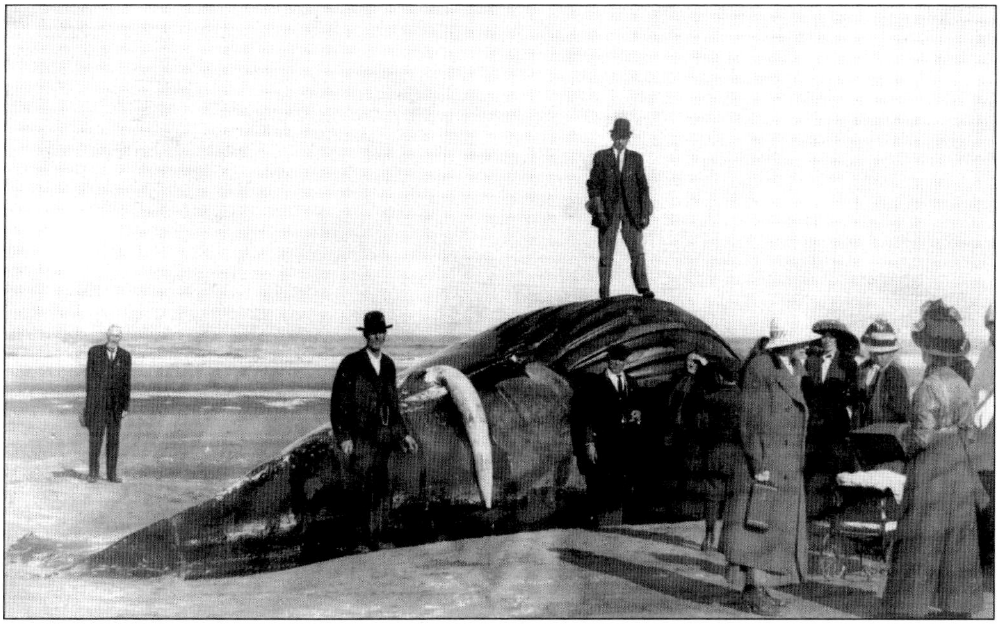

This photograph shows a male, black humpback whale on a beach. It likely dates to the 1920s.

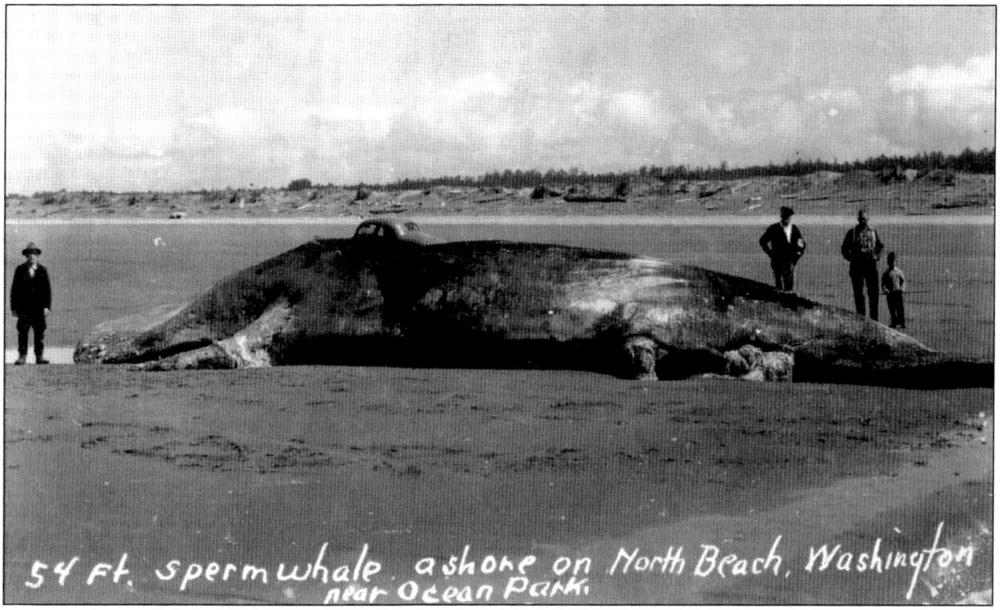

A 54-foot sperm whale is pictured here washed ashore near Ocean Park.

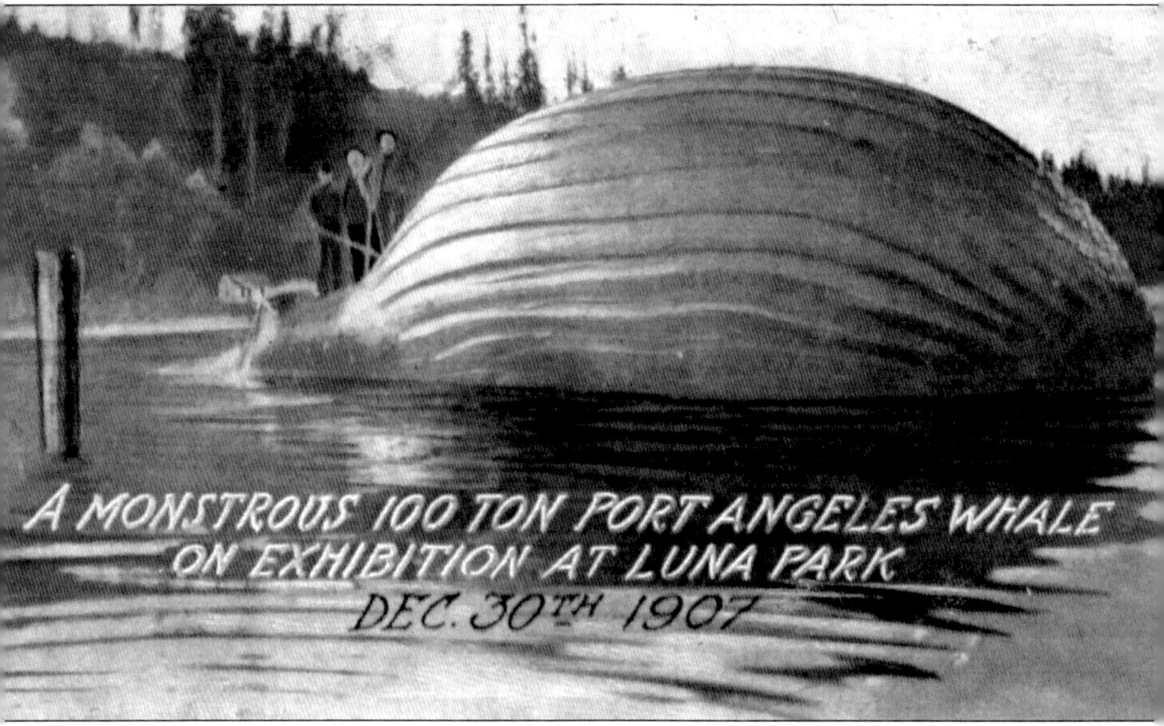

In 1907, a stranded whale was placed on exhibition at Luna Park.

Six

Western Whaling Company

The last phase of whaling in British Columbia was described as the first all Canadian-owned whaling company in British Columbia. The new company, incorporated in Vancouver with $500,000 of capital, consisted of a consortium of people and companies, including British Columbia Packers, Nelson Brothers Fisheries, and W.F. Gibson & Sons. The new company was called the Western Whaling Company.

The original intention of the company was to resurrect the old Rose Harbor whaling station, but thankfully, the enclosed aircraft hangars at the Royal Canadian Air Force's seaplane base at Coal Harbour became available. The enclosed hangars provided sufficient covered space for the entire set of processing equipment to be located inside and kept out of the elements. The downside to the location was the time and distance needed to reach the open ocean, as Coal Harbour is inside the Vancouver Harbor area. The company planned to deal with this problem by having the whales dropped off and brought to the station by tenders.

Plans for the purchase of all new equipment were made, including four Norwegian Kvaermer-type digesters, five Sharples "Super-D Canters," horizontal screen cookers, deep-bay cookers, a flame dryer, a "meal cyclone" meat press, four Sharples separators, a liver-oil plant, settling tanks, blowdown tanks, and separating tanks—all of which were kept in one hangar. The second hangar had an evaporator plant for the reduction of solubles, and a freezer for fresh meat storage. The equipment was the latest available, but still preserved the tried and true methods employed by previous British Columbia companies. With all of this equipment in place, the company now needed to pay attention to the ships necessary to bring in the whales.

The vessels were purchased for the start of the 1948 season. The first whaler purchased was the *James Carruthers*, a fishing trawler built in England in 1912. It was sent to B.C. Marine Engineers and Shipbuilders for its refit and the installation of the harpoon cannon that made it a real whaler. Her captain would be Louis Larsen, who had experience with many of the west coast whaling companies. The second vessel was the *Nahmint*, a four-year-old ex-minesweeper from San Francisco, captained by Johan "Big John" Bordewickj. The third vessel was an old whaler called the *Sebastian*, which had been fishing for 32 years after she stopped whaling. The fourth was the *Tahsis Chief*, which, unfortunately, failed sea trials.

The whaling company also had to deal with unions, most of which were just a few years old. Once an agreement was reached with the unions and the whaling company, whaling was allowed to commence. The season opened on May 30, 1948, and closed on September 24. The vessels operated between Cape Cook and Cape Scott, and took in 182 whales. The small number of whales caught was attributed to the company having to train personnel on the whalers and at the processing station, and to a bottleneck in the factory, which was only able to process three whales per day.

After the first season at Coal Harbour, the company got rid of the *James Carruthers* and the *Saanich* due to their poor performance. The first of the replacements was the *Kimisquit*, which was a 104-foot ex-Navy vessel—powered by a Cummins engine and built at Nanaimo in 1944—captained and owned by Jack Haan. The other vessel was the *Tahsis Chief*, which was reevaluated and accepted. By 1950, the Western Whaling Company was wholly owned by B.C. Packers, and had added the *Bouvet III*—a whaler from Antarctica and Labrador—to the fleet. At the time, *The Bouvet III*, which was built in 1932, was joining the *Nahmint* and the reworked *Tahsis Chief*. Additionally, two tenders, the *Speedmac* and *Towmac*, were being used to tow whales from the float where they were dropped in Winter Harbor to Coal Harbour.

For the 1951 season, Western Whaling added two catcher boats from the Antarctic and expanded the plant by 25 percent to handle the increased catch. The *Polar V* was a 112-foot catcher boat, which had been constructed by the Nylands ship works in Oslo in 1931. The vessel was purchased directly from service in Antarctica and was rerouted from Cape Town, South Africa, to British Columbia. The second new vessel, the *Globe VII*, was a 251-foot Antarctic whaler built by Moss in Germany in 1935, and was one of the most modern whalers available at the time. In 1954, the company acquired the *Lavallee*—built in Tacoma, Washington—which was originally a Navy minesweeper.

Every year became a dance between the whaling company and the unions. The unions were insisting that the companies were profitable, while the companies insisted that expenses were increasing and whaling was becoming less profitable each year. In 1959, the unions voted to stand by their demands, and even though mediation was attempted, an agreement could not be reached. Without an agreement, the whaling company prepared a letter explaining to the workers that there would be no whaling in 1960. After this, mediation was again attempted, and an agreement was reached.

The 1959 catch was a high one, with 868 whales caught, and the season was topped by a large 83-foot blue whale. Even so, profit per whale was very low. The worldwide prices for whale meat, oil, and sperm oil were extremely low. As a result, B.C. Packers announced that it would not go whaling in 1960. By not whaling—it was hoped—stocks of whale products would decrease and the prices for the next year should be more favorable. Shore whaling on the west coast of North America was restricted to two whaling companies in 1960, both operating out of San Francisco Bay. The two companies were the Del Monte Fishing Company and Golden Gate Fisheries, both of which whaled from Richmond, California.

The Coal Harbour station was reopened in 1961, but under new management. A series of talks had taken place between B.C. Packers and Taiyo Gyogyo Kadushki Kaisha—Japan's largest whaling and fishing combine. Whaling reopened under the name of Western Canada Whaling Company Limited. The association's main product was to be whale meat, which would be frozen, canned, and shipped to Japan for human consumption. The agreement called for a fully cooperative whaling operation to produce whale meat that met Japanese standards and was prepared by Japanese laborers who were skilled in its production. Western Whaling had produced whale meat before, but as chicken fodder and mink food. A portion had also been produced for human consumption, but it had been shipped fresh and in limited quantities.

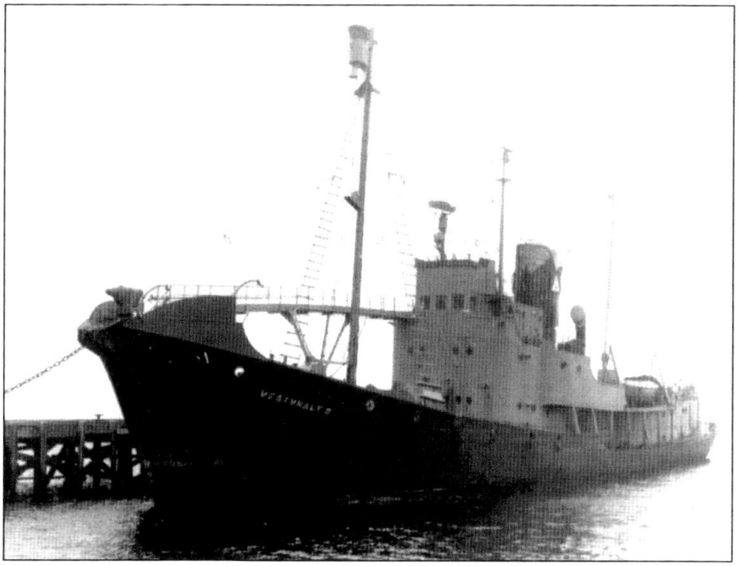

According to Robert Lloyd Webb in *On the Northwest*, B.C. Packers & Taiyo decided to upgrade their whaling fleet and set the older ships aside. Taiyo sent larger, more modern vessels to take the place of the older ships. In 1965, Western Whaling refitted the *Toshi Maru 22* (previously the *Suderoy XVII*), pictured here, and renamed it the *Westwhale 8*.

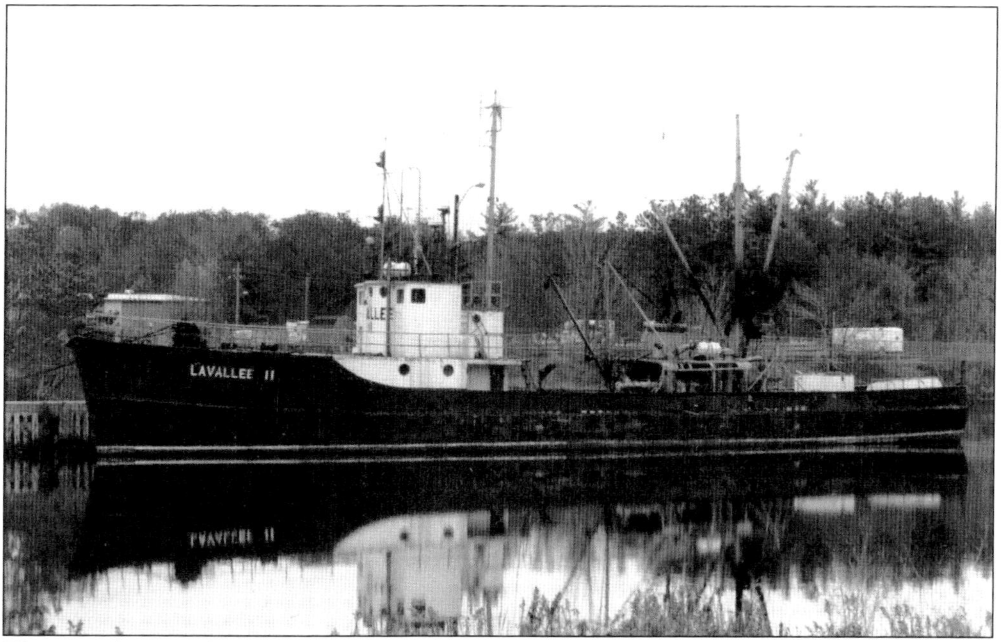

This is a photograph of the *Lavalee II*. Originally called the *Tahsis Chief*, she was purchased by Western Whaling in 1954. Diesel powered, and fitted with sonar and steel cabling for whaling, she was originally built in Tacoma, Washington, as a Navy minesweeper. Crewmembers said that a diesel whaler would never work, as the noise of the engines would scare off the whales, but the owners liked that the diesel engine required fewer firemen than the traditional coal-fired vessels. In the end, the diesel powered whaler worked just fine.

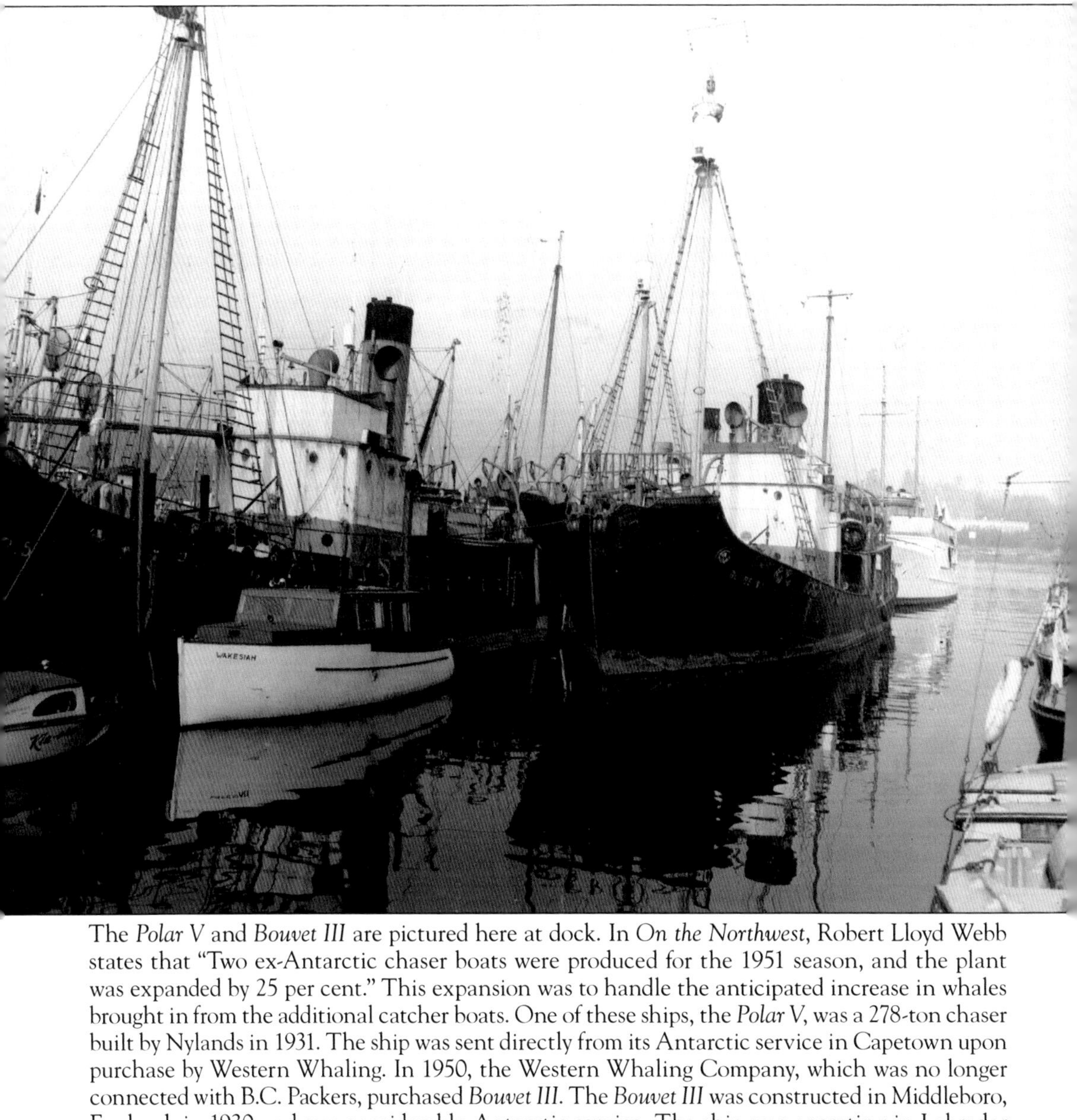

The *Polar V* and *Bouvet III* are pictured here at dock. In *On the Northwest*, Robert Lloyd Webb states that "Two ex-Antarctic chaser boats were produced for the 1951 season, and the plant was expanded by 25 per cent." This expansion was to handle the anticipated increase in whales brought in from the additional catcher boats. One of these ships, the *Polar V*, was a 278-ton chaser built by Nylands in 1931. The ship was sent directly from its Antarctic service in Capetown upon purchase by Western Whaling. In 1950, the Western Whaling Company, which was no longer connected with B.C. Packers, purchased *Bouvet III*. The *Bouvet III* was constructed in Middleboro, England, in 1930 and saw considerable Antarctic service. The ship was operating in Labrador when it was purchased by Western Whaling.

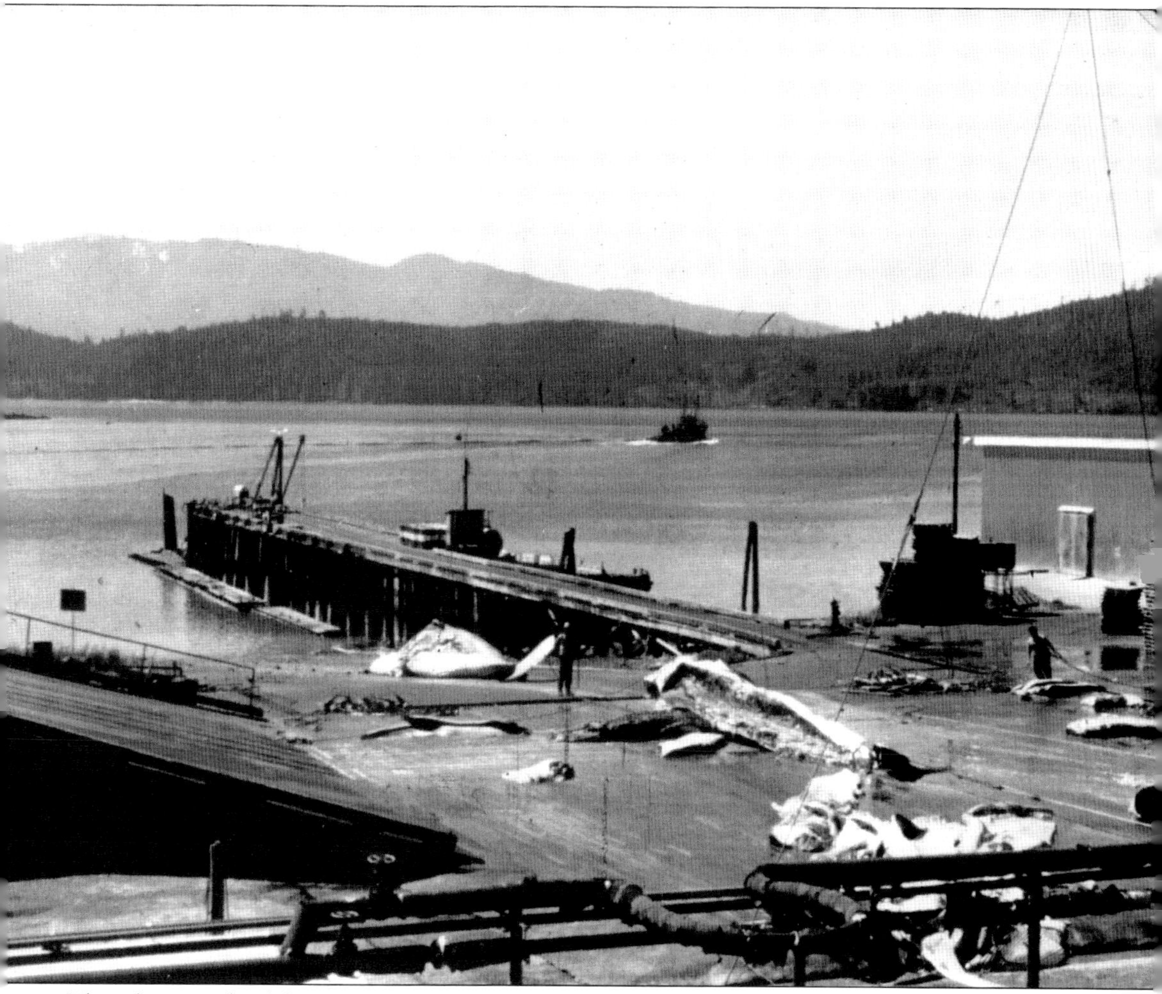

This photograph of the Coal Harbour whaling station in British Columbia shows the ramp and platform where the whales were flensed, cut up, and brought into the plant for processing.

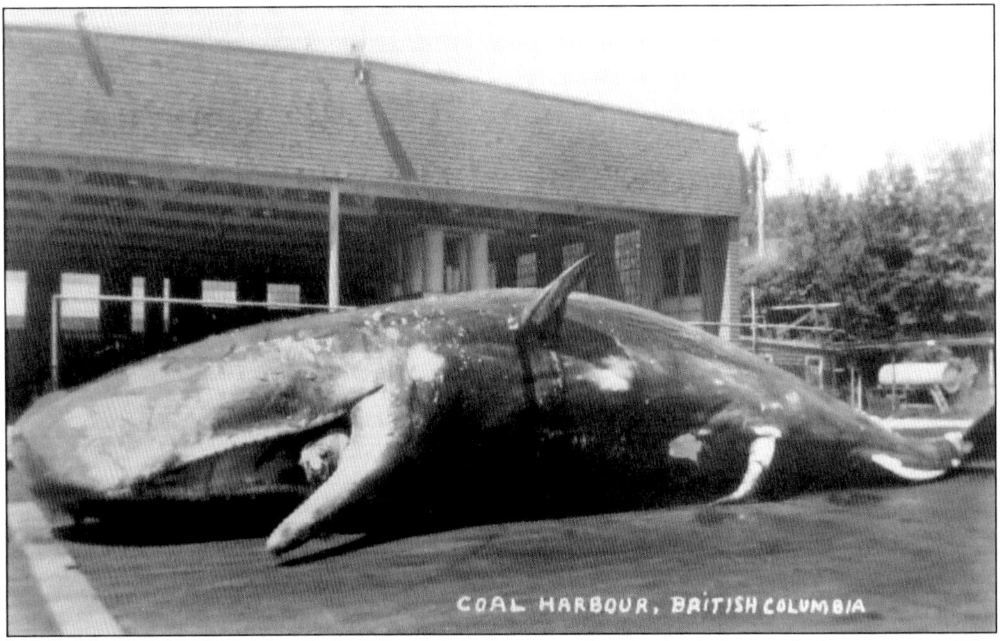

The body of a male sperm whale awaits processing at the Coal Harbour whaling station. The plant began as a seaplane port and was converted into a whaling factory. It offered considerable covered space, which offered protection from rain and other bad weather.

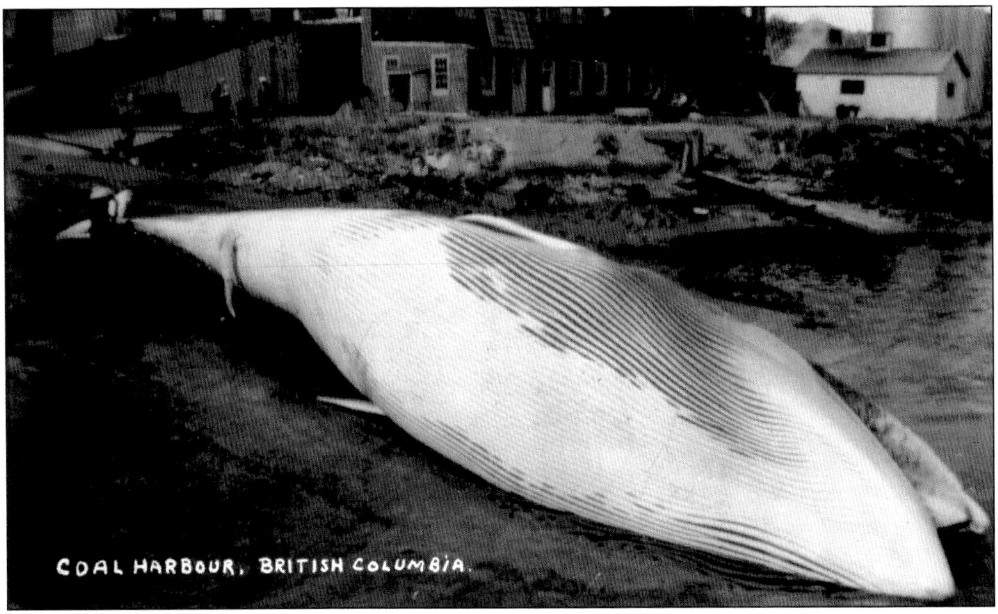

A fin whale is shown here on the ramp of the Coal Harbour whaling station, ready for flensing.

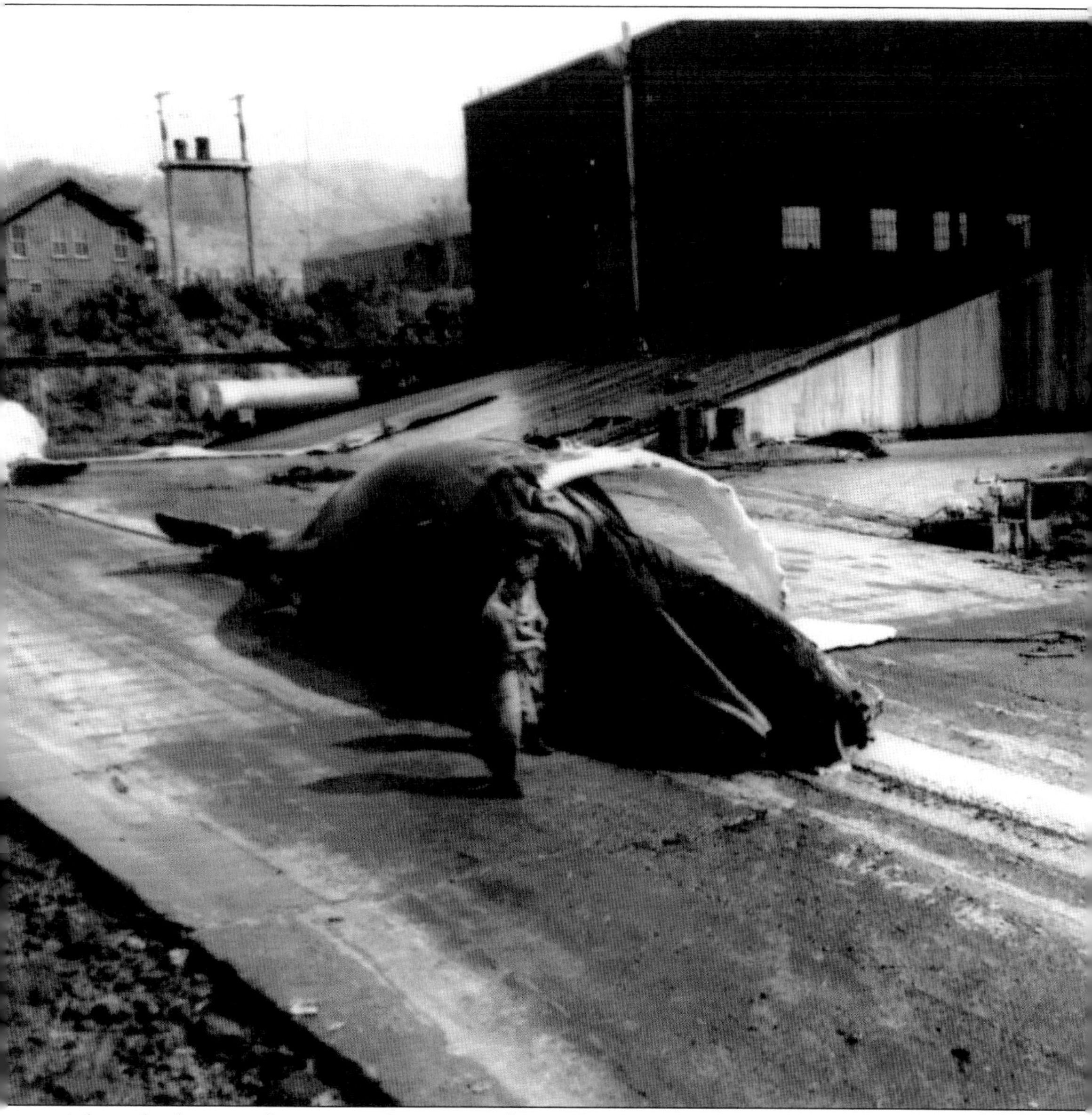

A humpback awaits flensing on the ramp at the Coal Harbour whaling station. The humpback is easy to recognize by its large, wing-like front flippers.

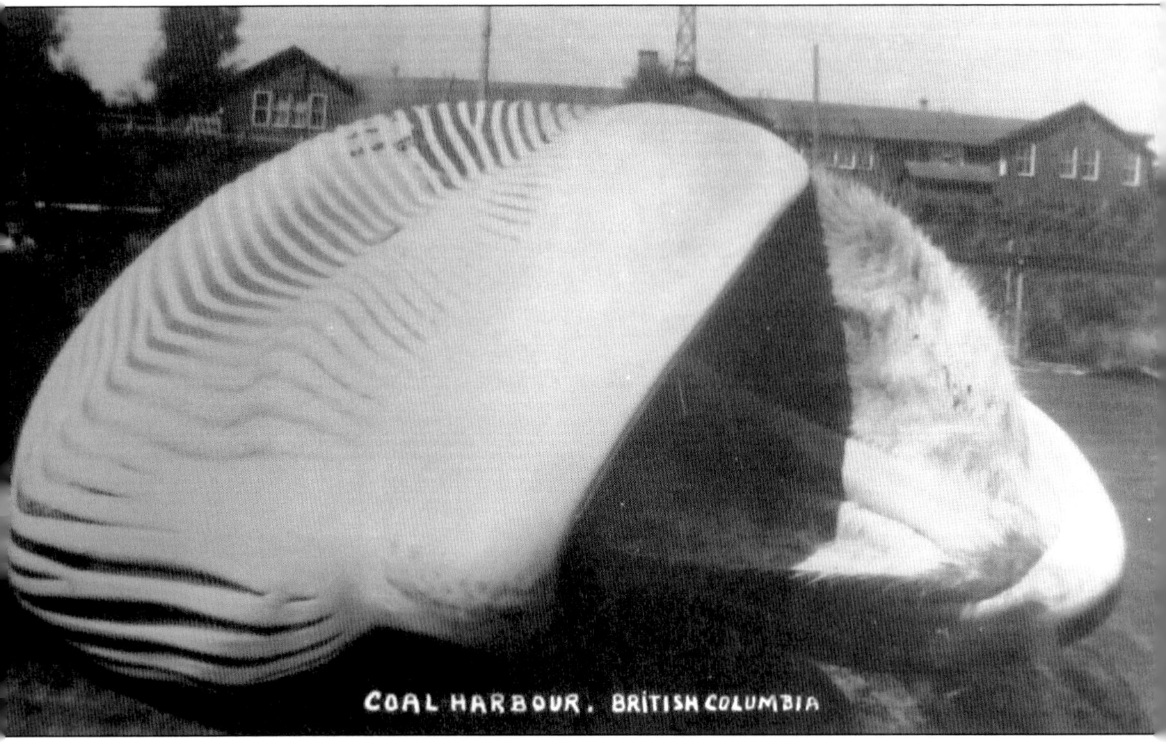

This close-up of a finback whale shows its mouth and baleen plates on the right, and the ventral grooves on its stomach to the left. The ventral grooves expand when the whale takes in large amounts of fish-laden water. The whale then expels the water through the baleen, filtering out the fish, which are quickly moved back by the whale's tongue and swallowed.

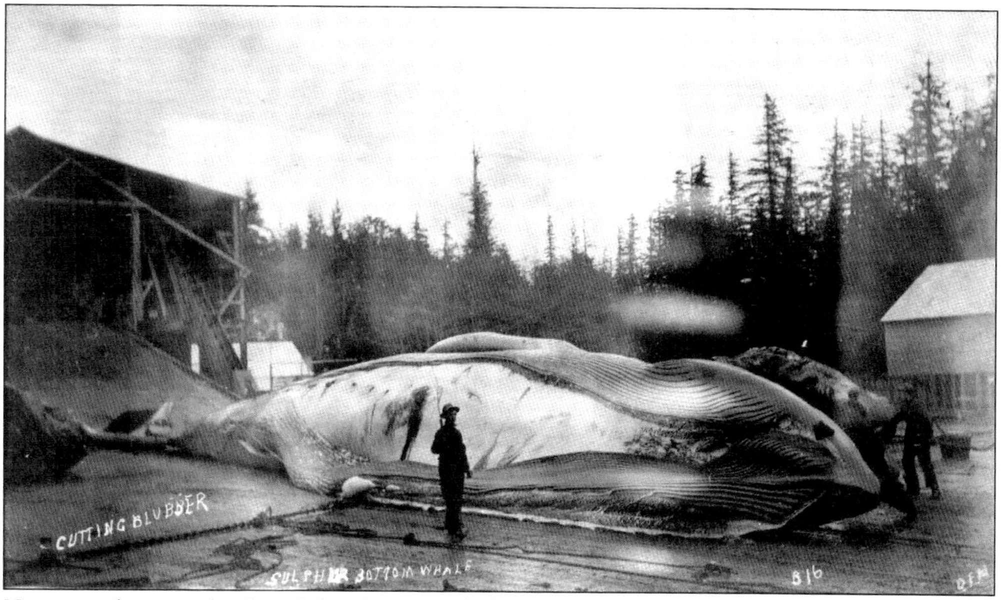

Here is a photograph of a sulphur bottom whale (or blue whale) on the ramp at Coal Harbour, near Vancouver, British Columbia.

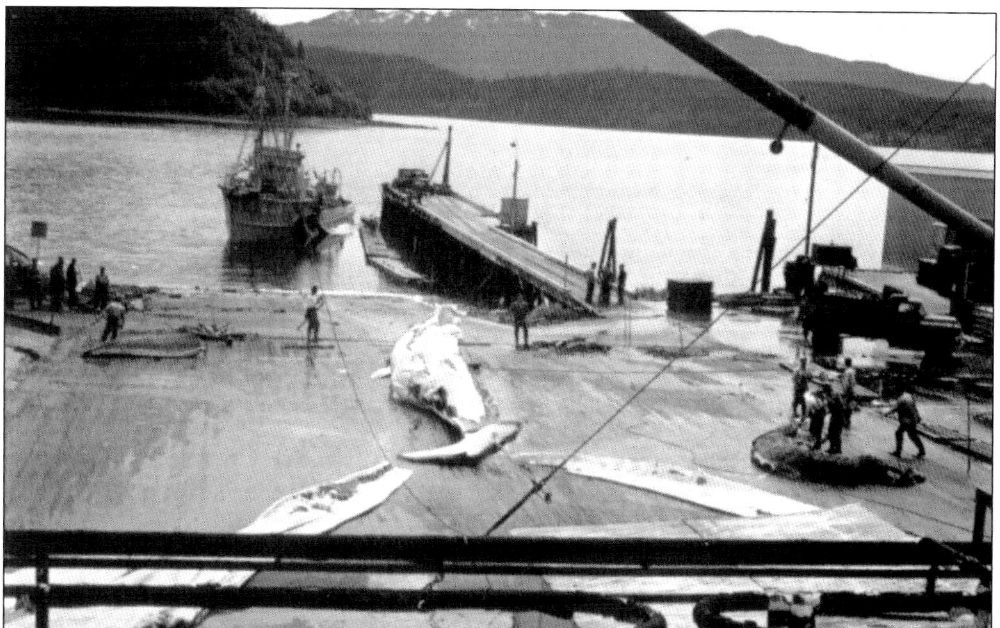

This view of the ramp of the Coal Harbour whaling station shows one of the whalers in the water at the dock.

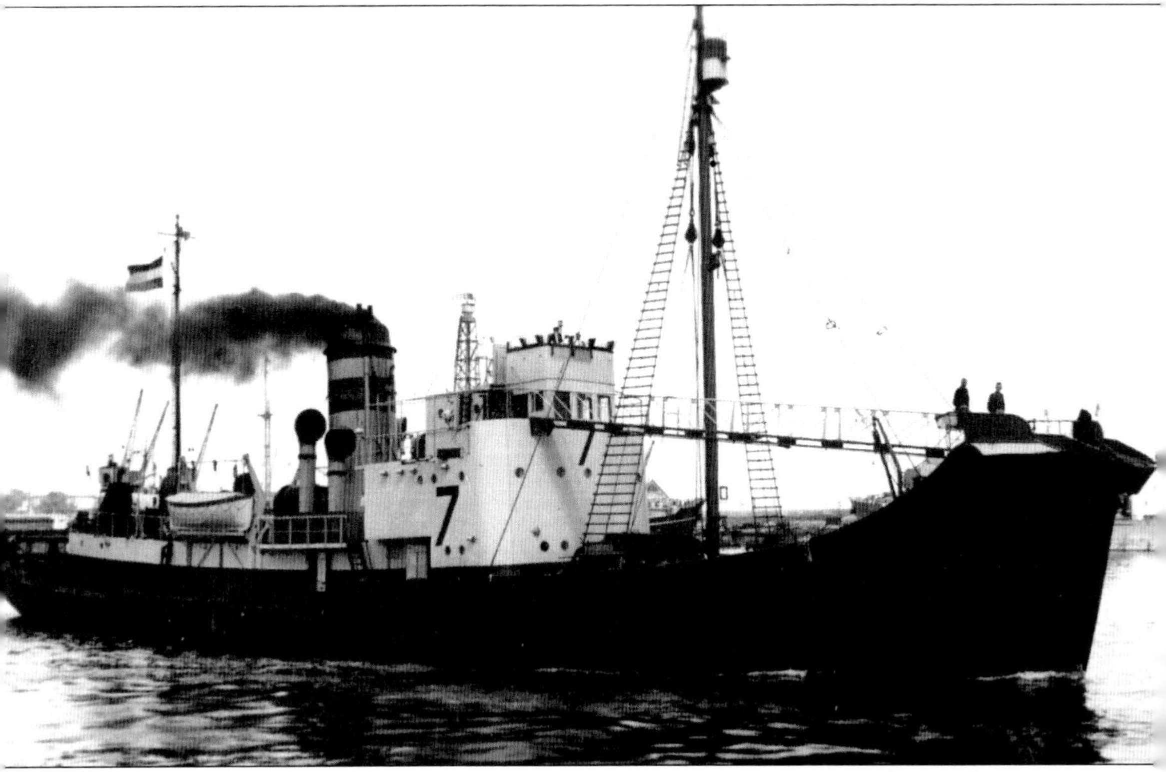

The *Toshi Maru 21* was the largest boat sent from Japan to the Western Whaling fleet. It was constructed in 1952 as the Norwegian *Suderoy XVI*. The *Toshi Maru 21* was renamed *Westwhale 7* in British Coumbia in 1963. She had been in Antarctica for the Suderoy Hvalfangstaktieselskapet and, for a short time, was named the *Kot 51*.

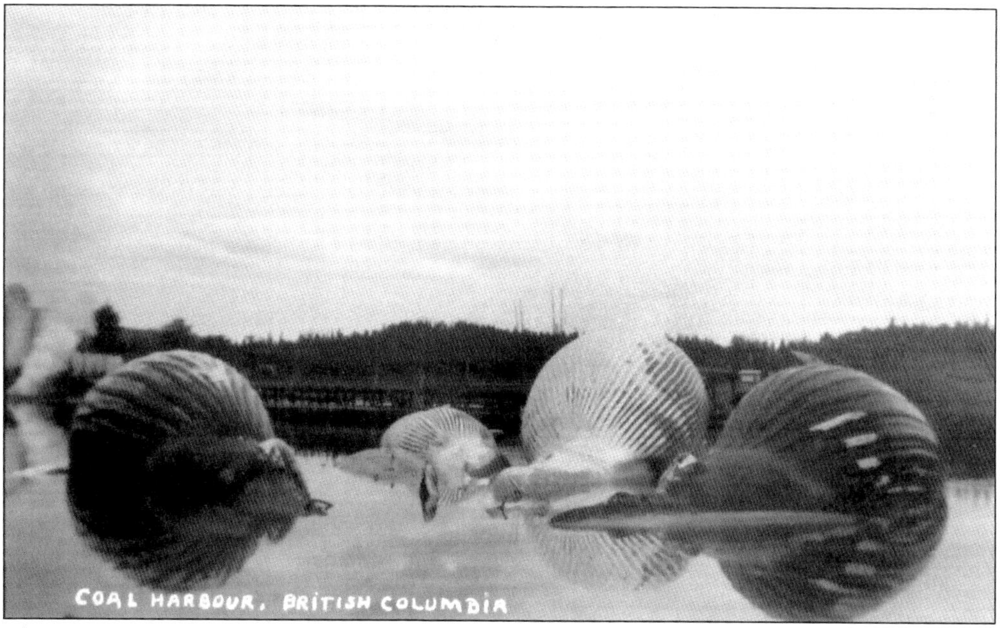

This view from the water shows several whales waiting to be flensed at Coal Harbour.

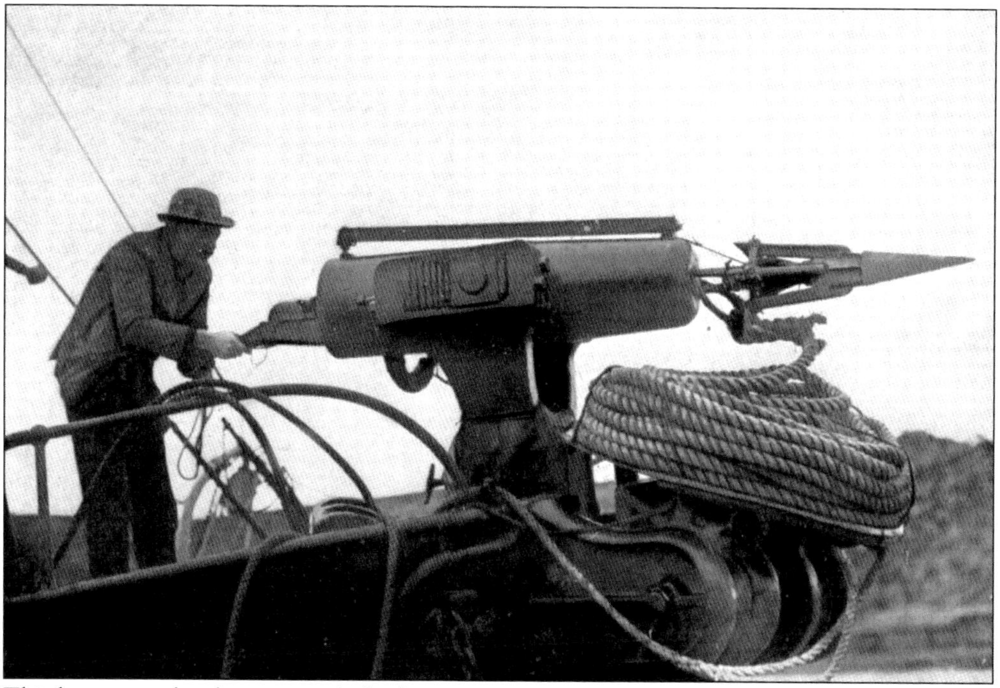

This harpooner has his gun ready for firing.

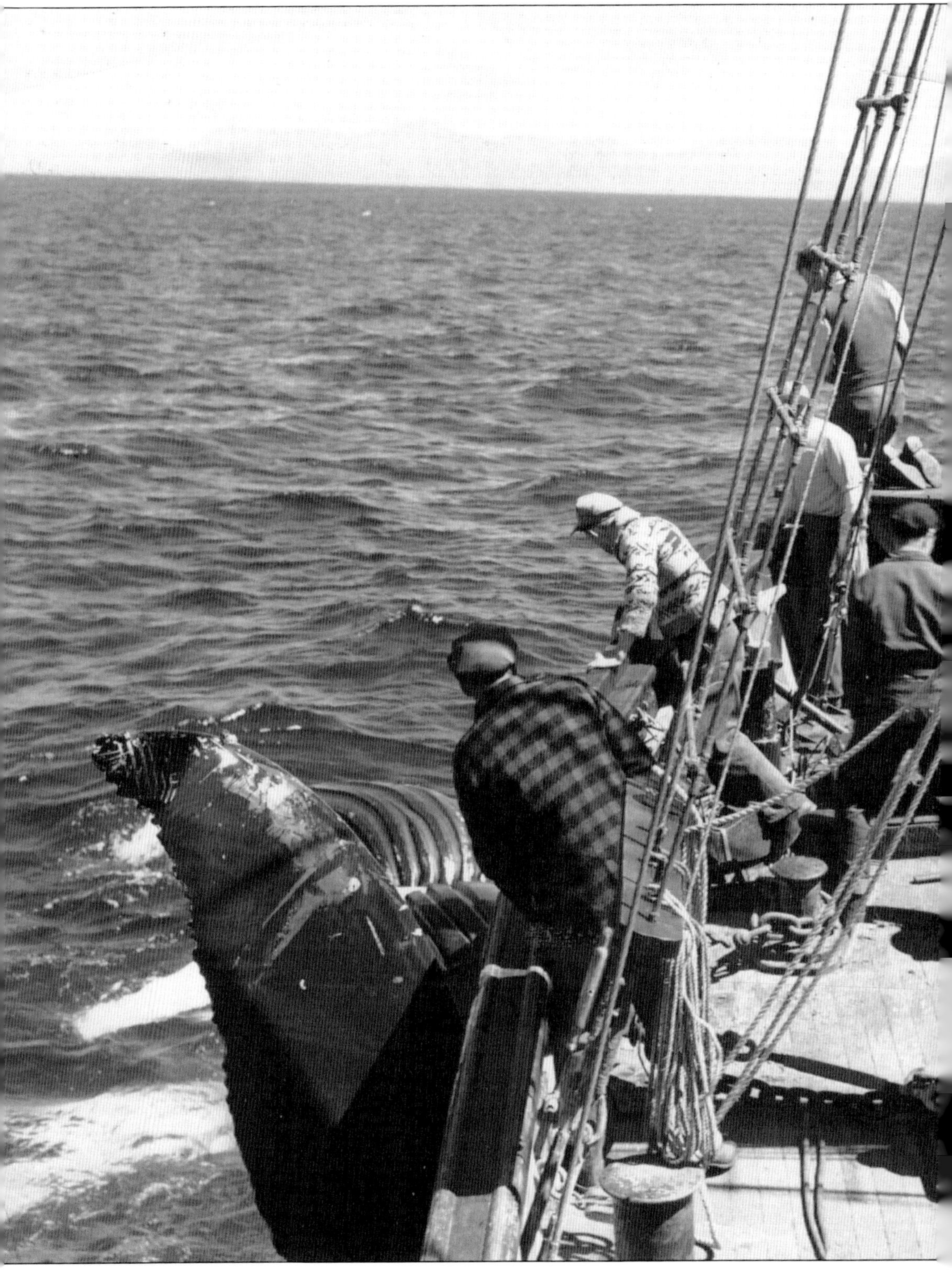

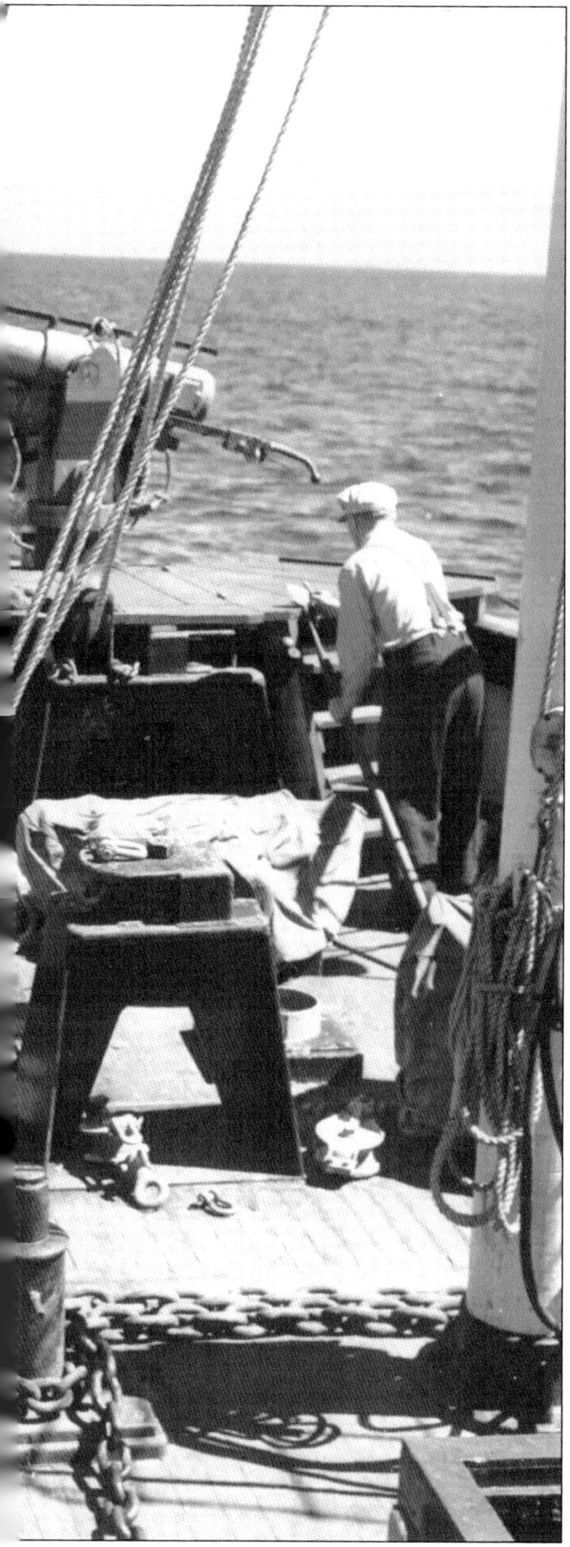

This photograph of the bow of the *Nahmint* shows the activity that surrounded tying a recently caught whale to the ship for towing. The *Nahmint* was a converted minesweeper. Western Whaling's ships were renamed for the new company in 1961, with the *Polar V*, the flagship of the fleet, becoming *Westwhale*; the *Bouvet III* becoming *Westwhale 2*; the *Globe VII* becoming *Westwhale 3*; and the *Lavallee* becoming *Westwhale 4*. Two new whaling ships arrived from Japan: the *Katsu Maru*, a 1,600 horsepower 14-knot chaser that was renamed *Westwhale 5*; and the *Seki Maru No. 2*, which was renamed *Westwhale 6*. Later, for the 1964–1965 season, the *Toshi Maru 21* was renamed *Westwhale 7*, and the *Toshi Maru 22* became *Westwhale 9*. The whale catch began to decline in the mid-1960s, and, at the end of the 1967 season, Western Whaling's management made the announcement that the Coal Harbour station would not reopen for the 1968 season. Men, ships, and equipment were dispersed around the world for fishing and whaling, or sold for scrap.

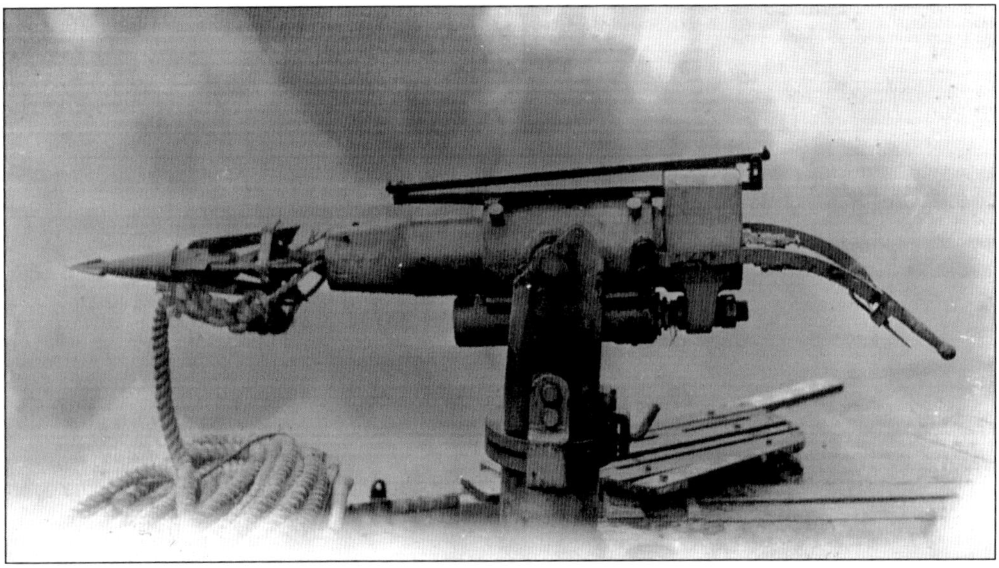

Here are two more examples of a harpooner and gun ready for firing. The bottom photograph was taken in Victoria, British Columbia, in 1961. Under new ownership, the boats arrived with Japanese captain-gunners and mates, which caused additional problems with the local unions. Previous contracts called for three-man crews consisting of a captain, a gunner, and a mate. Under the Japanese system, however, one man was eliminated.

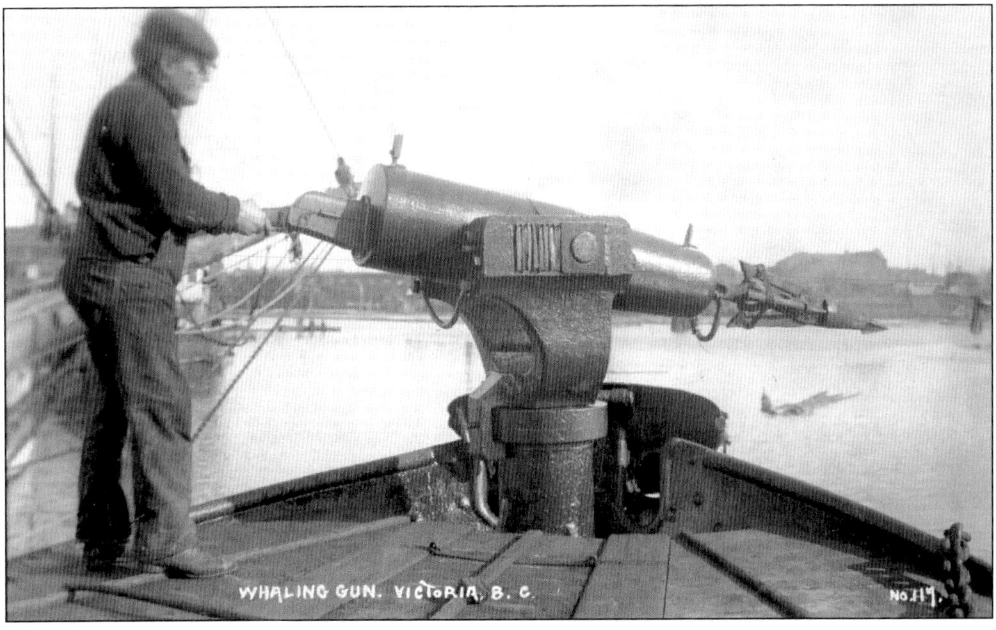

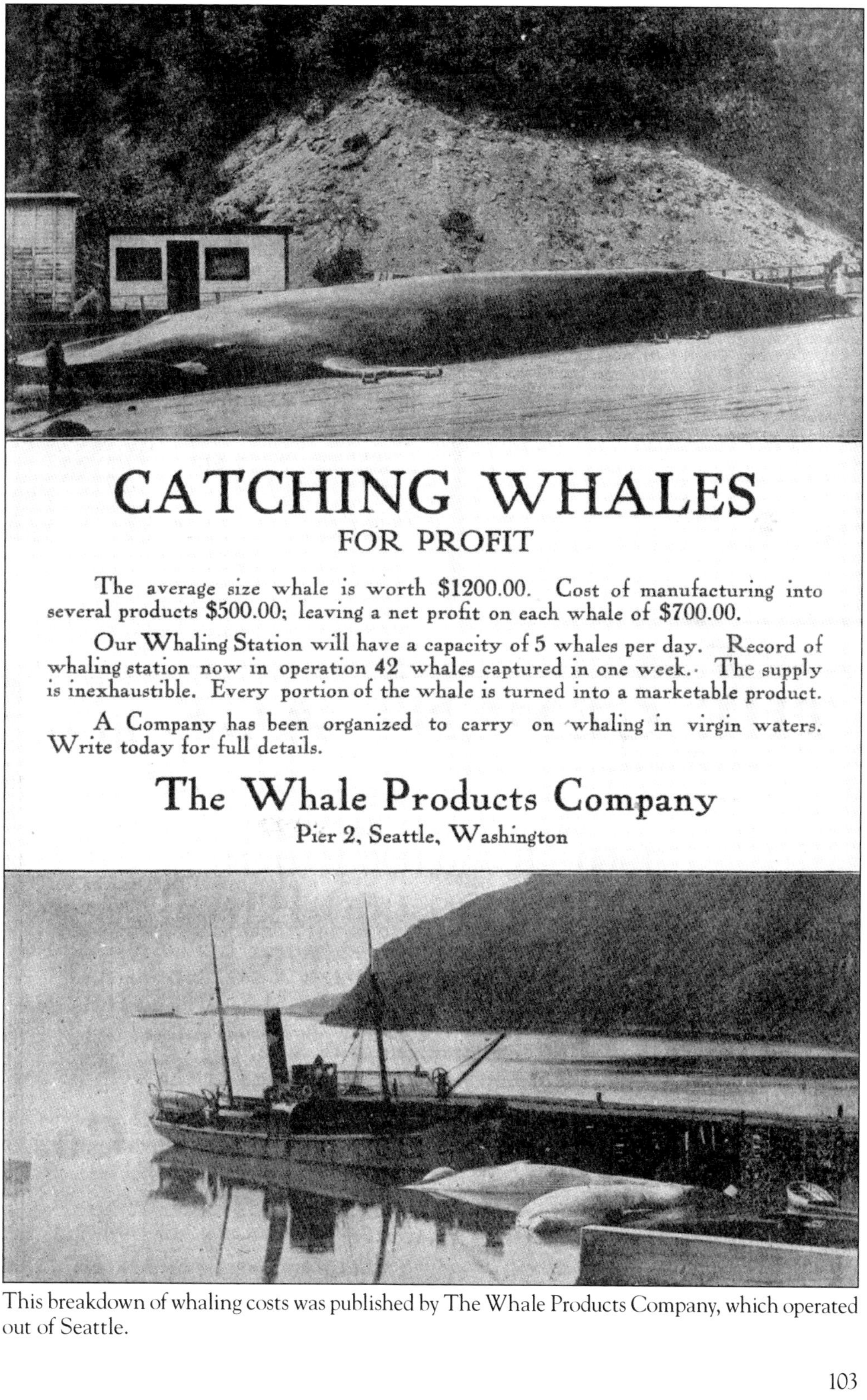

This breakdown of whaling costs was published by The Whale Products Company, which operated out of Seattle.

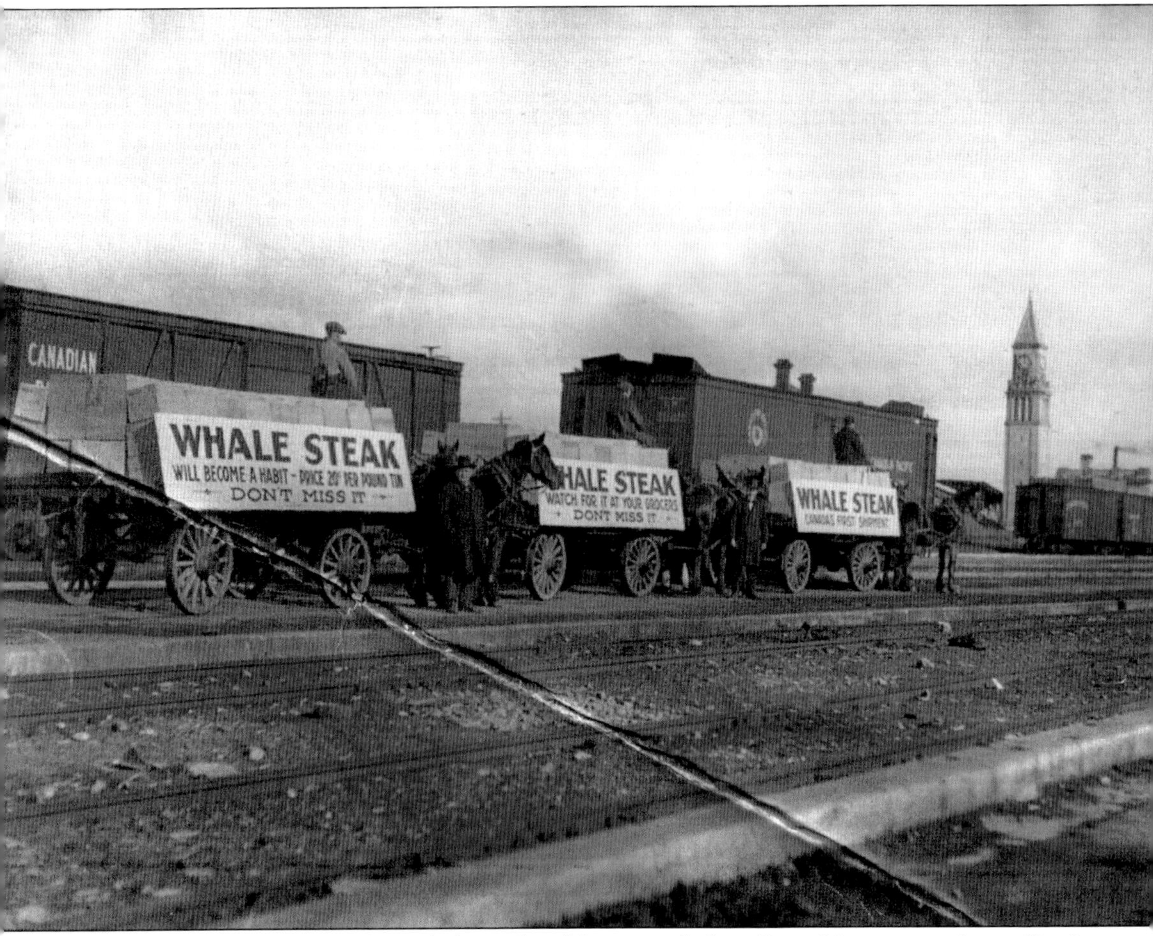

The first of these signs reads, "Whale steak will become a habit – Price 20¢ per pound tin – Don't miss it," while the second reads, "Whale steak – Watch for it at your grocers," and the third reads, "Whale steak – Canada's first shipment."

Seven

SOUTHERN ALASKA WHALING

The Tyee Whaling Company incorporated in 1907 on Admiralty Island near Sitka, Alaska. The owners were the Norwegian-American founder, John Barneson, and Capt. I.N. Hibbard of San Francisco. The company contracted the Moran Company of Seattle to construct a whaler named the *Tyee Jr.* The Tyee station was able to operate without many restrictions, where the Canadian stations were restricted from having more than one catcher per station. Further, Tyee could ship to the favorable markets of the United States without paying import duties. The company operated from 1907 until 1912, during which time it only took 61 whales. This stood in comparison to two new stations built in 1912 that had taken about 300 whales each. In 1911, the steamer *Fearless*, working out of the station with the whalers *Tyee Jr.* and *Resolute*, caught an 86-foot whale. This was the largest whale taken by any vessel in the fleet.

When the Tyee Whaling Company closed, the *Tyee Jr.* was sold to the American Pacific Whaling Company—operating out of Akutan, Alaska—and was renamed the *Tanginak*. The station equipment was brought down on the company vessels to Seattle.

With initial success at the first British Columbia station at Sechart, Norwegian whaling financiers visited the plant and began to look for other locations that might be used to start a competitive whaling operation. Peter Bogen of Norway raised $3 million to start a plant near Sitka, Alaska. The company was called the United States Whaling Company, and the station was built at a place called Port Armstrong, not far from Sitka and Juneau. The Seattle Construction and Drydock Company built three whaling ships in time for the 1912 season, named *Star 1*, *Star 2*, and *Star 3*. The station opened and whaling began on May 2, 1912. A factory ship, the *Sommerstad*, was used as a floating station while construction was being completed. The *Sommerstad* was moved around during the first year because there were fewer whales near Port Armstrong than expected. Even though the whalers took 314 whales in the first season, it was a disappointment in terms of revenue.

In 1913, the United States Whaling Company took 75 sperm whales, which was a record for a single whaling station. However, the catch for baleen whales—including humpback and fin whales—was below expectations, and this resulted in another disappointing season. After the 1915 season, storms damaged the station and it needed to be rebuilt. Capt. E. Earling, the harpooner on the *Star I*, performed a survey, and workmen spent a month repairing the station prior to the season's opening.

With the start of World War I, the *Star I* was drafted into naval service. The vessel was assigned the identification number 1351 and served as a minesweeper until February 12, 1919. In 1918, the two sister ships—which the Navy had not claimed—were back on the job. The company took 121 whales, making 1918 another in the long list of mediocre seasons. The catches did not improve, and 1922 was the last season for the United States Whaling Company. In 1922, the station was recommissioned to produce herring meal and oil. The boats were sold to the Ross Sea Whaling Company, sailed for Seattle, and then on to New Zealand. The vessels operated in the Ross Sea for the Norwegian company and were repaired each year at Paterson Inlet on Stewart Island, New Zealand. The *Star 2* was sold to the fishing service and later ended up on Spencer's Island, near Green Point, New Zealand. Her harpoon gun is at the Southland Museum at Invercargill, New Zealand.

A second Norwegian whaling station was established by Lars Christensen at Akutan, Alaska—on the Aleutian chain—and operated as the Alaska Whaling Company. This firm also used a factory ship, the *Admiralen*, as whaling began before the land station was completed. The station operated for one season, and lost about $100,000. While this amount was not bad for a first year, the company encountered so many problems that it decided to stop whaling. It was sold to Americans and renamed the North Pacific Sea Products Co. of Minneapolis. Akutan was idle in 1913, but operations began under the new management in 1914. After ceasing production during the war, the company began again in 1918, but the owner had reorganized. The new parent company for the station, the Victoria Whaling Company, was owned by Knut B. Birkeland.

One of the new products that the station attempted to capitalize on was whale meat sold for human consumption. The company produced whale meat at the Akutan station and at Rose Harbor on Vancouver Island. In early 1907, Joya Shokai—a Japanese company from Nagasaki—had come to Victoria to contract the monthly production of 500 tons of food-quality whale meat. When whale meat was not diverted for food, it normally ended being converted into fertilizer.

In 1917, whale meat was brought onto the market, and newspapers across the country carried headlines such as "Sell Whale Meat," "Whale Meat On Sale In Markets, Whale Meat Is Good," "Northwest Declares, Whale Meat Good," and "Whale Steak the Latest; It's Palatable and Cheap." The articles would announce that a large quantity of whale meat was available in the local markets at 9 or 10¢ a pound. The meat was from the loin of the whale, and resembled beef in both color and general appearance. Whale meat was said to have been eaten in all countries where whales were caught, except in North America.

One article said that the Indians of the Washington coast had always regarded whale meat as a delicacy. This new food was endorsed by the US Bureau of Fisheries and Secretary of Commerce Redfield as being wholesome. At that time, most whale meat was manufactured into fertilizer, as the flesh was considered a by-product of the oil. The price of whale meat was bucking the high cost of living during the war, according to Henry Schupp, who was manager of the by-products plant of the American Pacific Whaling Company. About a ton of whale meat was brought to Seattle and other cities that accepted deliveries into their local markets.

The Bureau of Fisheries promoted the sale of the meat, and went so far as to publish a book of recipes that featured delicacies like fried whale steak, and whale pot roast. Whale meat was also introduced on the east coast, and found a good market there. Housewives could buy whale meat and have a cheap, fairly good-tasting substitute for beef when they could not buy that staple with their ration coupons. When the ration coupons went away, however, and beef went back on the market, people returned to it in spite of the lower price of whale meat. It was estimated that 100 million pounds of whale meat could be supplied to the people of the American continent from British Columbia, annually, at a price of about 12.5¢ per pound. Whale meat was sold again in 1918 and 1919, but not in great quantities. It was not sold at all after 1919, except for a supply of whale meat that was canned in 1923 and sold in West Africa in 1924.

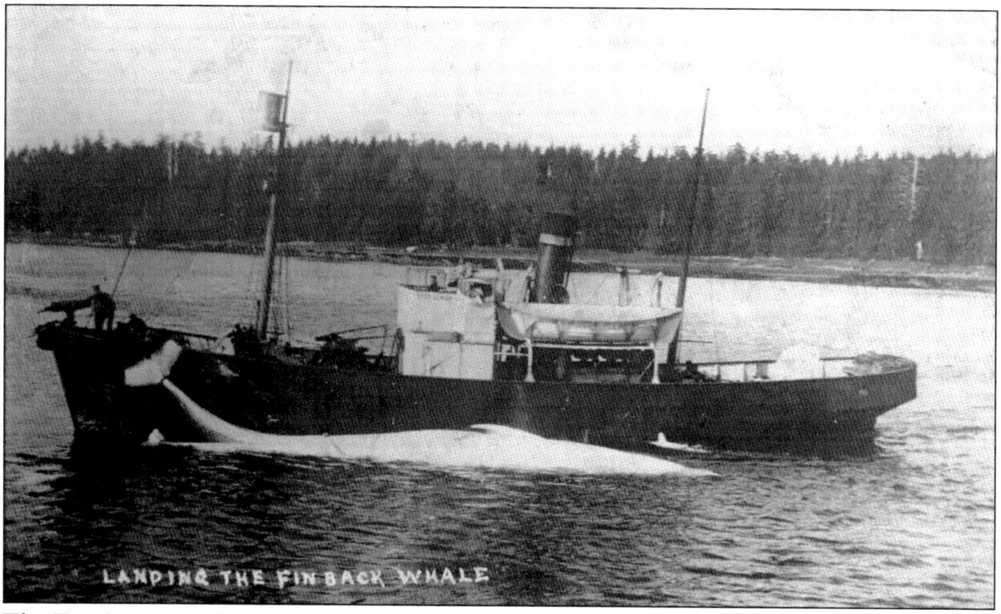

The *Tyee Jr.* operated on behalf of the Tyee Whaling Company, and then as the *Tanginak* for the American Pacific Whaling Company, in Akutan. She was the first modern, steel whaling chaser boat built in America. The *Tyee Jr.* was built by the Moran Shipbuilding Company in Seattle. She was 97.9 feet long and weighed 71 tons. This photograph shows her towing a finback whale into port.

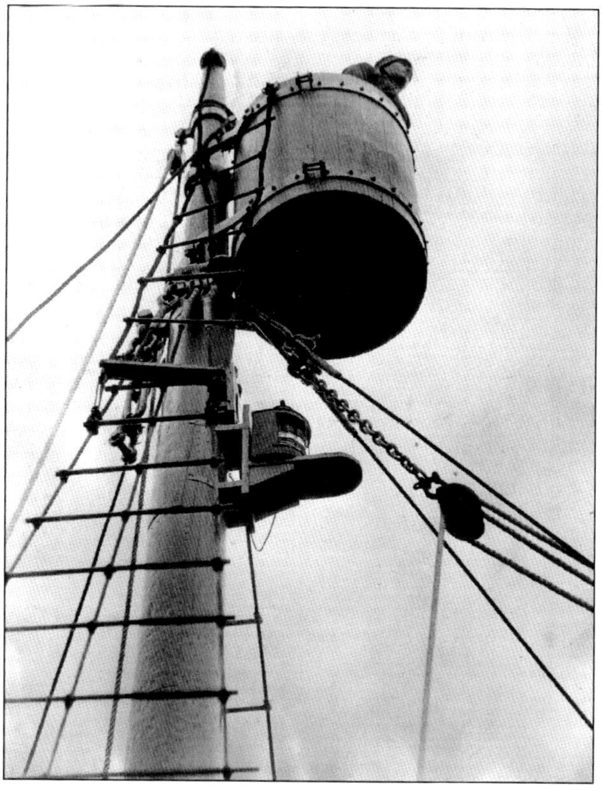

Here is a photograph of the *Tyee Jr.*'s crow's nest with a lookout watching for whales. The whaler had its name changed to the *Tanginak* when it was sold to the American Pacific Whaling Company in 1914.

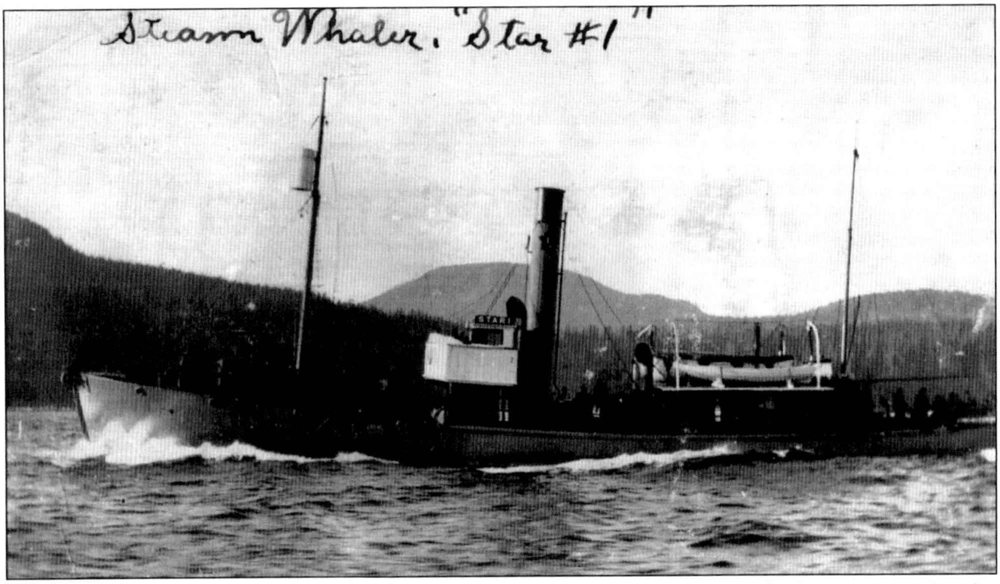

The *Star I*, pictured here, was built by the Seattle Construction and Drydock Company for the United States Whaling Company. The vessel was 106 feet long—making it some 18 feet longer than its sister ships, the *Star II* and *Star III*.

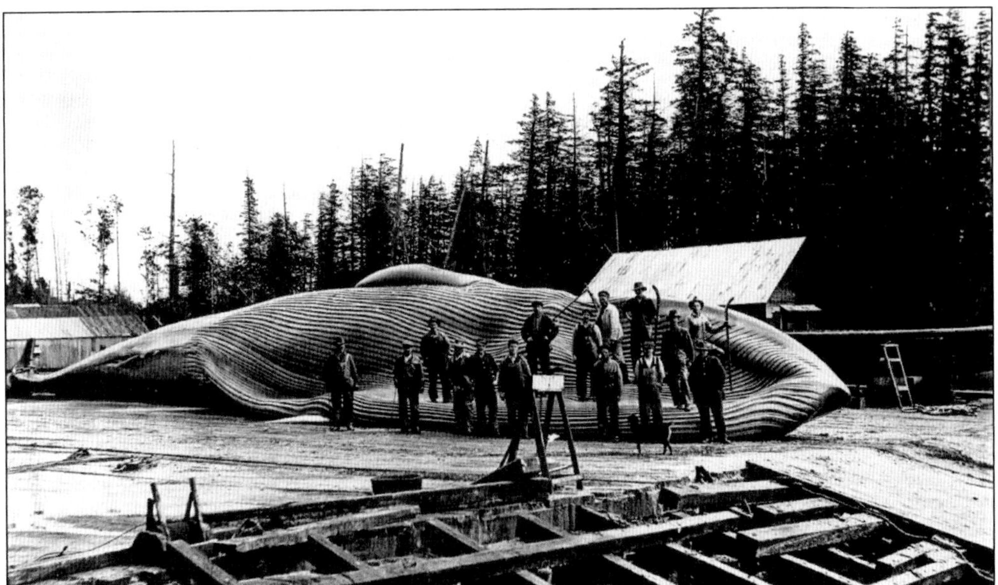

A baleen whale is pictured here at the Port Armstrong whaling station. The photograph was taken with the station's entire crew. The head flenser is at center, with his flensing blade. Most of the time, he would pose on top of the whale for pictures.

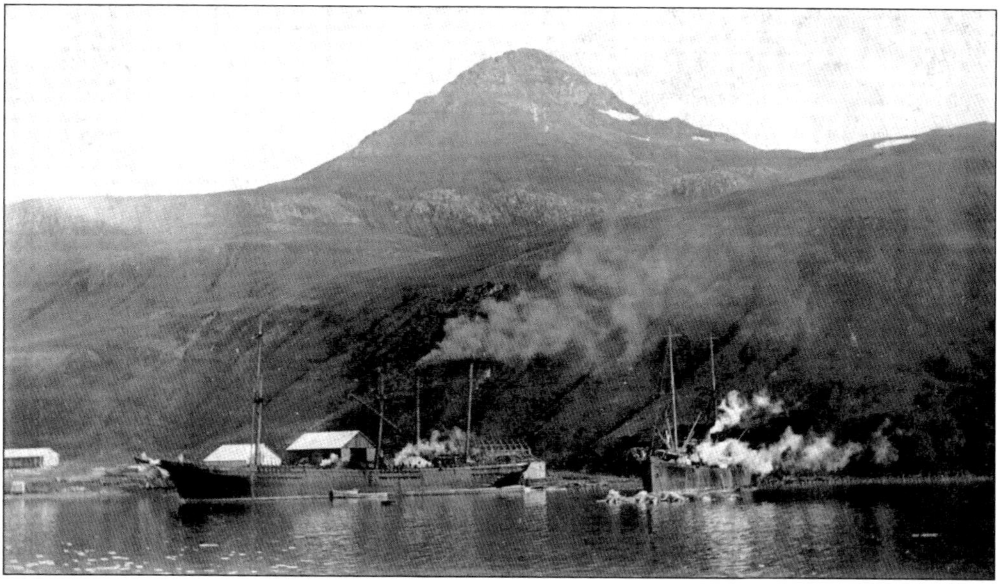

This early photograph of Akutan, Alaska, was probably taken between 1912 and 1914. It shows the barque *Fresno*, at right, being used as a whaling station to boil oil and perform other tasks. Most of the construction at Akutan has not yet begun.

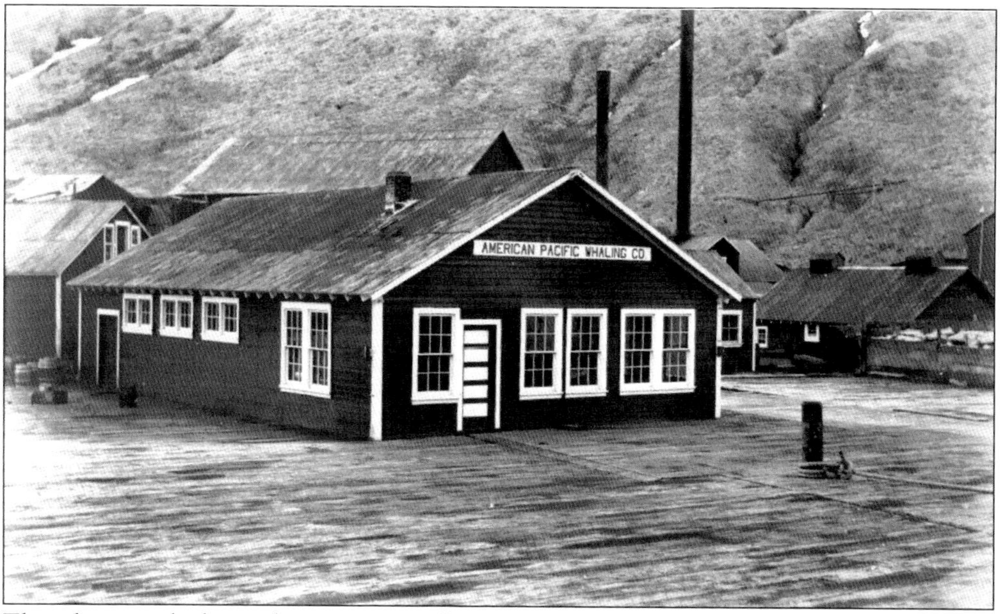

This photograph shows the manager's office at the American Pacific Whaling Company in Akutan, Alaska. The APWC was the second whaling company to operate at Akutan. The first lasted only a year before selling to the APWC, which operated for about 30 years.

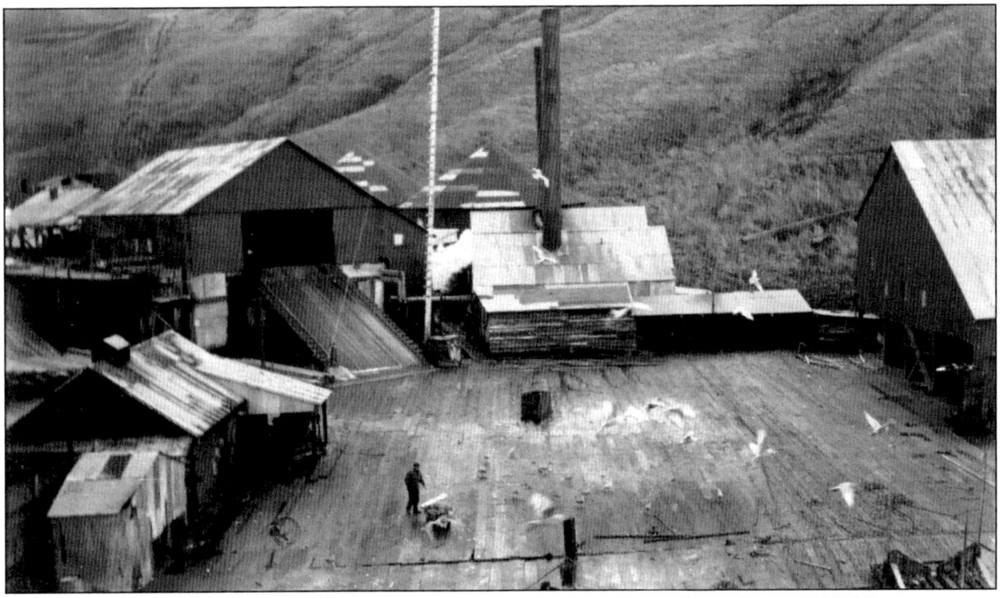

This is the main flensing area at Akutan. Whales came in from the right, and blubber went out to the right while bones and meat went to the upper left.

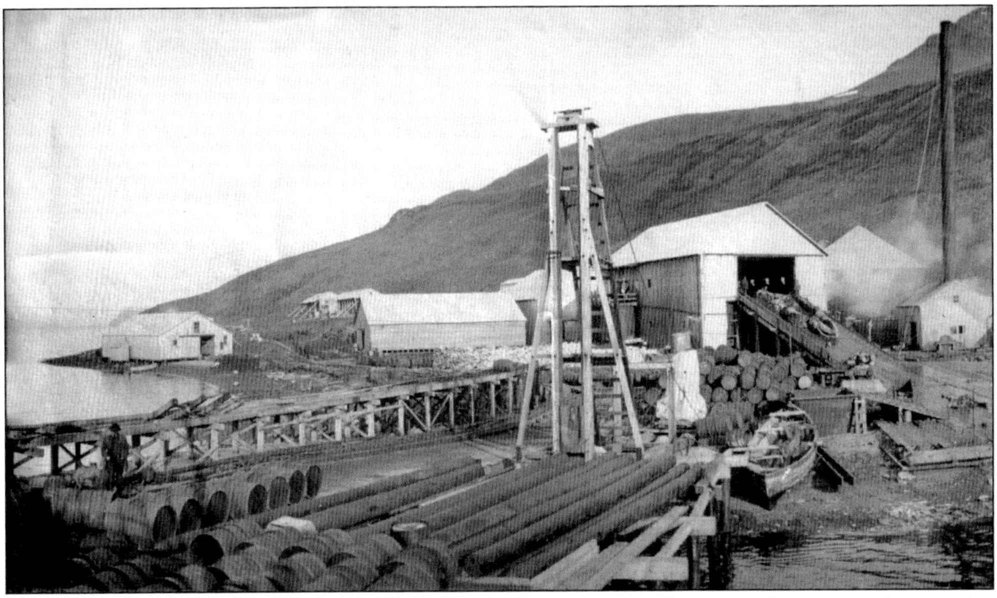

This photograph of the Akutan whaling station shows a partially stripped carcass going up the large ramp, while to the left, construction of a crew quarters is visible. The other buildings at the station were completed by the early 1920s.

This photograph shows Gus Wester, harpooner for the *Aberdeen*. The harpoon gun would be loaded with an explosive head when it was ready to be fired. Ropes were tied around the barbs to prevent them from opening until the harpoon entered the whale.

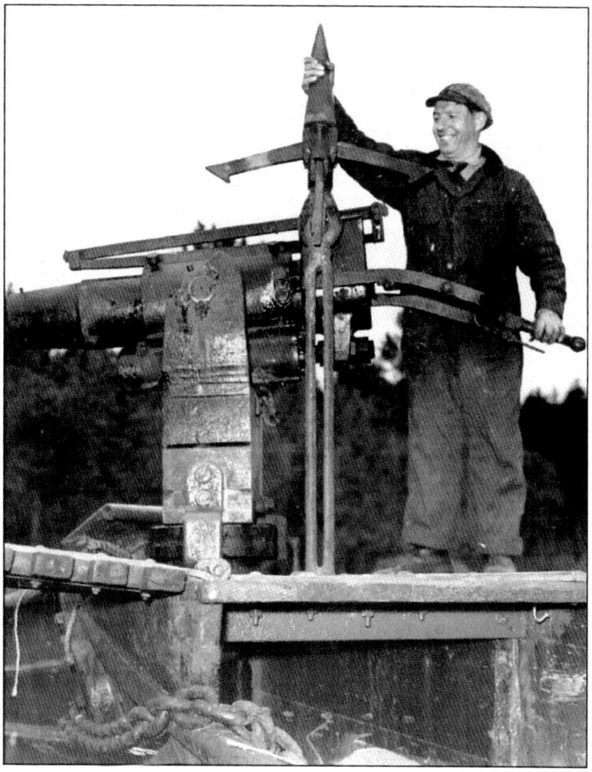

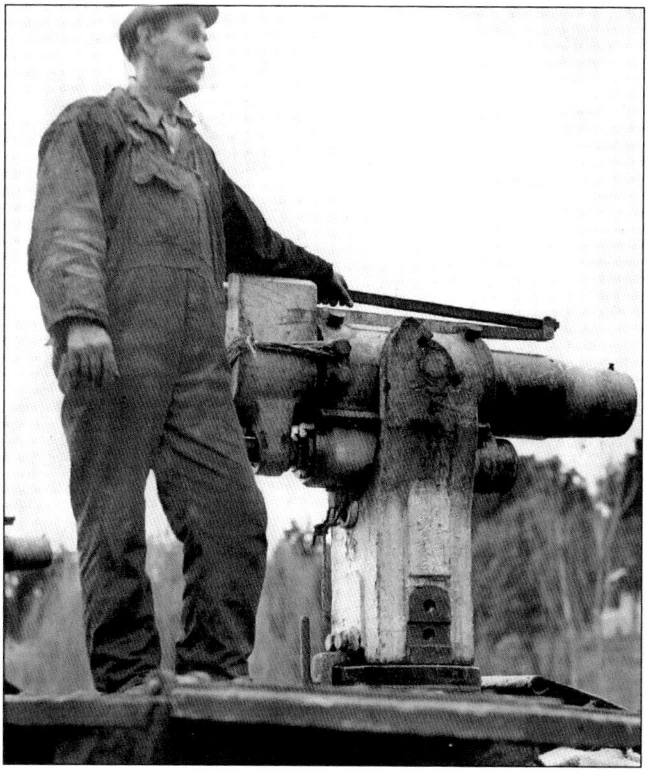

Frank Christianson, seen here, was the harpooner aboard the *Paterson*.

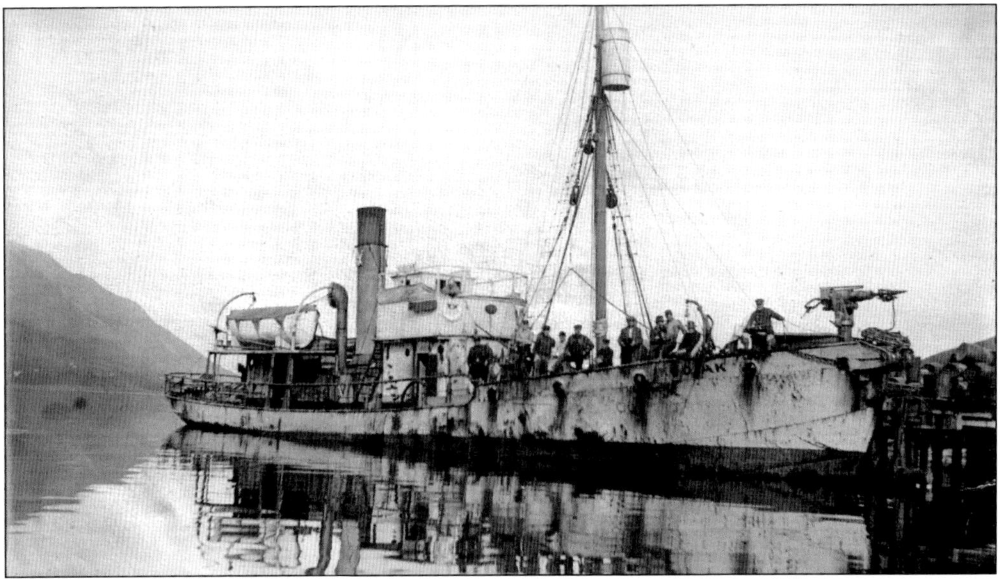

The whaler *Kodiak*, seen here at the end of a season, has had the paint worn off her sides by towing whales. She will be repainted before the start of the new season.

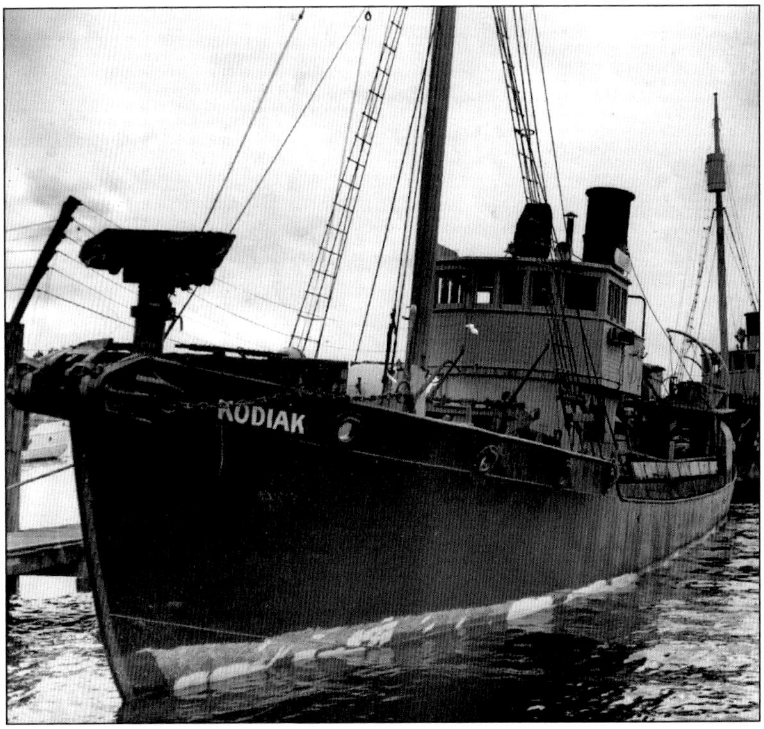

Here, the *Kodiak* has been repainted black, which was not her normal color. Some of the original paint is visible near the waterline. The reason for this color change has not been determined.

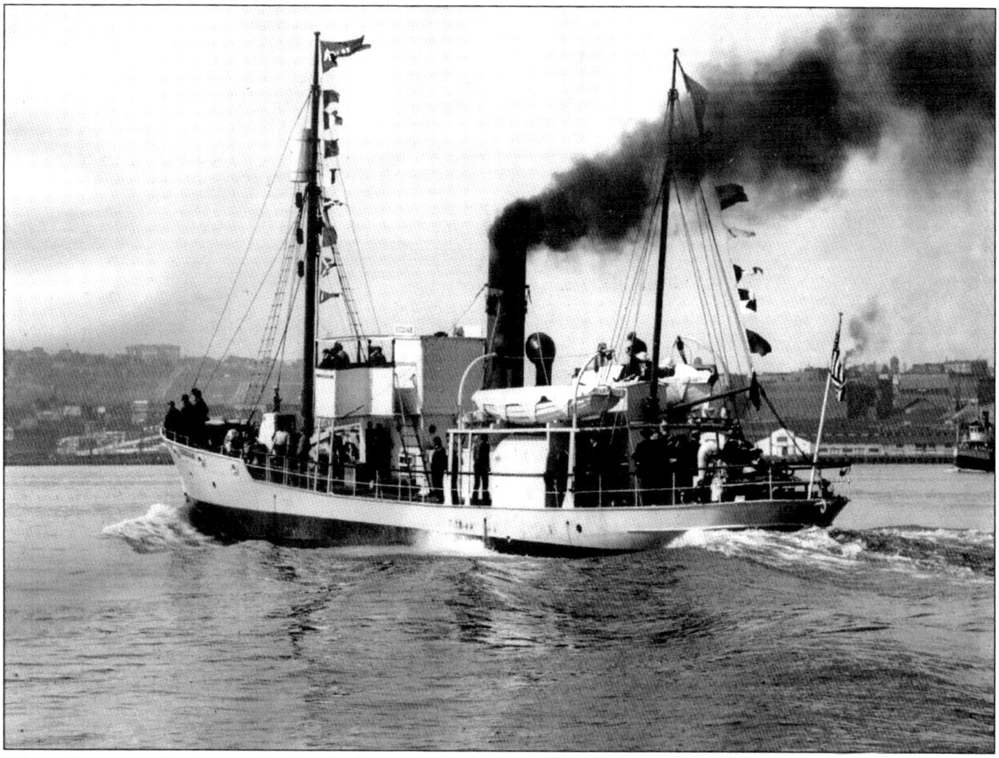

This photograph shows the Kodiak painted in her normal colors and flying flags. She may have been part of a parade celebrating the start of the whaling season, or simply arriving at the station from Seattle.

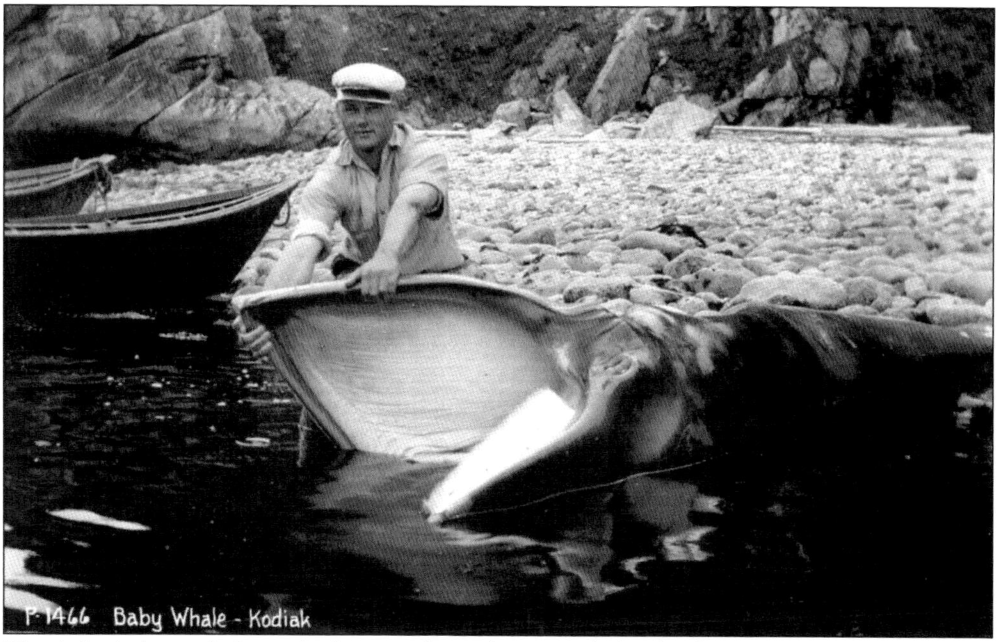

This baby baleen whale washed up on the rocks on Kodiak Island. It is possible that the baby came from a whale that was being towed to a whaling station.

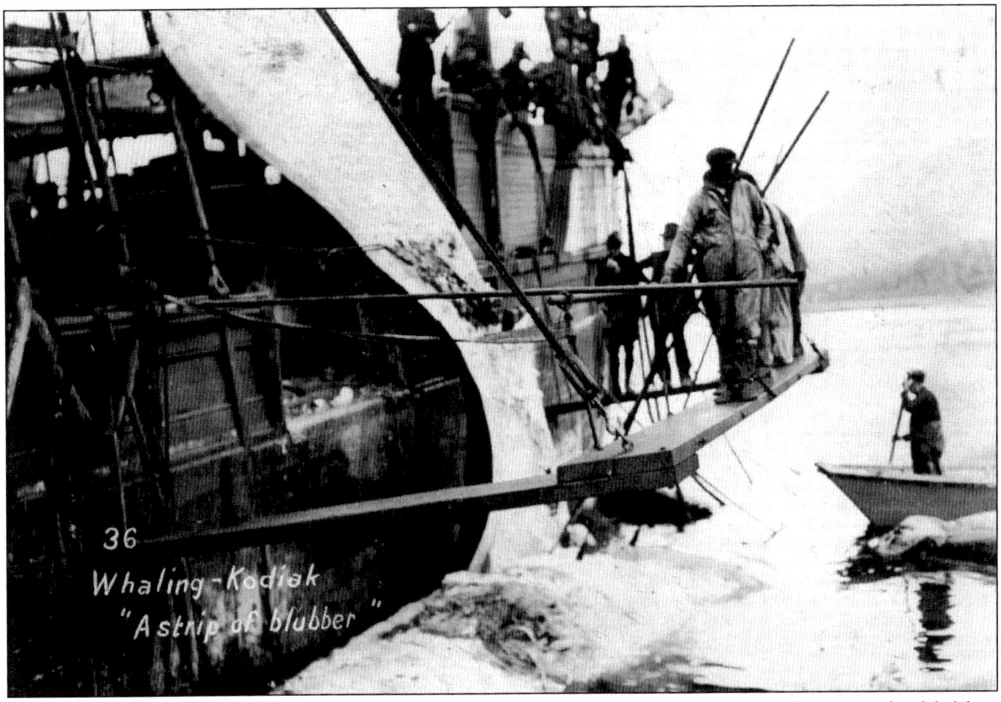

This photograph is part of a set that shows the whaling operations at Kodiak. Here, the blubber is being cut off of the whale. As the process continues, the whale will be rolled over in the water to cut a vertical strip around its body. On shore, the flensers will remove a horizontal strip of blubber from half of the whale's body.

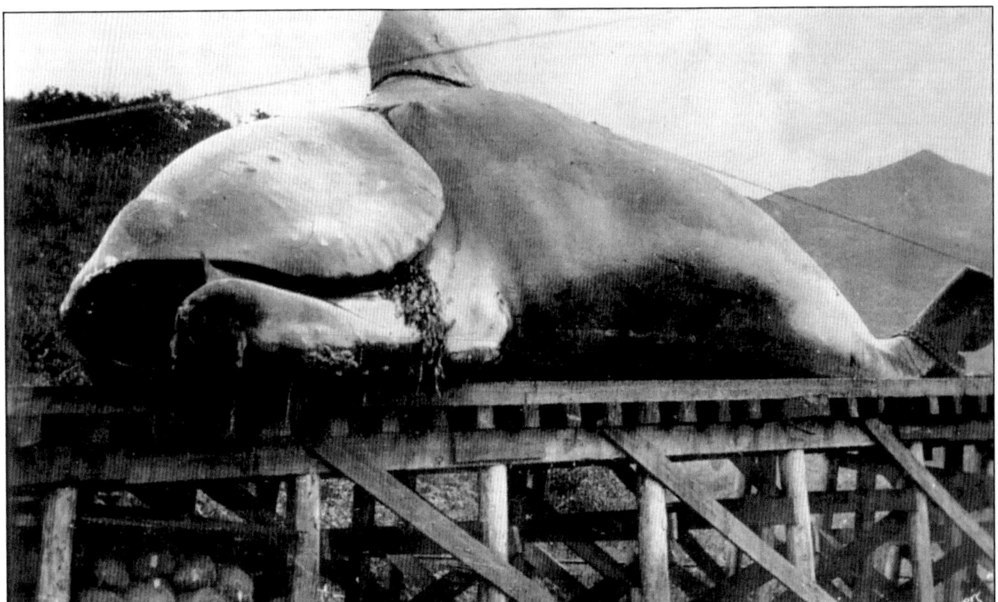

This photograph shows a right whale, left on the ramp for processing at the Port Hobron whaling station near Kodiak, Alaska.

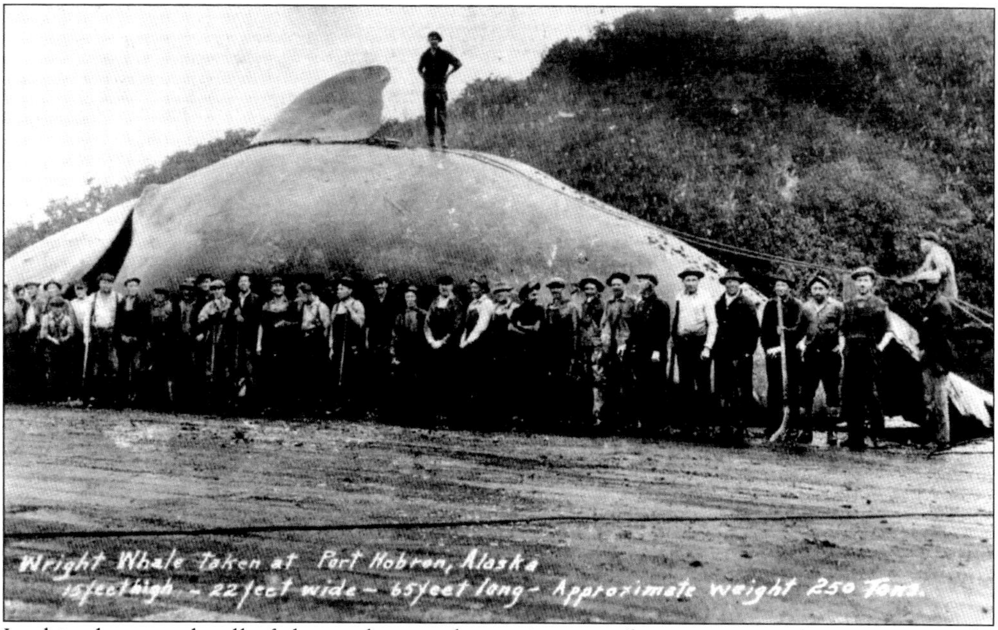

In this photograph, all of the workers at the station pose for a picture with a very rare right whale. The whale was 65 feet long, 15 feet high, 22 feet wide, and weighed an estimated 250 tons. Spectators were allowed to walk around the whale and touch it.

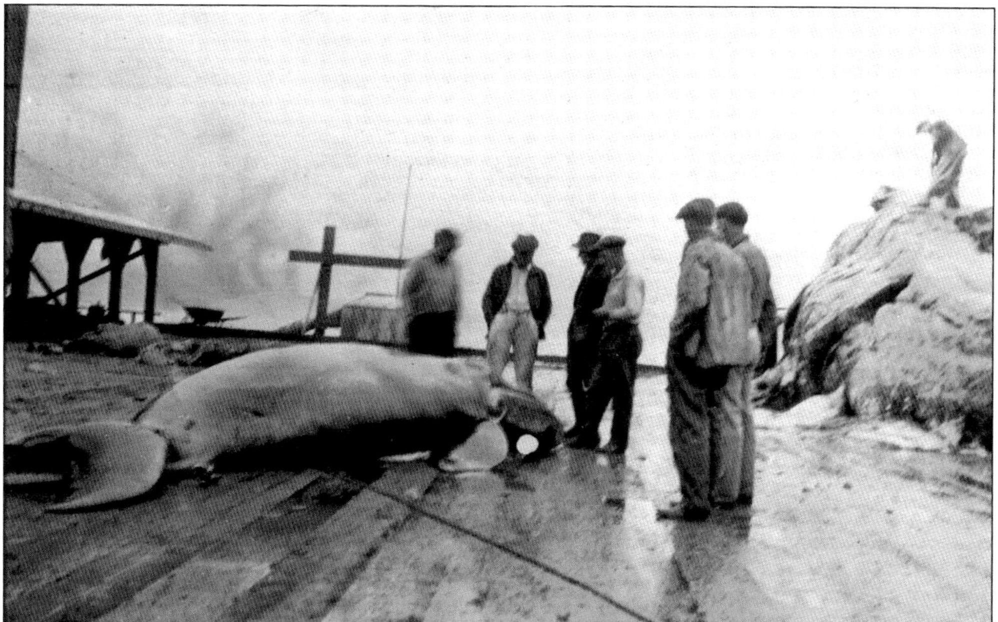

These men are looking at a small whale or dolphin, while in the background another worker has finished extracting the baleen from a whale and is starting to work on removing the meat.

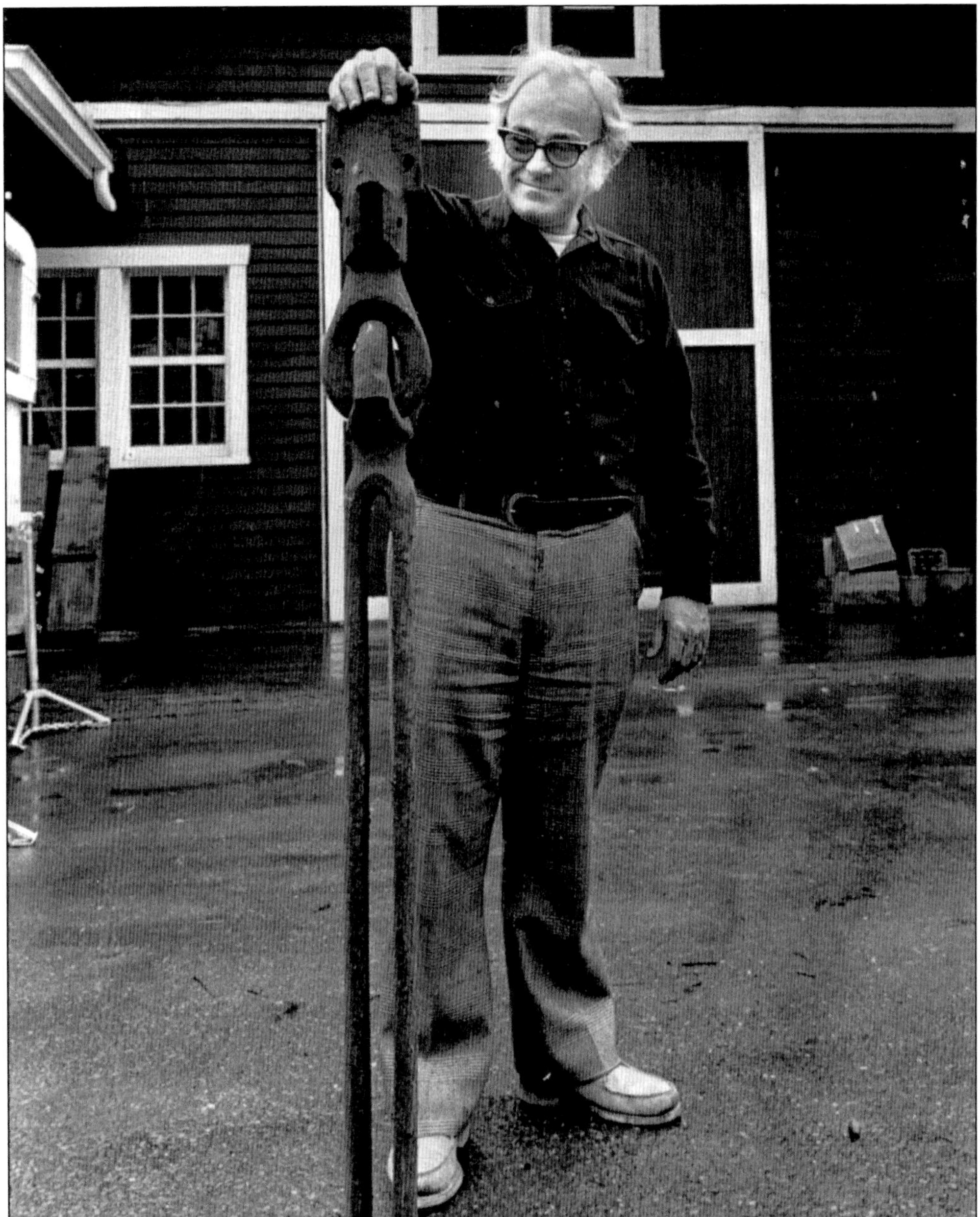

William Lagen, the son of station manager Marc Lagen, shows off a harpoon in this photograph. This was taken after several items were stolen from his collection.

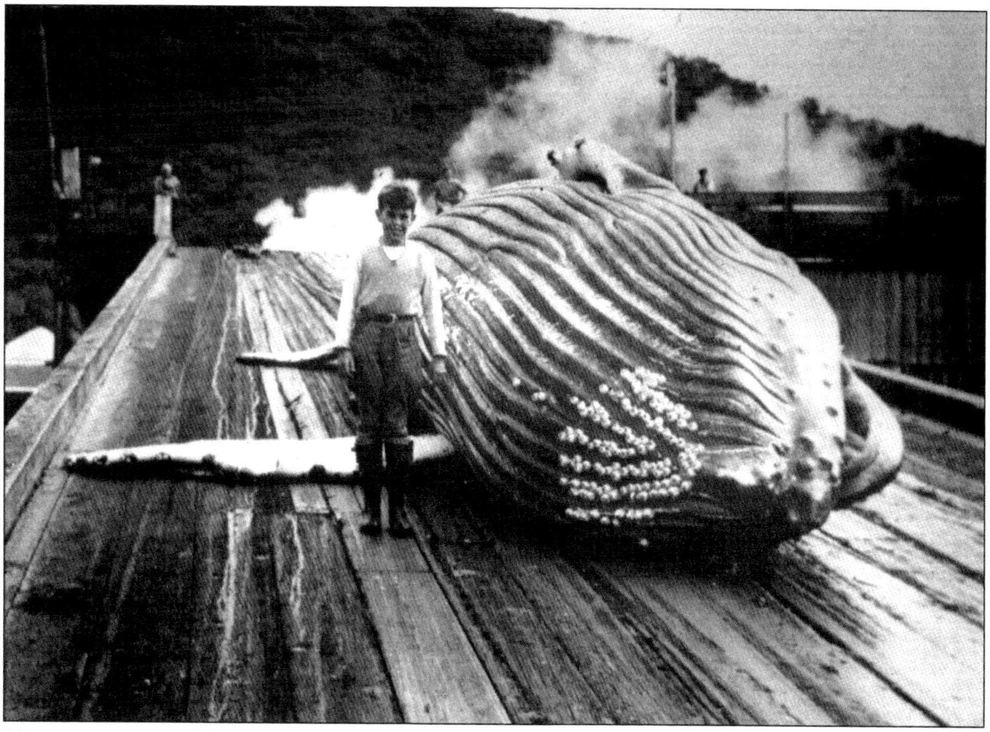

Here, a young William Lagen poses at the Point Hobron station. He is 10 years old in this photograph. The grandson of Henry Schupp, William's father, Marc Lagen, was in charge of operations at Port Hobron.

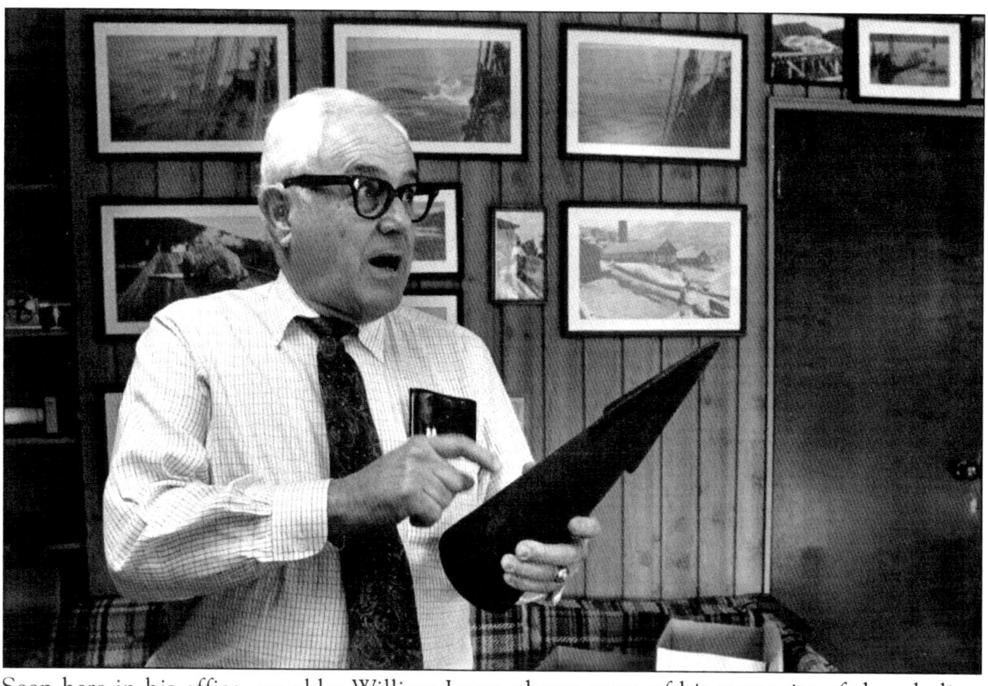

Seen here in his office, an older William Lagen shares some of his memories of the whaling industry. Port Hobron closed permanently after 1937.

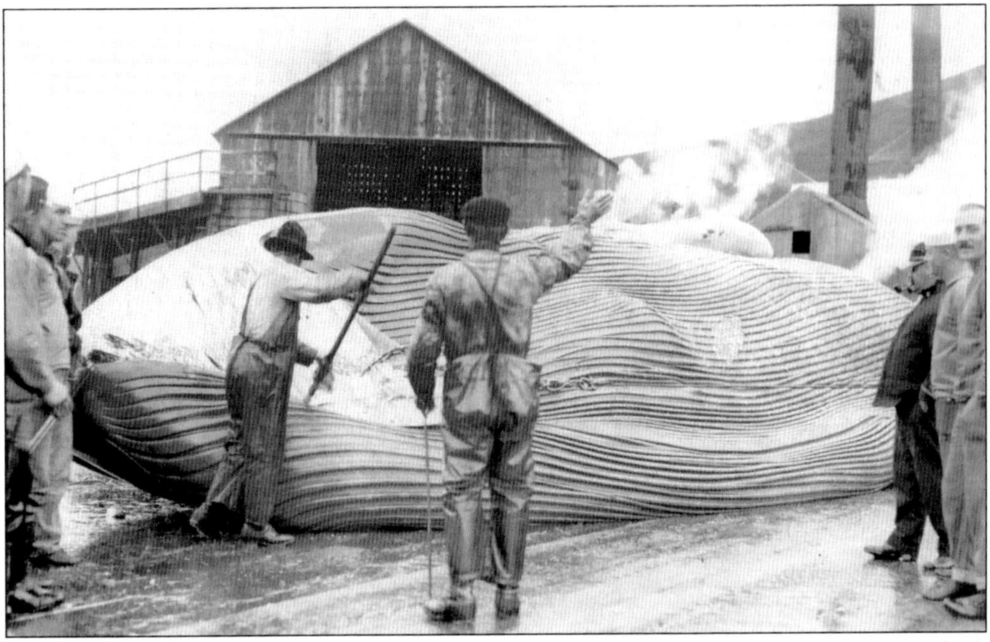

Here, workers are making the first cuts into a whale to remove the baleen. A few spectators look on. Small rocks often got embedded in the whale, which could cause problems—such as dulling the knives and other equipment—if they were not cleared away.

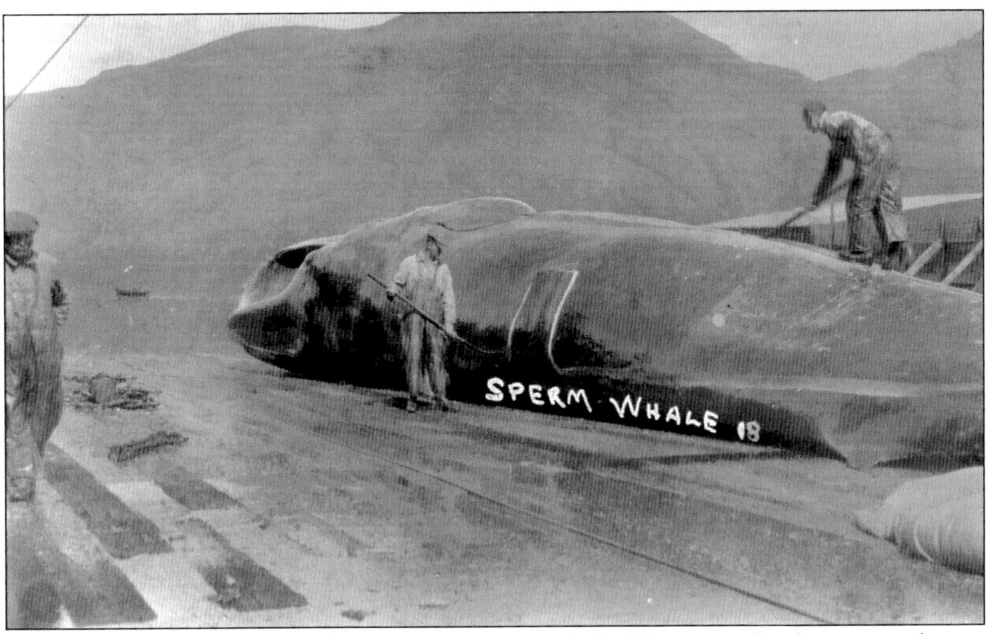

These whalers are making the first cuts into a sperm whale. The reason for the rectangular cut seen in many of these pictures is not fully understood today. It may be for disarticulating the whale—to make it easier for later processing—as the cut seems to most often be made at the high point of the back.

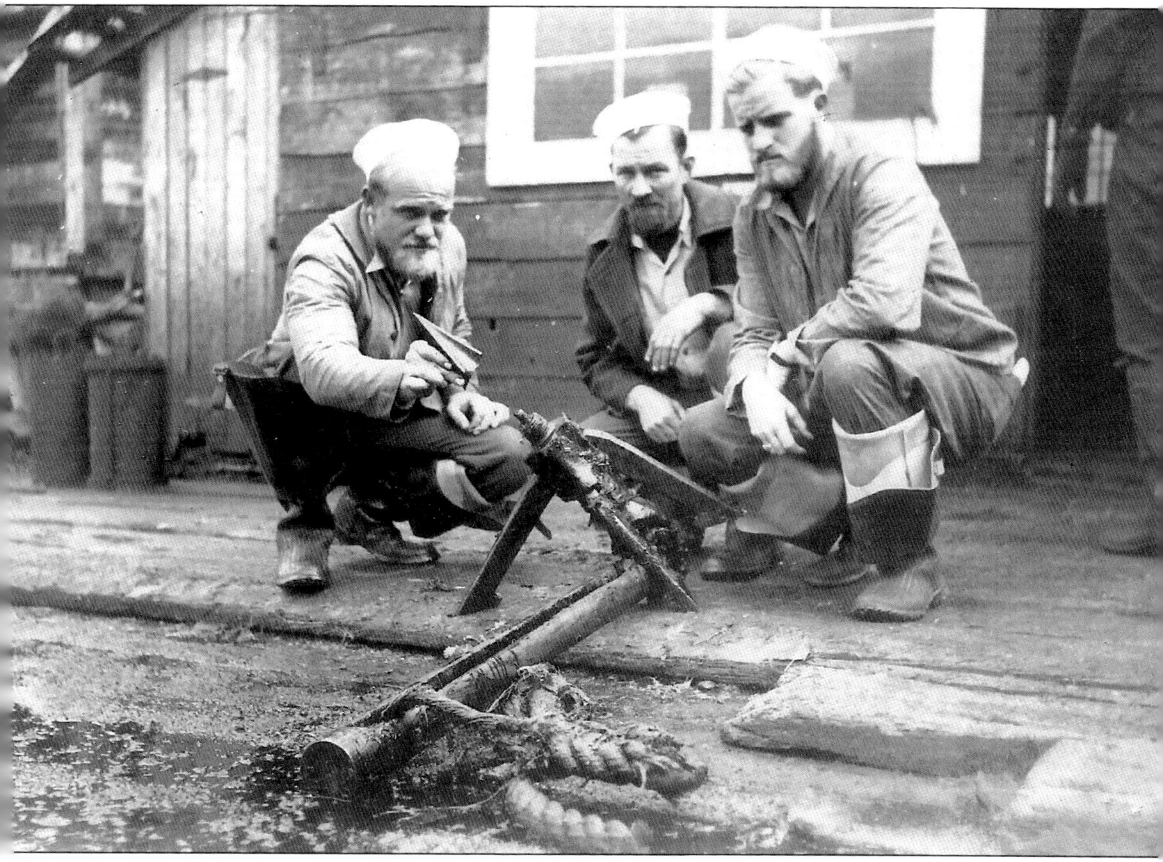

These sailors are inspecting the head of a harpoon that was used to kill a whale. The man on the left is holding the tip of the harpoon. The space between the tip and the rest of the harpoon shows the location and size of the explosive part of the tip. When the harpoon entered the whale, the explosive charge detonated. The barbs designed to hold the whale, and the rest of the harpoon, were mangled by the whale's tremendous strength in its attempt to get away.

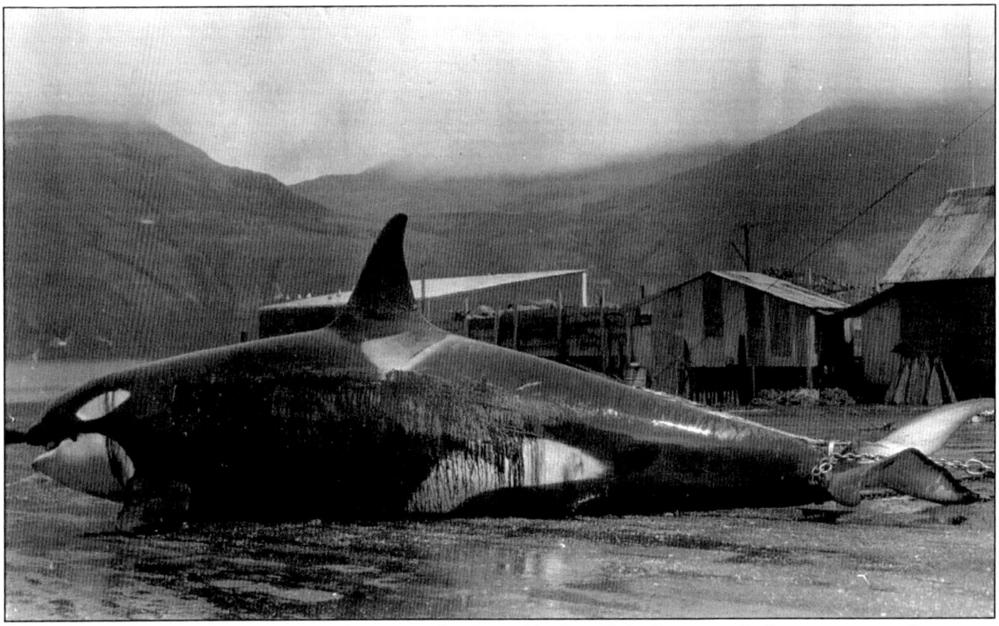

This killer whale, or orca, was taken at Akutan, Alaska. Whalers needed a permit to shoot an orca, so this one was probably caught for scientific purposes.

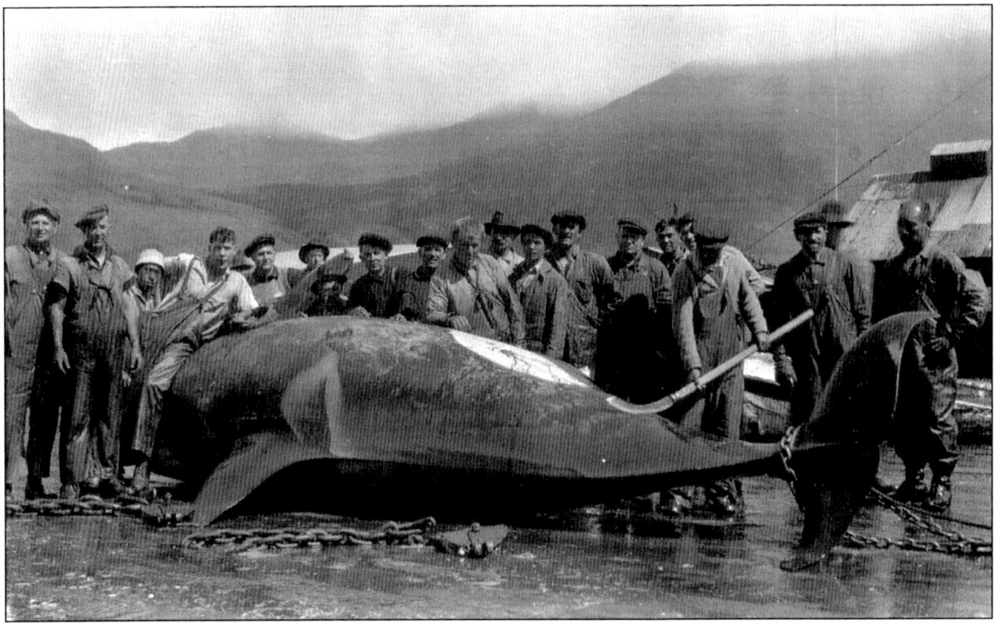

The same orca is shown here, as the crew of the whaling station looks on.

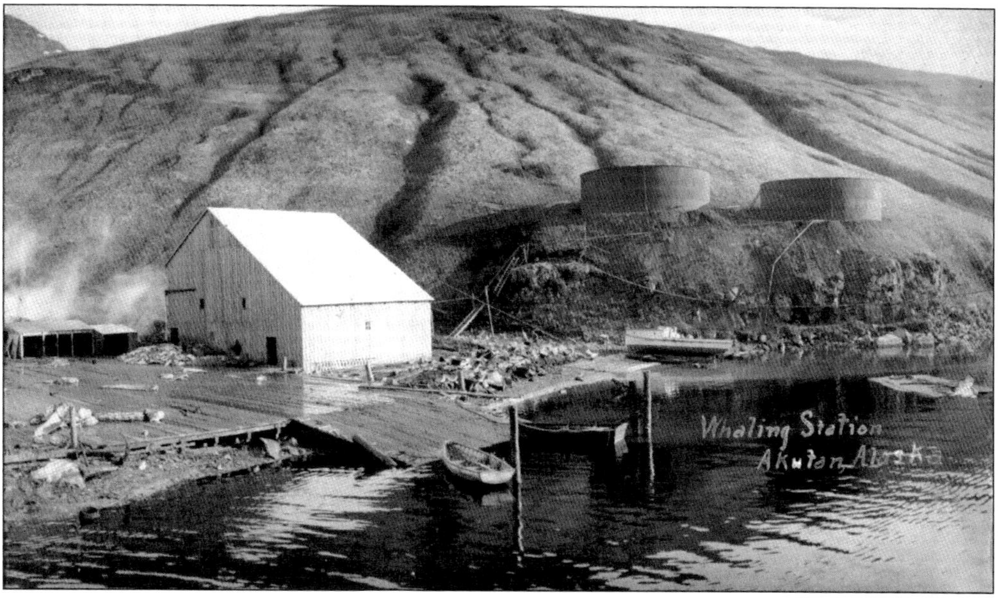

This is a photograph of the Akutan whaling station showing the slipway to the left, and the storage tanks to the right. Whales would be winched out of the water to be flensed on the platform to the left. Whale oil would be boiled out of the blubber and then stored in the large tanks on the hill. This photograph was probably taken before 1920, as many more tanks were eventually built behind this part of the station.

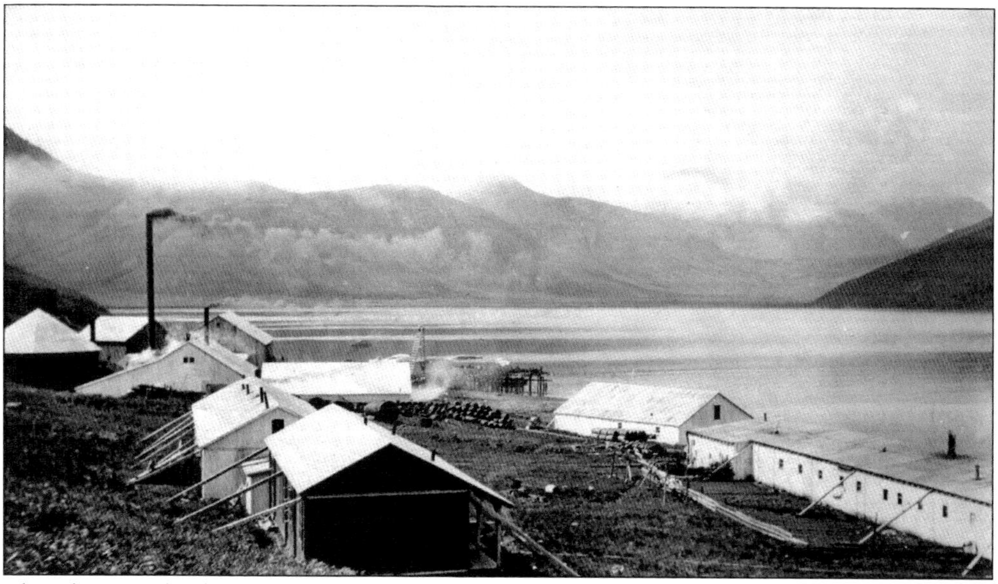

This photograph of the station shows the living area for the workers. On the left are cabins for the Americans, and on the right are the cafeteria and quarters for the Japanese workers. The American workers did not want to live and eat with the Japanese.

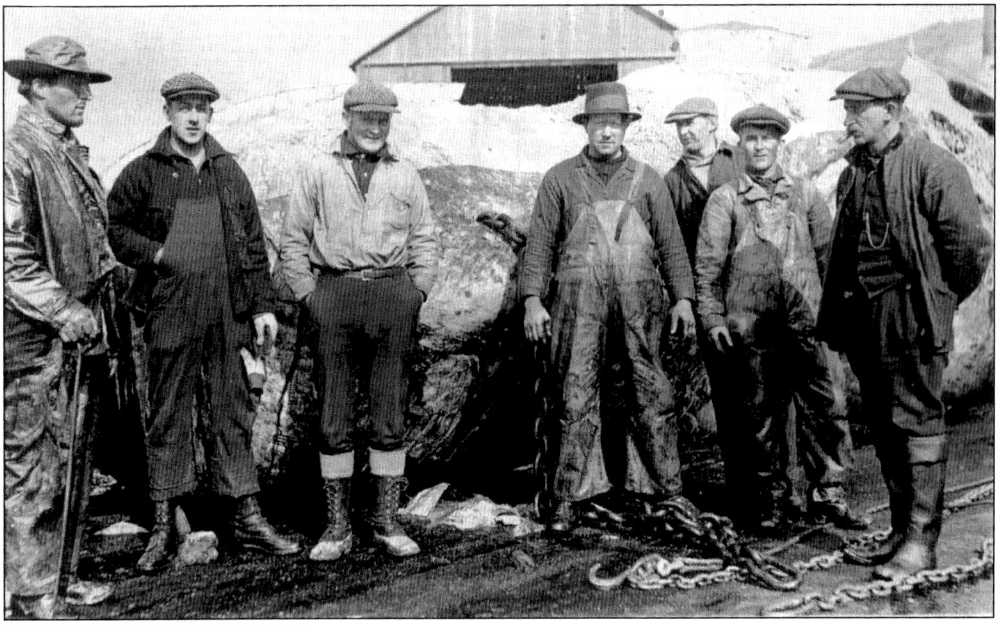

The man at the center of this photograph, with his hands in his pockets, appears to be a visitor. The man on the far left looks very serious and is likely in charge of flensing the whale.

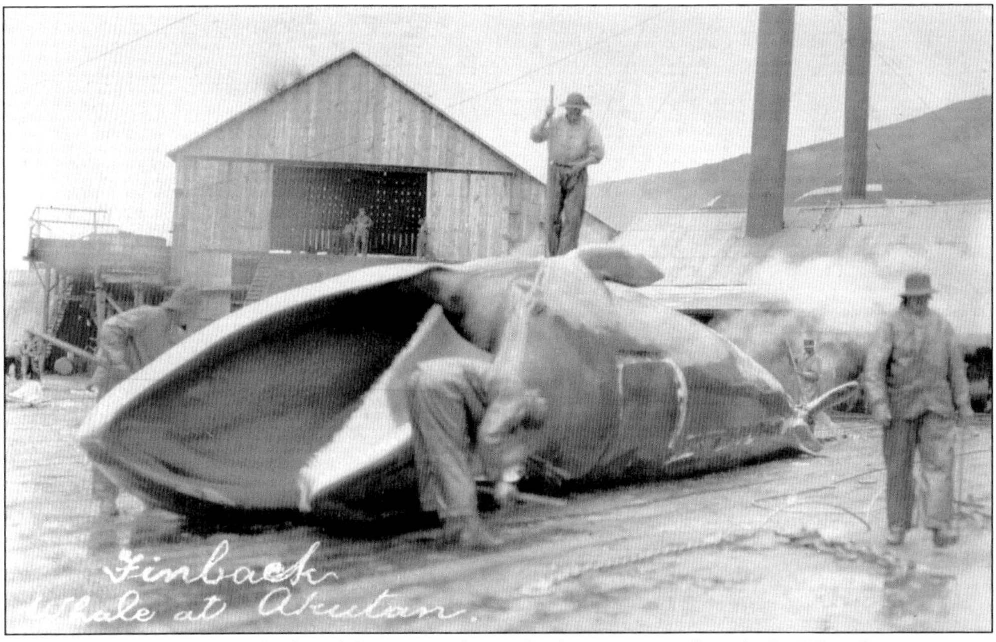

This photograph shows the head flenser making the last cut in a fin whale. The flensing crew seems to have made a cut around what appears to be a bone mass under the blubber. It appears to have been done to let them take the whole blubber blanket from the whale without the difficulty of cutting through the bone.

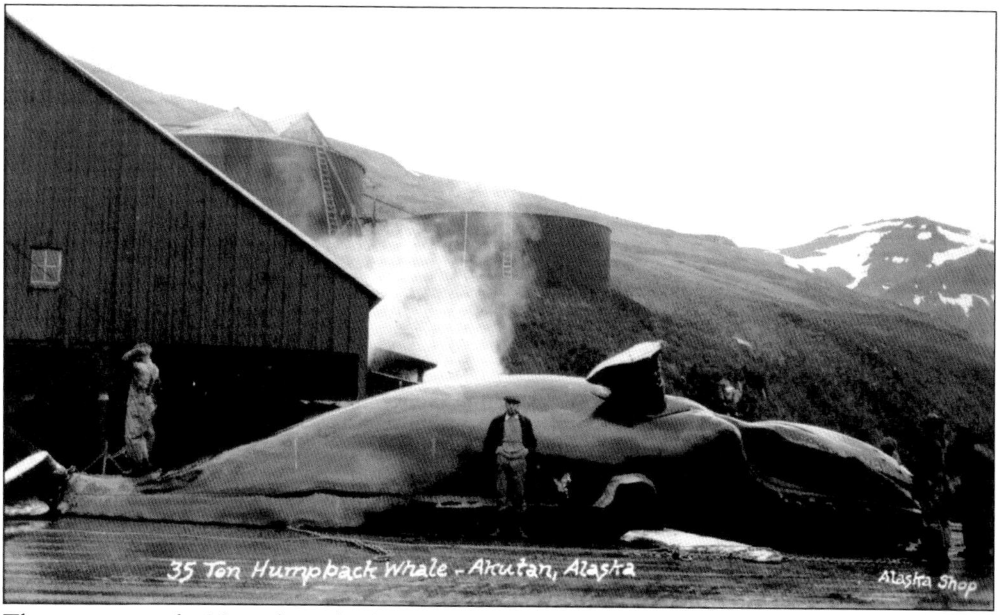

This picture is of a 35-ton humpback whale. Note that one fin and the tail fluke have been cut. This is done to reduce drag, so that the animal tows better in the water.

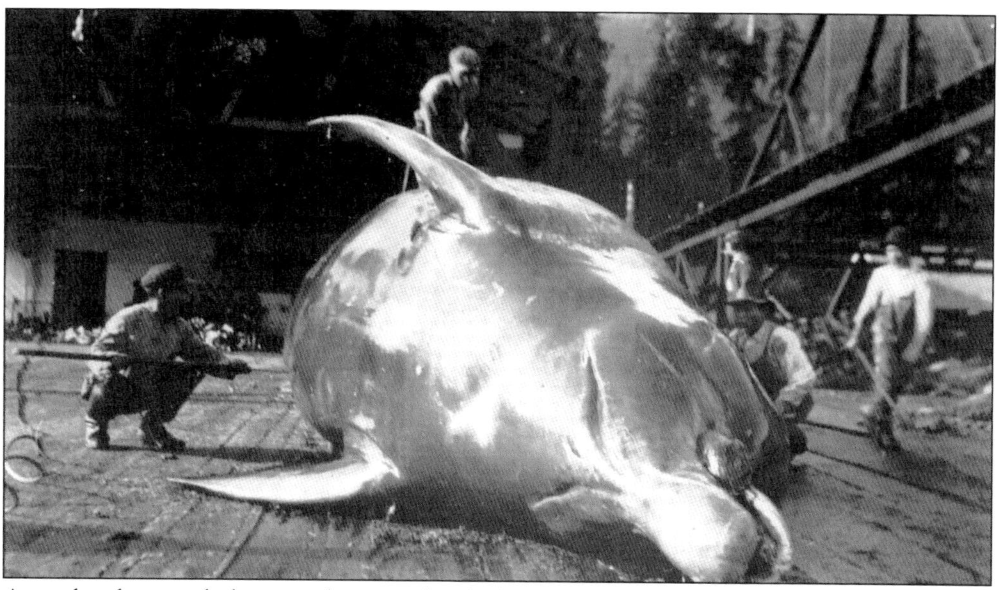

A rare bottlenose whale is seen lying on the platform at the Akutan whaling station. Harpooners generally know the species, sex, and approximate weight and length of a whale before they shoot it. Bringing down this whale could not have been an accident.

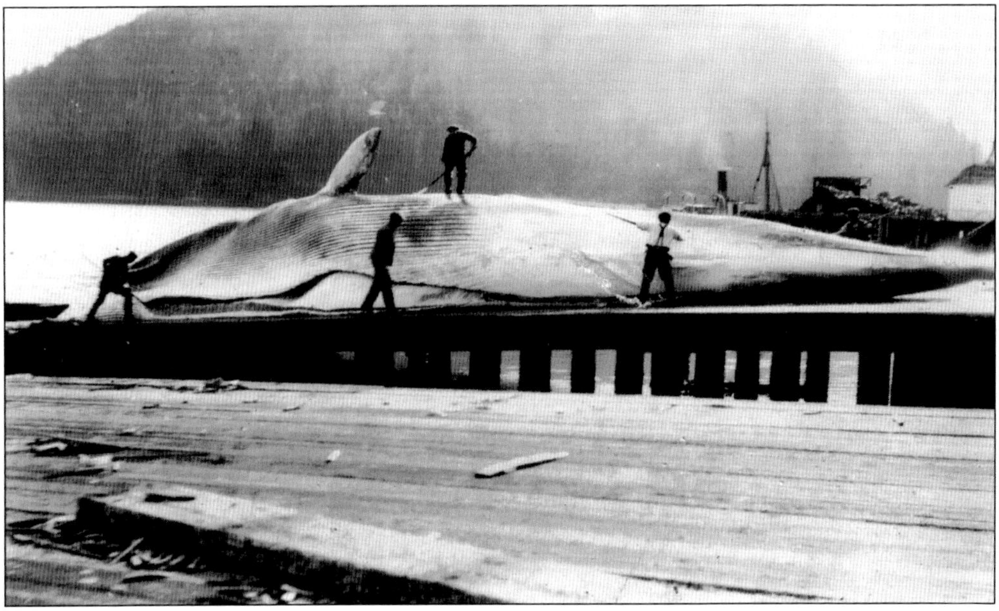

This picture shows the largest of the whale species taken in whaling—a blue whale. The methods for taking and processing a blue whale are the same as for other whales, though the animal may be 10 to 20 feet longer than other whales. While blue whales have been known to be 100 feet or more in length, it would be rare to see one over 85 feet in length today.

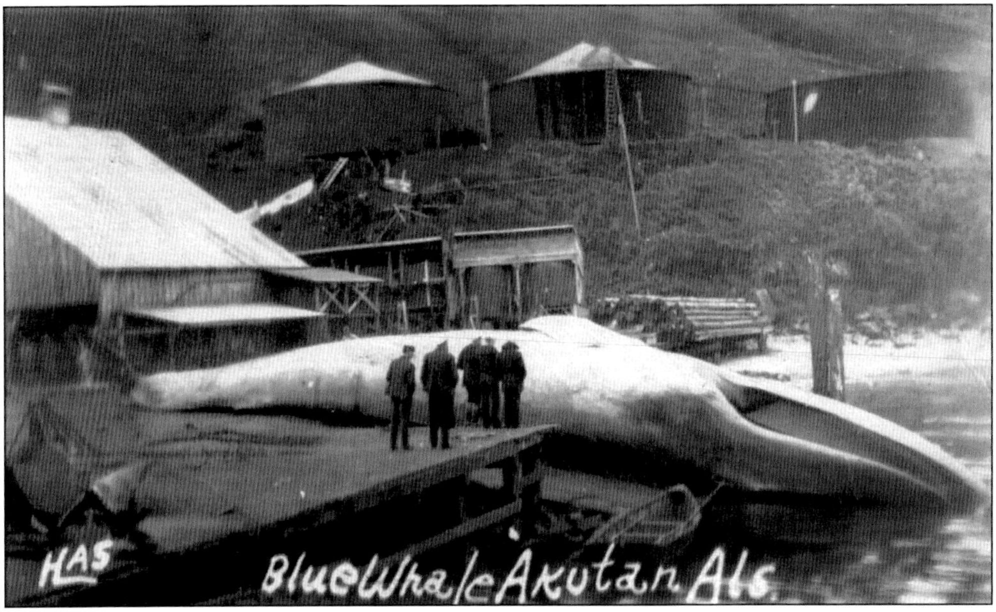

Another large blue whale is shown here at the whaling station in Akutan, Alaska. This image also shows the development of the facilities at Akutan. A third large storage tank is under construction on the hill. The station would eventually have 15 of these tanks.

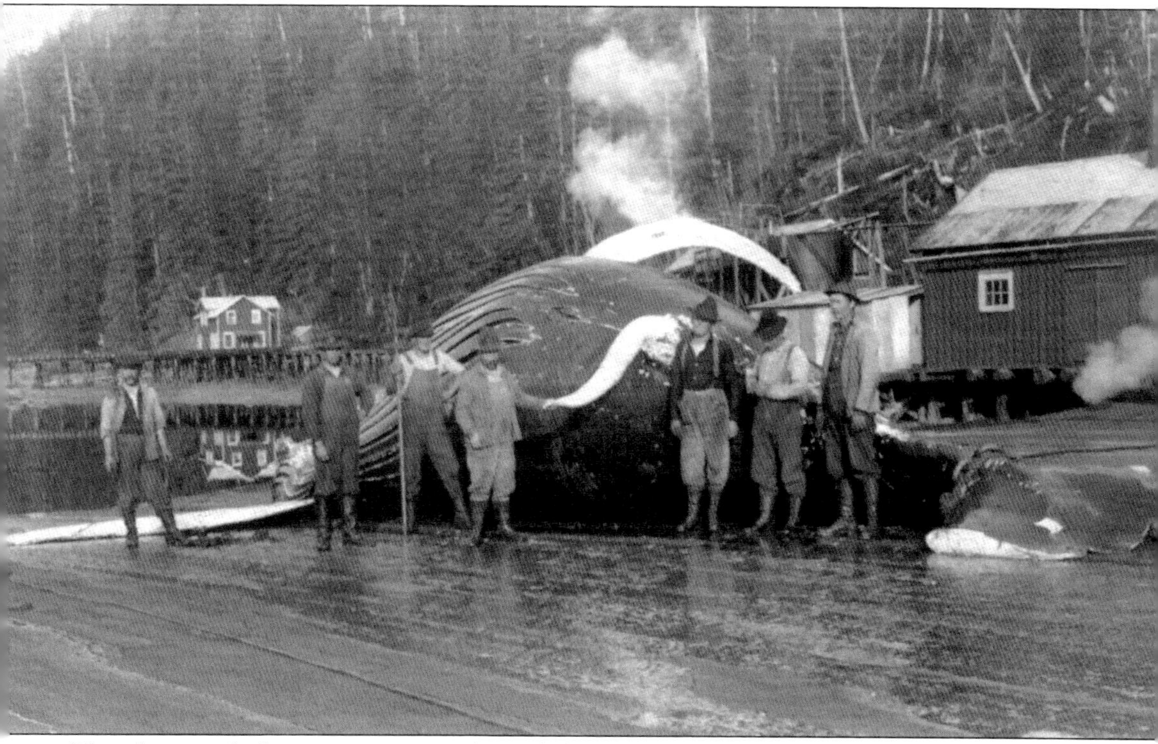

This photograph shows seven men and a male humpback whale. The whale probably measures 35 to 50 feet in length.

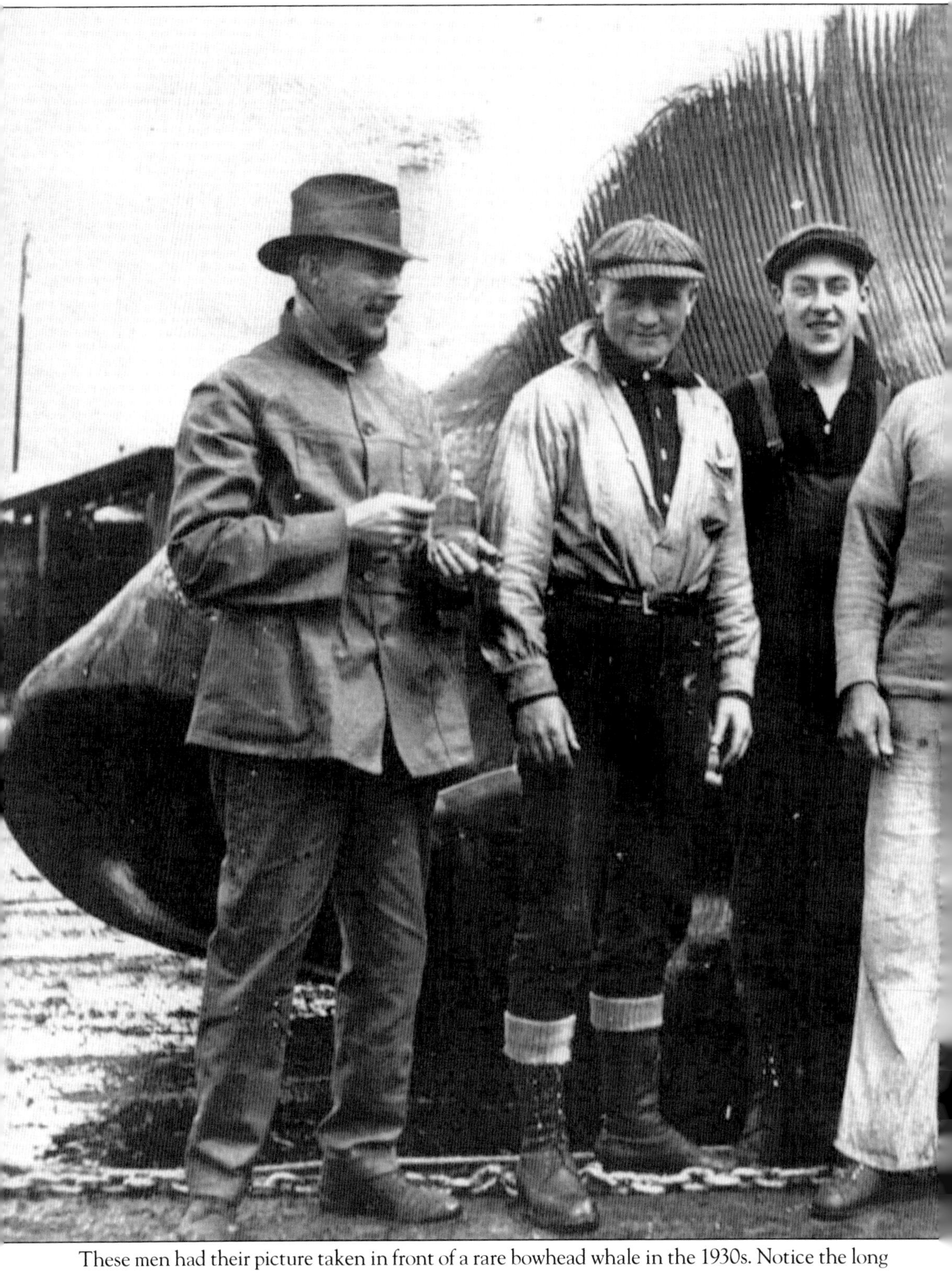

These men had their picture taken in front of a rare bowhead whale in the 1930s. Notice the long

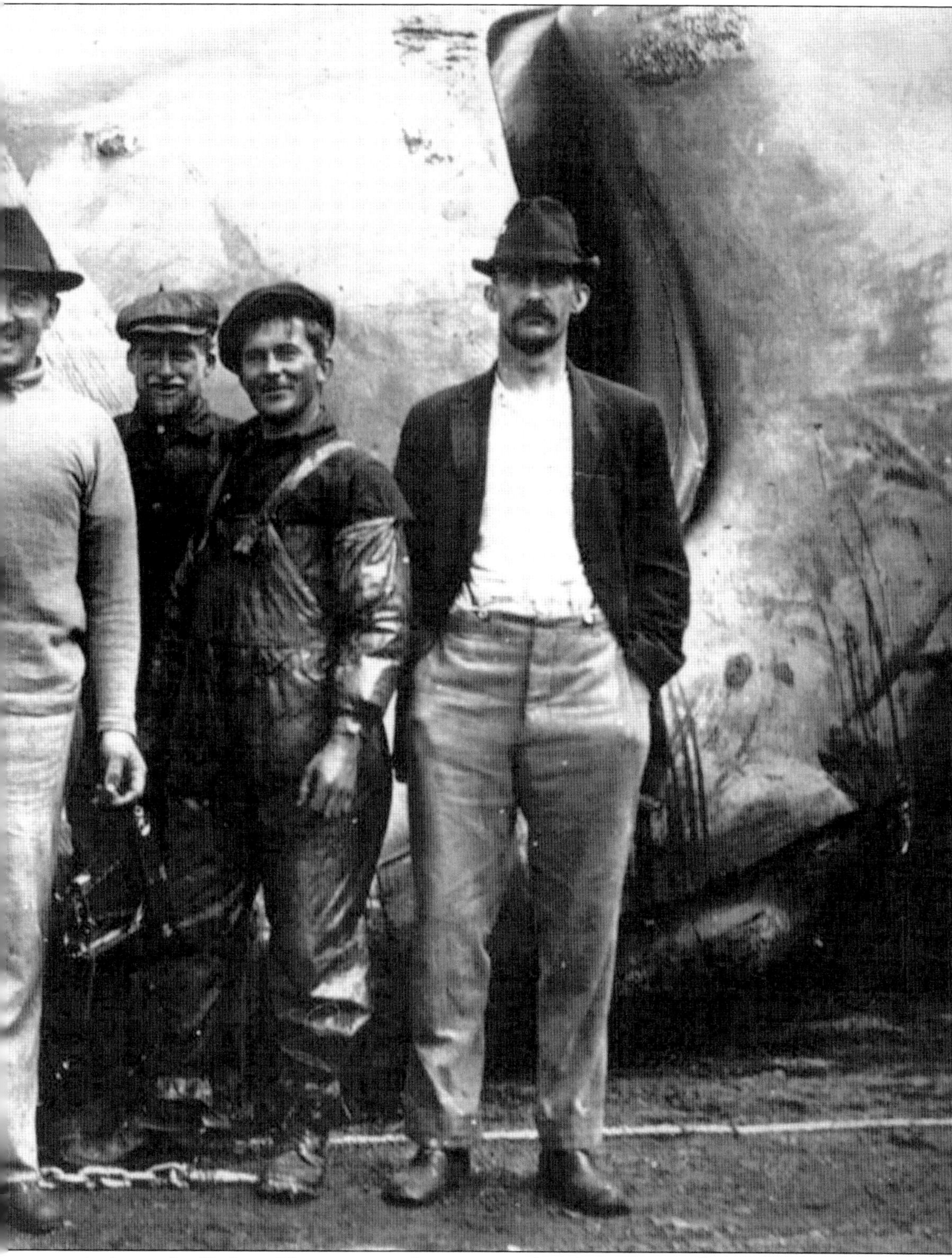

vertical strands of baleen. They appear to be visitors and workers in coveralls.